Math Fundamentals

GRADE 1

Manufacturer Evan-Moor Corporation
10 Harris Court, Suite C-3 Monterey, CA 93940, USA
www.evan-moor.com

EU Rep. Authorised Rep Compliance Ltd., Ground Floor,
71 Lower Baggot Street, Dublin, D02 P593, Ireland
www.arccompliance.com

Writing: Marti Beeck
Content Editing: Lisa Vitarisi Mathews
Copy Editing: Cathy Harber
Laurie Westrich
Art Direction: Yuki Meyer
Cover Design: Yuki Meyer
Art Manager: Kathy Kopp
Illustration: Ann Iosa
Design/Production: Yuki Meyer
Jessica Onken

Evan-Moor Educational Publishers

EMC 3081

Visit *teaching-standards.com* to view a correlation of this book.

Correlated to Current Standards

Congratulations on your purchase of some of the finest teaching materials in the world.

For information about other Evan-Moor products, call 1-800-777-4362, fax 1-800-777-4332, or visit our website, www.evan-moor.com.

10 Harris Court, Suite C-3, Monterey, CA 93940-5773. Printed in USA.

005

CPSIA: Sheridan Saline, Inc., Saline, MI, USA [6/2025]

Contents

What's in This Book

Math Fundamentals is your comprehensive resource for grade-level problem-solving and analysis practice. The broad scope of math skills ranges in difficulty on skill practice pages, allowing you to precisely target specific skills for each student.

- Each unit is divided into concept sections that include a student reference page showing multiple strategies and models, skill practice pages that progress from foundational to challenging, and a culminating problem-solving activity. These activities offer opportunities to investigate and analyze the concept, improve computational fluency, and apply the skill in student-friendly real-world contexts.
- The student pages may be assigned as individual practice or homework. They can also be used for small-group work or a whole-class lesson.
- If you wish to use this book as a core resource, we suggest using the units in the order shown on page 8.

Teacher Page

Unit Overview

This page shows at a glance the concepts and math process skills in the unit.

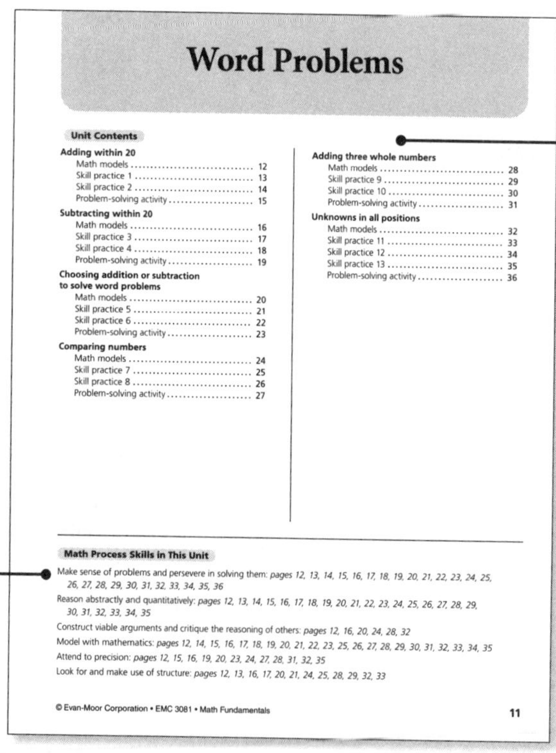

Word Problems

Unit Contents

Math Process Skills in This Unit

Make sense of problems and persevere in solving them: *pages 12, 13, 14, 15, 16, 17, 18, 19, 20, 21, 22, 23, 24, 25, 26, 27, 28, 29, 30, 31, 32, 33, 34, 35, 36*

Reason abstractly and quantitatively: *pages 12, 13, 14, 15, 16, 17, 18, 19, 20, 21, 22, 23, 24, 25, 26, 27, 28, 29, 30, 31, 32, 33, 34, 35*

Construct viable arguments and critique the reasoning of others: *pages 12, 16, 20, 24, 28, 32*

Model with mathematics: *pages 12, 14, 15, 16, 17, 18, 19, 20, 21, 22, 23, 25, 26, 27, 28, 29, 30, 31, 32, 33, 34, 35*

Attend to precision: *pages 12, 15, 16, 19, 20, 23, 24, 27, 28, 31, 32, 35*

Look for and make use of structure: *pages 12, 13, 16, 17, 20, 21, 24, 25, 28, 29, 32, 33*

© Evan-Moor Corporation • EMC 3081 • Math Fundamentals 11

Unit Contents
This area shows the concepts included in the unit and how many pages are included in each concept.

Math Process Skills in This Unit
This section lists the math process skills that students will use in the unit, along with the specific page numbers for each skill.

Student Pages

Math Models

These reference pages help students with each concept.

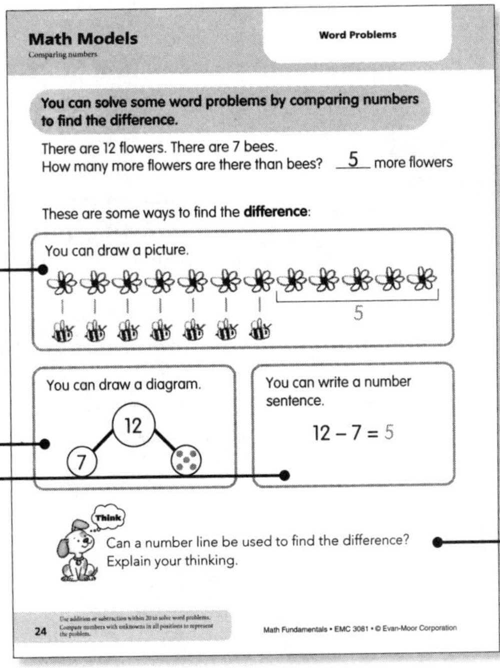
Math Models — Word Problems
Comparing numbers

You can solve some word problems by comparing numbers to find the difference.

There are 12 flowers. There are 7 bees.
How many more flowers are there than bees? 5 more flowers

These are some ways to find the **difference**:

You can draw a picture.

You can draw a diagram.

You can write a number sentence.
12 – 7 = 5

Think
Can a number line be used to find the difference? Explain your thinking.

24 Math Fundamentals • EMC 3081 • © Evan-Moor Corporation

Multiple solving strategies with examples
Several example problems are shown, along with all work and answers so students can follow the steps. Multiple strategies or models are used so students can choose what best fits their thinking or the type of problem.

Reference page with many uses
- Introduce students to the types of problems they'll encounter.
- Print, project, or post it for reference as you teach the unit.
- Send it home as a resource for homework so parents can connect what they know with current methodology.

"Think" questions
"Think" questions help students apply what they have learned to a similar problem. The questions provide students an opportunity to talk about math strategies and to explain their thinking.

Skill Practice

These pages help students analyze concepts, gain fluency, and apply skills.

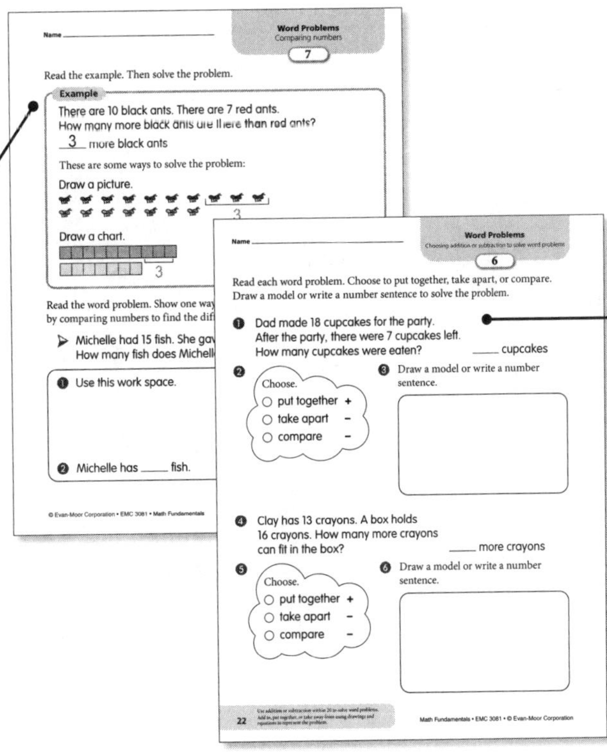
Name ______ Word Problems Comparing numbers 7

Read the example. Then solve the problem.

Example
There are 10 black ants. There are 7 red ants.
How many more black ants are there than red ants?
3 more black ants
These are some ways to solve the problem:
Draw a picture.
Draw a chart.

Read the word problem. Show one way ... by comparing numbers to find the dif...
Michelle had 15 fish. She ga...
How many fish does Michell...
1 Use this work space.
2 Michelle has ___ fish.

Name ______ Word Problems Choosing addition or subtraction to solve word problems 6

Read each word problem. Choose to put together, take apart, or compare. Draw a model or write a number sentence to solve the problem.

1 Dad made 18 cupcakes for the party. After the party, there were 7 cupcakes left. How many cupcakes were eaten? ___ cupcakes
2 Choose. ○ put together + ○ take apart – ○ compare –
3 Draw a model or write a number sentence.
4 Clay has 13 crayons. A box holds 16 crayons. How many more crayons can fit in the box? ___ more crayons
5 Choose. ○ put together + ○ take apart – ○ compare –
6 Draw a model or write a number sentence.

22 Math Fundamentals • EMC 3081 • © Evan-Moor Corporation

Example problem
The first skill practice page in each section includes an example to show students how to mark the answer and show their work.

Practice problems
Students practice math skills and work toward fluency.

Student Pages, *continued*

Problem-Solving Activity

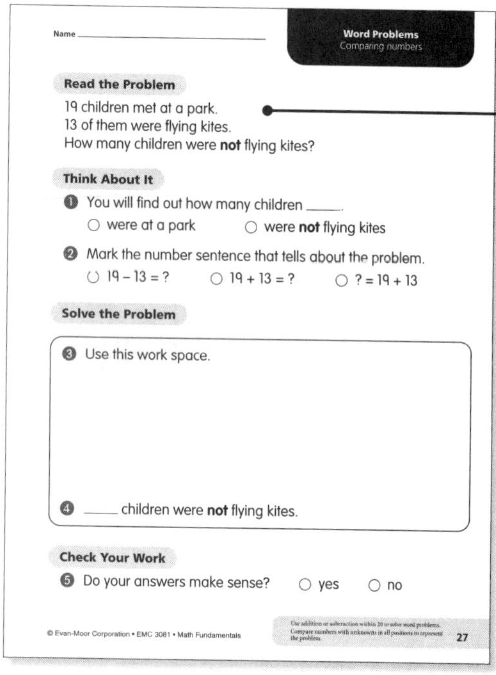
Name ______________________

Word Problems
Comparing numbers

Read the Problem

19 children met at a park.
13 of them were flying kites.
How many children were **not** flying kites?

Think About It

1. You will find out how many children ____.
   ○ were at a park ○ were **not** flying kites
2. Mark the number sentence that tells about the problem.
   ○ 19 – 13 = ? ○ 19 + 13 = ? ○ ? = 19 + 13

Solve the Problem

3. Use this work space.
4. ____ children were **not** flying kites.

Check Your Work

5. Do your answers make sense? ○ yes ○ no

© Evan-Moor Corporation • EMC 3081 • Math Fundamentals

Use addition or subtraction within 20 to solve word problems. Compare numbers with unknowns in all positions to represent the problem.

27

Real-world problem
Students tackle a real-world problem. The activity leads students through unpacking the problem: analyzing what the problem asks for, figuring out what information is needed to calculate the answer, showing their work or model, arriving at a solution, and checking their work.

Answer Key

Correct Answers or Examples

The correct response or an exemplar response is shown on a reduced version of the actual page.

Teachers may establish their own criteria for evaluating and scoring work shown leading to an answer.

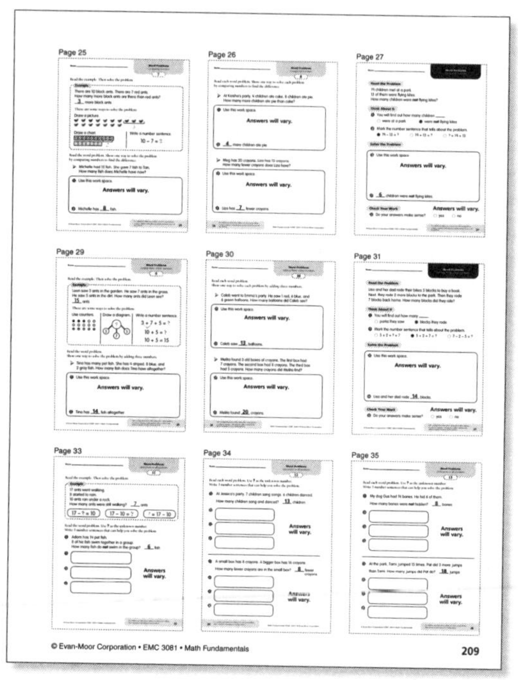

Math Models

Small-Group Instruction

The Math Models pages are intended to be used in a small-group instruction setting. Consider the following approach:

1. Read aloud the concept statement to students.
2. Guide students through each example. Lead them in a discussion about the strategies.
3. Read aloud and discuss the "Think" question at the bottom of the page. Encourage students to participate in the discussion and explain their thinking. This is an opportunity for you to check students' understanding of the math concept.

The models included are suggestions. A variety of widely used models are represented in the book, but feel free to add additional models or integrate those used in class. Where counters are pictured, you may have students use actual manipulative counters or work with representations of them, as you see fit.

Parent Education

Send home Math Models pages for parent education.

Many parents may have questions about the new math strategies their children are learning. The math models will help them better understand the concepts so they can support their children's math education.

Suggested Teaching Path

If you wish to use this book as a core resource, we suggest using the units in the following order:

1. **Counting and Number Sequences (page 83)**
   Counting from zero
   Counting on: 1 to 50
   Counting on: 51 to 120
   Skip counting
   Counting back
2. **Add and Subtract Within 20 (page 51)**
   Counting on to add
   Counting back to subtract
   Making a ten
   Leading to a ten
   Using equivalent or known sums
3. **Equivalency and Unknown Numbers (page 73)**
   Determining equivalency
   Finding unknown numbers
4. **Place Value: Two-Digit Numbers (page 105)**
   Tens
   Tens and ones
   Comparing two-digit numbers
5. **Place Value: Addition and Subtraction (page 119)**
   Adding two-digit numbers within 100
   Ten more or ten less
   Subtracting multiples of ten
6. **Operations and Number Relationships (page 37)**
   Addition: Changing the order (commutative property)
   Addition: Changing the grouping (associative property)
   Subtraction: Using the unknown addend
7. **Word Problems (page 11)**
   Adding within 20
   Subtracting within 20
   Choosing addition or subtraction to solve word problems
   Comparing numbers
   Adding three whole numbers
   Unknowns in all positions
8. **Time (page 143)**
   Telling time by the hour
   Telling time by the half-hour
9. **Money (page 171)**
   Identifying coins
   Writing the value of coins
   Counting coins
10. **Measuring Length (page 133)**
    Ordering objects by length
    Measuring and writing the length of objects
11. **Charts and Graphs (page 153)**
    Understanding charts and graphs
    Tally charts
    Picture graphs
    Bar graphs
12. **Geometry (page 185)**
    Identifying two- and three-dimensional shapes
    Identifying defining and nondefining attributes
    Creating composite shapes
    Partitioning shapes into equal shares
    Partitioning shapes into fractional shares

Strategies for Solving Word Problems and Activities

❶ **Read**  **or listen to**  **the problem** carefully.
Think about what it says.

❷ **Draw**  **a model** of the problem. It can be a picture, a diagram, or a chart of data.

❸ **Think about**  **what you need** to do to solve it.

Do you need to:

- add  or subtract 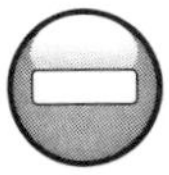?
- skip count **2, 4, 6** ?
- measure  something?
- write 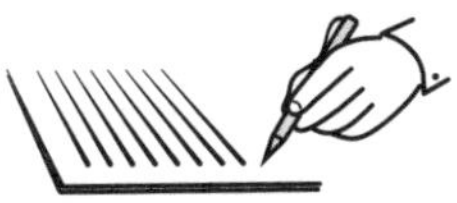 an equation?
- figure out  a piece of information before you solve the problem?

❹ **Solve**  **the problem.** Hint: Sometimes it will take two steps.

❺ **Check**  **your work.** Does your answer make sense?

Use *Math Fundamentals* to Reteach and Reinforce

The perfect companion to Evan-Moor's *Daily Math Practice*

Thousands of grade 1 through 6 classrooms use *Daily Math Practice* for focused practice and review. Multiple studies show that this type of distributed, or spaced, practice is a powerful strategy for achieving proficiency and retention of skills.

Student responses on the *Daily Math Practice* items will indicate which skills need additional practice or remediation. Use *Math Fundamentals* to provide the reteaching and additional practice. For example:

A student makes errors in week 24 of *Daily Math Practice*. Your assessment is that the student needs more practice with these skills.

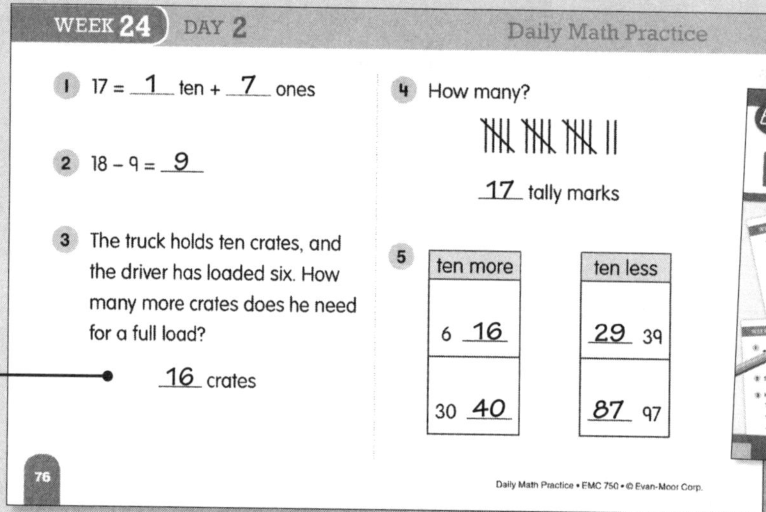

WEEK 24 DAY 2 Daily Math Practice

1. 17 = 1 ten + 7 ones
2. 18 − 9 = 9
3. The truck holds ten crates, and the driver has loaded six. How many more crates does he need for a full load? 16 crates
4. How many? 17 tally marks
5.

ten more	ten less
6 16	29 39
30 40	87 97

76 Daily Math Practice • EMC 750 • © Evan-Moor Corp.

The student does not know whether to add or subtract.

Use these pages from *Math Fundamentals* to reteach and practice the skills the student has not mastered.

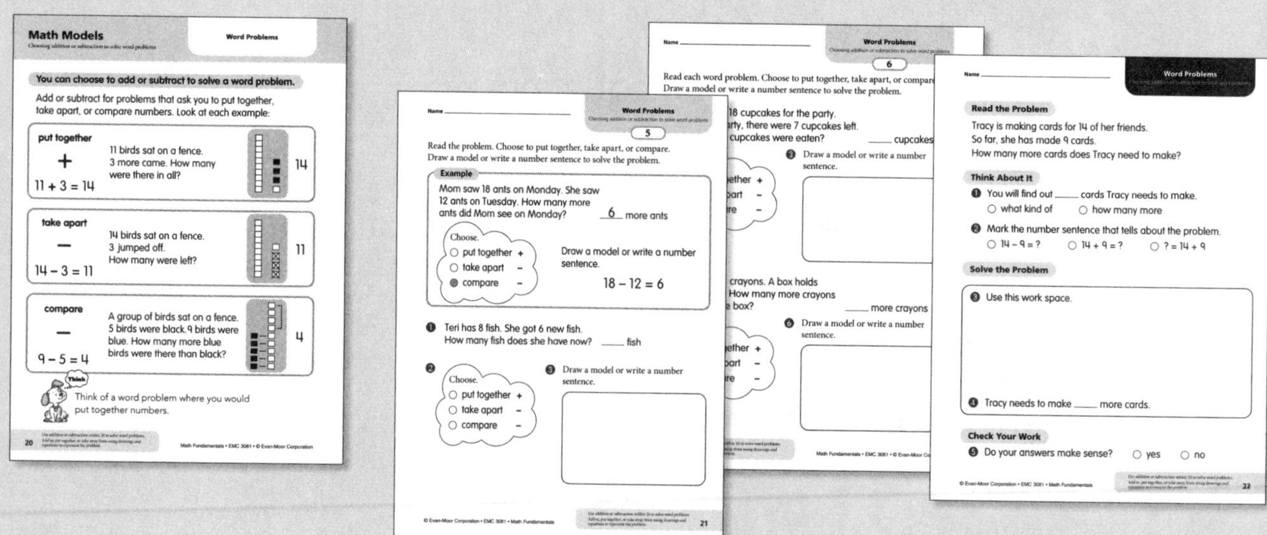

Word Problems

Unit Contents

Math Process Skills in This Unit

Make sense of problems and persevere in solving them: *pages 12, 13, 14, 15, 16, 17, 18, 19, 20, 21, 22, 23, 24, 25, 26, 27, 28, 29, 30, 31, 32, 33, 34, 35, 36*

Reason abstractly and quantitatively: *pages 12, 13, 14, 15, 16, 17, 18, 19, 20, 21, 22, 23, 24, 25, 26, 27, 28, 29, 30, 31, 32, 33, 34, 35*

Construct viable arguments and critique the reasoning of others: *pages 12, 16, 20, 24, 28, 32*

Model with mathematics: *pages 12, 14, 15, 16, 17, 18, 19, 20, 21, 22, 23, 25, 26, 27, 28, 29, 30, 31, 32, 33, 34, 35*

Attend to precision: *pages 12, 15, 16, 19, 20, 23, 24, 27, 28, 31, 32, 35*

Look for and make use of structure: *pages 12, 13, 16, 17, 20, 21, 24, 25, 28, 29, 32, 33*

You can solve some word problems with addition.

Dan has 8 white socks and 2 gray socks.
How many socks does he have in all? 10 socks

These are some ways you can **put together** numbers:

You can draw a picture.

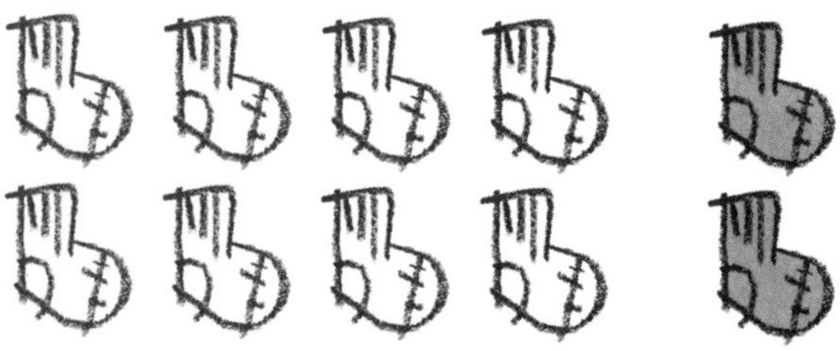

You can use counters.

You can draw a diagram.

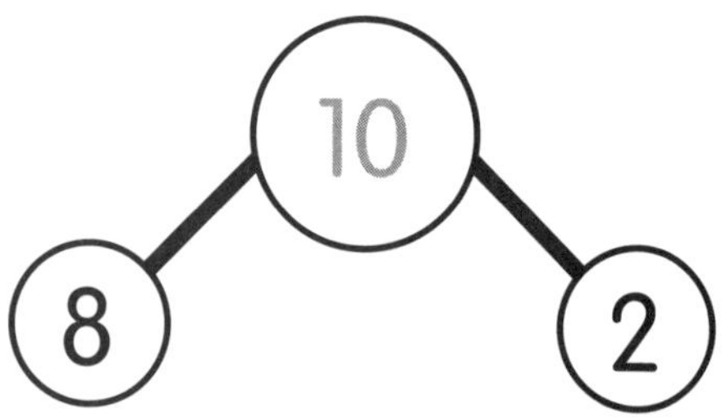

You can write a number sentence.

$8 + 2 = 10$

Jesse solved the word problem. He wrote **8 + 2 = 10**.
Do you agree? Explain your thinking.

Use addition within 20 to solve word problems.
Add to or put together using objects, drawings, and equations to represent the problem.

Name ______________________________

Read the example. Then solve the problem.

Example

6 ants sat on a log.
4 more ants came.
How many ants were there in all? <u>10</u> ants

These are some ways to solve the problem:

Draw a picture.

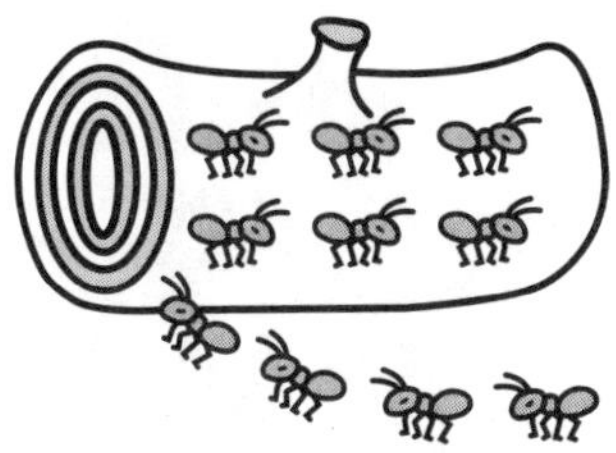

Draw a diagram.

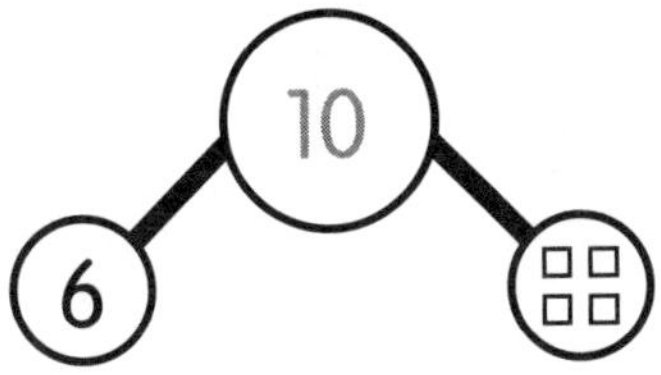

Write a number sentence.

$6 + 4 = ?$

Read the word problem.
Show one way to solve the problem by adding.

▶ Luis has 8 fish. Tia has 7 fish.
How many fish do they have in all?

❶ Use this work space.

❷ They have _____ fish in all.

Use addition within 20 to solve word problems.
Add to or put together using objects, drawings, and equations to represent the problem.

Name ______________________________

Read each word problem.
Show one way to solve each problem by adding.

➤ There were 3 girls and 9 boys at Emma's party.
How many children were at the party?

❶ Use this work space.

❷ _____ children were at the party.

➤ Liz had 10 crayons. I gave her 5 more.
How many crayons does Liz have now?

❸ Use this work space.

❹ Liz has _____ crayons.

Use addition within 20 to solve word problems.
Add to or put together using objects, drawings, and equations to represent the problem.

Name ______________________________

Read the Problem

Lily saw children flying kites at the park.
She counted 6 yellow and 7 blue kites.
How many kites did she see altogether?

Think About It

1. You will find out how many _____ Lily saw.
   ○ children ○ parks ○ kites

2. Mark the number sentence that tells about the problem.
   ○ 7 – 6 = ? ○ 6 + 7 = ? ○ 6 + ? = 7

Solve the Problem

3. Use this work space.

4. Lily saw _____ kites altogether.

Check Your Work

5. Do your answers make sense? ○ yes ○ no

Use addition within 20 to solve word problems.
Add to or put together using objects, drawings, and equations to represent the problem.

Math Models

Subtracting within 20

You can solve some word problems with subtraction.

15 apples were in the tree.
Jen picked 5 apples.
How many apples were left? 10 apples

These are some ways you can **take apart** numbers:

You can draw a picture.

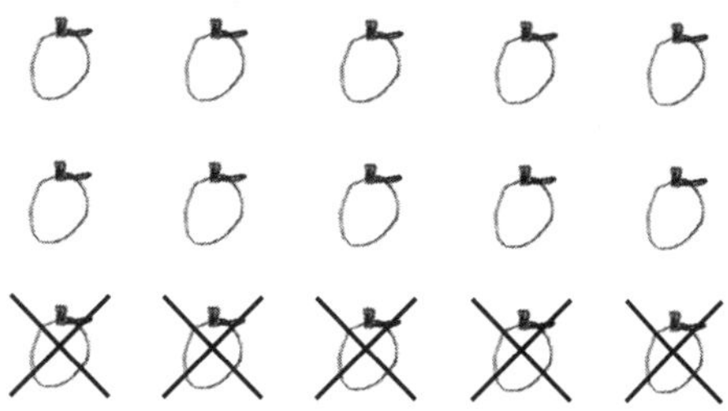

You can use counters.

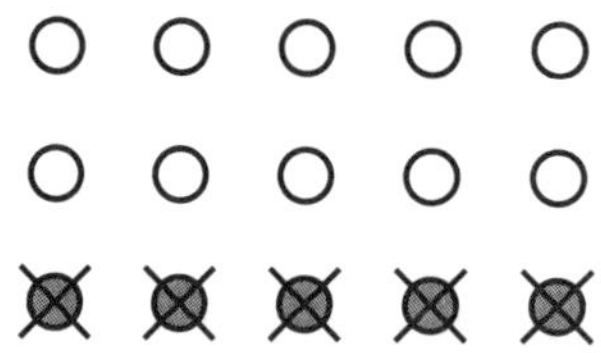

You can draw a diagram.

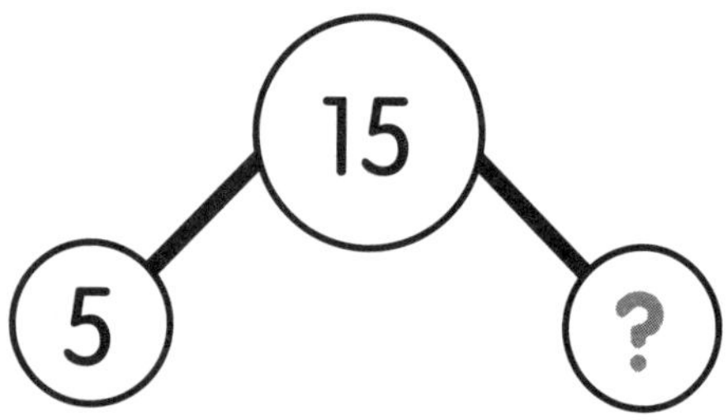

You can write a number sentence.

$$15 - 5 = ?$$

What is your favorite math model to use for this problem? Explain your answer.

Use subtraction within 20 to solve word problems.
Take away from or take apart using objects, drawings, and equations to represent the problem.

Name ______________________________

Read the example. Then solve the problem.

Example

10 ants sat on a log.
4 ants went away.
How many ants were left? __6__ ants

These are some ways to solve the problem:

Draw a picture.	Draw a diagram.	Write a number sentence.
	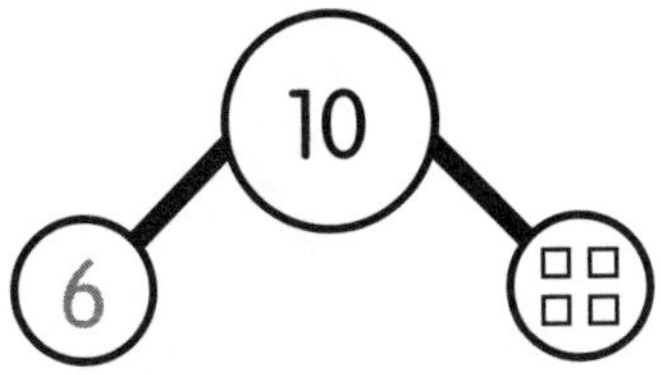	10 – 4 = 6

Read the word problem.
Show one way to solve the problem by subtracting.

➤ Mike had 15 fish. He gave 7 fish to Jan.
How many fish does Mike have now?

❶ Use this work space.

❷ Mike has _____ fish.

Name ______________________________

Read each word problem.
Show one way to solve each problem by subtracting.

➤ There were 12 children at Alisa's party. 9 children played games. How many children did **not** play games?

❶ Use this work space.

❷ _____ children did **not** play games.

➤ Carlos had 15 crayons. He lost 2 crayons. How many crayons does Carlos have left?

❸ Use this work space.

❹ Carlos has _____ crayons left.

Use subtraction within 20 to solve word problems.
Take away from or take apart using objects, drawings, and equations to represent the problem.

Name ____________________

Read the Problem

At the park, Harold saw 13 kites flying.
Then 3 kites got stuck in trees.
How many kites were still flying?

Think About It

1. You will find out how many _____ were still flying.
   - ○ kites ○ trees ○ birds

2. Mark the number sentence that tells about the problem.
   - ○ ? – 13 = 3 ○ 13 + 3 = ? ○ 13 – 3 = ?

Solve the Problem

3. Use this work space.

4. _____ kites were still flying.

Check Your Work

5. Do your answers make sense? ○ yes ○ no

Use subtraction within 20 to solve word problems.
Take away from or take apart using objects, drawings, and equations to represent the problem.

Math Models

Choosing addition or subtraction to solve word problems

You can choose to add or subtract to solve a word problem.

Add or subtract for problems that ask you to put together, take apart, or compare numbers. Look at each example:

put together

+

11 + 3 = 14

11 birds sat on a fence.
3 more came. How many were there in all?

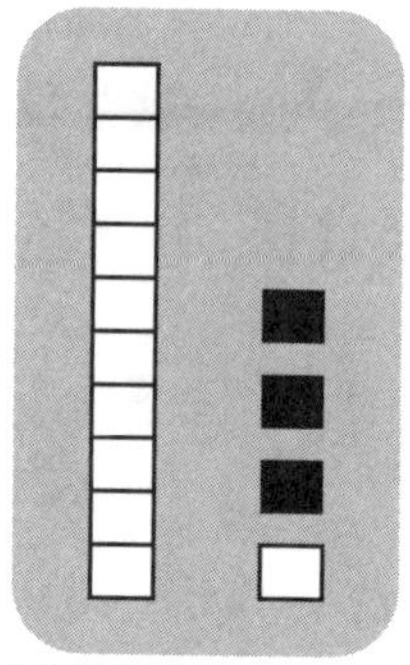

14

take apart

−

14 − 3 = 11

14 birds sat on a fence.
3 jumped off.
How many were left?

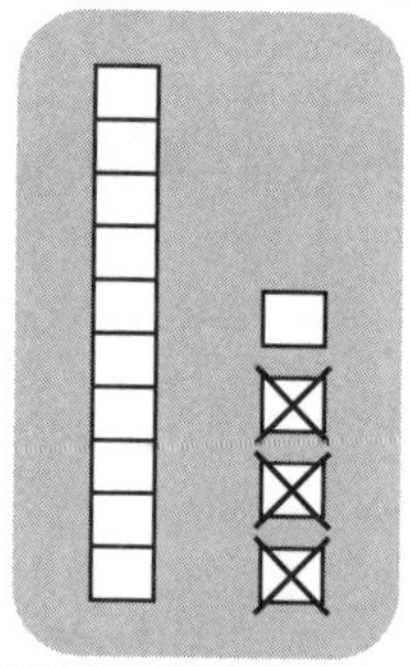

11

compare

−

9 − 5 = 4

A group of birds sat on a fence.
5 birds were black. 9 birds were blue. How many more blue birds were there than black?

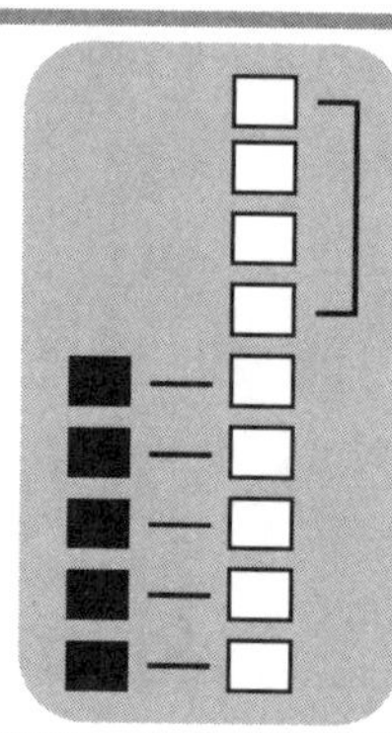

4

Think of a word problem where you would put together numbers.

Use addition or subtraction within 20 to solve word problems.
Add to, put together, or take away from using drawings and equations to represent the problem.

Name ______________________________

Read the problem. Choose to put together, take apart, or compare. Draw a model or write a number sentence to solve the problem.

Example

Mom saw 18 ants on Monday. She saw 12 ants on Tuesday. How many more ants did Mom see on Monday? __6__ more ants

Choose.

- ○ put together +
- ○ take apart –
- ● compare –

Draw a model or write a number sentence.

$18 - 12 = 6$

1 Teri has 8 fish. She got 6 new fish. How many fish does she have now? _____ fish

2 Choose.

- ○ put together +
- ○ take apart –
- ○ compare –

3 Draw a model or write a number sentence.

Use addition or subtraction within 20 to solve word problems. Add to, put together, or take away from using drawings and equations to represent the problem.

Name ______________________________

Read each word problem. Choose to put together, take apart, or compare. Draw a model or write a number sentence to solve the problem.

1. Dad made 18 cupcakes for the party. After the party, there were 7 cupcakes left. How many cupcakes were eaten? ______ cupcakes

2. Choose.
   - ○ put together +
   - ○ take apart −
   - ○ compare −

3. Draw a model or write a number sentence.

4. Clay has 13 crayons. A box holds 16 crayons. How many more crayons can fit in the box? ______ more crayons

5. Choose.
   - ○ put together +
   - ○ take apart −
   - ○ compare −

6. Draw a model or write a number sentence.

Use addition or subtraction within 20 to solve word problems. Add to, put together, or take away from using drawings and equations to represent the problem.

Name ______________________________

Read the Problem

Tracy is making cards for 14 of her friends.
So far, she has made 9 cards.
How many more cards does Tracy need to make?

Think About It

1. You will find out _____ cards Tracy needs to make.
   - ○ what kind of
   - ○ how many more

2. Mark the number sentence that tells about the problem.
   - ○ $14 - 9 = ?$
   - ○ $14 + 9 = ?$
   - ○ $? = 14 + 9$

Solve the Problem

3. Use this work space.

4. Tracy needs to make _____ more cards.

Check Your Work

5. Do your answers make sense? ○ yes ○ no

Use addition or subtraction within 20 to solve word problems. Add to, put together, or take away from using drawings and equations to represent the problem.

Math Models

Comparing numbers

You can solve some word problems by comparing numbers to find the difference.

There are 12 flowers. There are 7 bees.
How many more flowers are there than bees? __5__ more flowers

These are some ways to find the **difference**:

You can draw a picture.

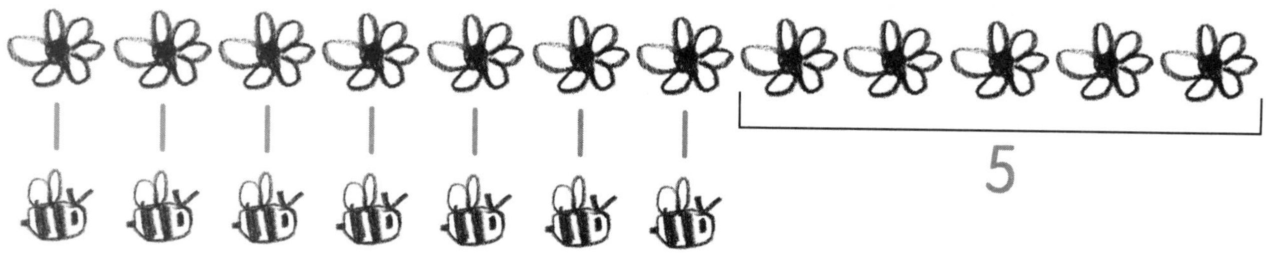

You can draw a diagram.

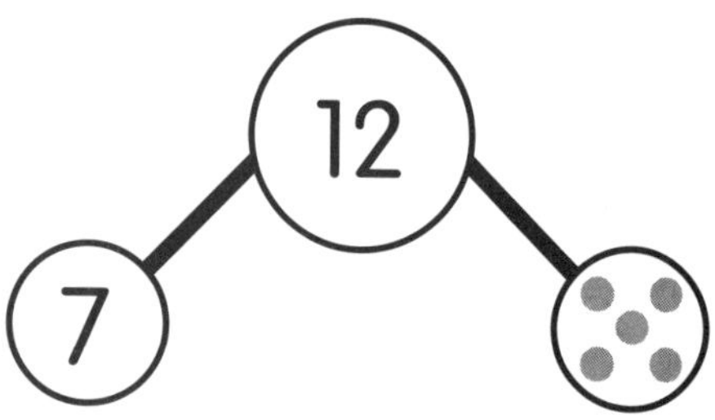

You can write a number sentence.

$$12 - 7 = 5$$

Can a number line be used to find the difference? Explain your thinking.

Use addition or subtraction within 20 to solve word problems.
Compare numbers with unknowns in all positions to represent the problem.

Name ____________________

Read the example. Then solve the problem.

Example

There are 10 black ants. There are 7 red ants.
How many more black ants are there than red ants?

__3__ more black ants

These are some ways to solve the problem:

Draw a picture.

Draw a chart.

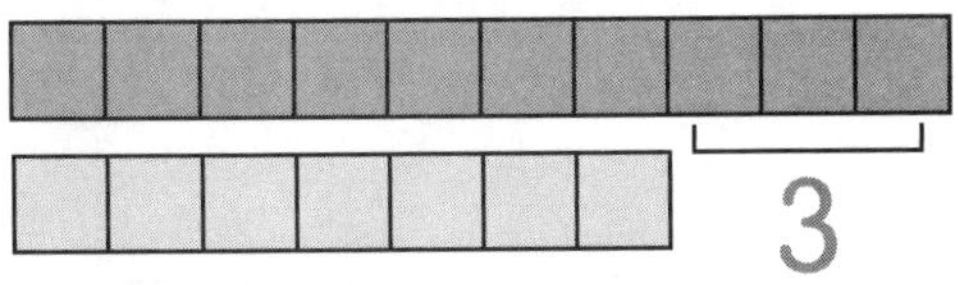

Write a number sentence.

$10 - 7 = 3$

Read the word problem. Show one way to solve the problem by comparing numbers to find the difference.

Michelle had 15 fish. She gave 7 fish to Tan.
How many fish does Michelle have now?

1. Use this work space.

2. Michelle has ______ fish.

Name ______________________________

Read each word problem. Show one way to solve each problem by comparing numbers to find the difference.

➤ At Keisha's party, 4 children ate cake. 8 children ate pie. How many more children ate pie than cake?

❶ Use this work space.

❷ _____ more children ate pie.

➤ Meg has 20 crayons. Liza has 13 crayons. How many fewer crayons does Liza have?

❸ Use this work space.

❹ Liza has _____ fewer crayons.

Use addition or subtraction within 20 to solve word problems.
Compare numbers with unknowns in all positions to represent the problem.

Name ______________________________

Read the Problem

19 children met at a park.
13 of them were flying kites.
How many children were **not** flying kites?

Think About It

1. You will find out how many children ____.
   - ○ were at a park
   - ○ were **not** flying kites

2. Mark the number sentence that tells about the problem.
   - ○ 19 – 13 = ?
   - ○ 19 + 13 = ?
   - ○ ? = 19 + 13

Solve the Problem

3. Use this work space.

4. ____ children were **not** flying kites.

Check Your Work

5. Do your answers make sense? ○ yes ○ no

Use addition or subtraction within 20 to solve word problems. Compare numbers with unknowns in all positions to represent the problem.

You can solve some word problems by adding three numbers.

Carla went to a farm.
She saw 5 cows, 6 goats, and 2 horses.
How many animals did she see? 13 animals

These are some ways to add three numbers:

You can use counters.

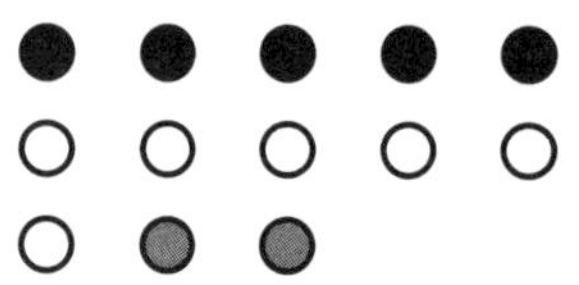

You can draw a diagram.

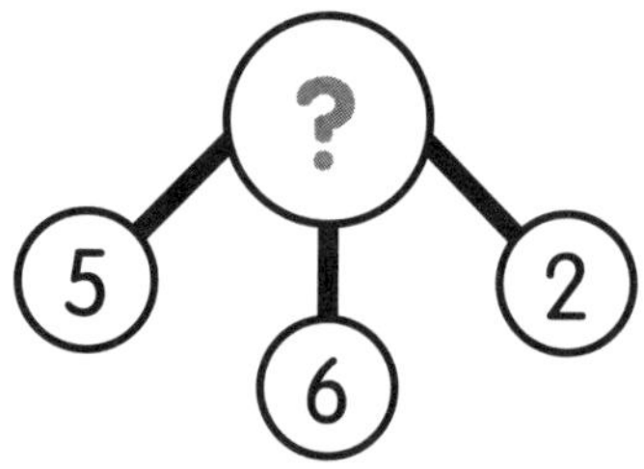

You can write a number sentence.

$$5 + 6 + 2 = ?$$

$$11 + 2 = 13$$

Explain some ways to choose which numbers to add first.

Solve word problems that call for adding three whole numbers. Use objects, drawings, and equations with a symbol for the unknown number to represent the problem.

Name ____________________

Word Problems
Adding three whole numbers

9

Read the example. Then solve the problem.

Example

Leon saw 3 ants in the garden. He saw 7 ants in the grass. He saw 5 ants in the dirt. How many ants did Leon see?

__15__ ants

These are some ways to solve the problem:

Use counters.

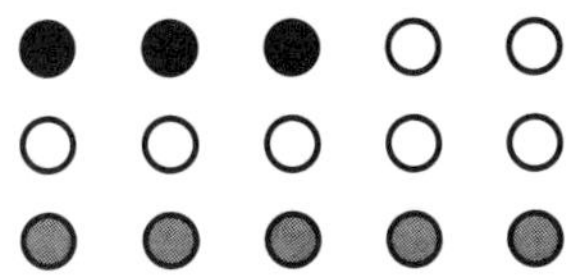

Draw a diagram.

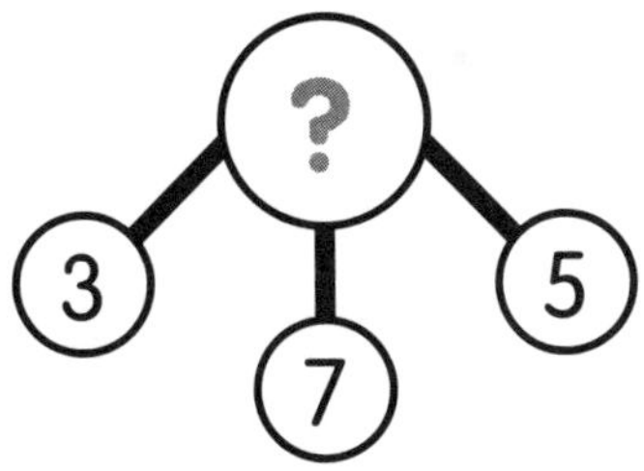

Write a number sentence.

$3 + 7 + 5 = ?$

$10 + 5 = ?$

$10 + 5 = 15$

Read the word problem.
Show one way to solve the problem by adding three numbers.

➢ Tina has many pet fish. She has 4 striped, 8 blue, and 2 gray fish. How many fish does Tina have altogether?

❶ Use this work space.

❷ Tina has ______ fish altogether.

Solve word problems that call for adding three whole numbers. Use objects, drawings, and equations with a symbol for the unknown number to represent the problem.

Name ______________________

Read each word problem.
Show one way to solve each problem by adding three numbers.

➤ Caleb went to Emma's party. He saw 1 red, 6 blue, and 6 green balloons. How many balloons did Caleb see?

1. Use this work space.

2. Caleb saw _____ balloons.

➤ Melita found 3 old boxes of crayons. The first box had 7 crayons. The second box had 8 crayons. The third box had 5 crayons. How many crayons did Melita find?

3. Use this work space.

4. Melita found _____ crayons.

Solve word problems that call for adding three whole numbers. Use objects, drawings, and equations with a symbol for the unknown number to represent the problem.

Name ____________________

Read the Problem

Lisa and her dad rode their bikes 5 blocks to buy a book. Next, they rode 2 more blocks to the park. Then they rode 7 blocks back home. How many blocks did they ride?

Think About It

❶ You will find out how many ____.

○ parks they saw ○ blocks they rode

❷ Mark the number sentence that tells about the problem.

○ 5 + 2 + ? = 7 ○ 5 + 2 + 7 = ? ○ 7 – 2 – 5 = ?

Solve the Problem

❸ Use this work space.

❹ Lisa and her dad rode ____ blocks.

Check Your Work

❺ Do your answers make sense? ○ yes ○ no

Solve word problems that call for adding three whole numbers. Use objects, drawings, and equations with a symbol for the unknown number to represent the problem.

You can use a symbol to stand for an unknown number in a number sentence. The symbol can be in different places.

There were 19 bugs.
A bird ate 6 of them.
How many bugs were left? 13 bugs

These are some ways to write a number sentence to help you solve the problem:

Kim

I wrote 19 − 6 = ?

19	−	6	=	?
bugs in all		eaten		unknown

Ben

I wrote 6 + ? = 19

6	+	?	=	19
eaten		unknown		bugs in all

Juana

I wrote ? = 19 − 6

?	=	19	−	6
unknown		bugs in all		eaten

Explain how Kim, Ben, and Juana might tell about each number sentence. What models could they use?

Name ______________________

Read the example. Then solve the problem.

Example

17 ants went walking.
It started to rain.
10 ants ran under a rock.
How many ants were still walking? 7 ants

17 – ? = 10 | 17 – 10 = ? | ? = 17 – 10

Read the word problem. Use **?** as the unknown number.
Write 3 number sentences that can help you solve the problem.

1. Adam has 14 pet fish.
   8 of his fish swim together in a group.
   How many fish do **not** swim in the group? _____ fish

2.

3.

4.

Use addition and subtraction within 20 to solve word problems.
Show situations with unknowns in all positions.

Name ______________________________

Read each word problem. Use **?** as the unknown number.
Write 3 number sentences that can help you solve the problem.

1. At Jessica's party, 7 children sang songs. 6 children danced.

   How many children sang and danced? _____ children

2.

3.

4.

---

5. A small box has 8 crayons. A bigger box has 16 crayons.

   How many fewer crayons are in the small box? _____ fewer crayons

6.

7.

8.

Name ______________________

Read each word problem. Use **?** as the unknown number.
Write 3 number sentences that can help you solve the problem.

1. My dog Gus had 14 bones. He hid 6 of them.

   How many bones were **not** hidden? _____ bones

2. [ ]

3. [ ]

4. [ ]

---

5. At the park, Tami jumped 15 times. Pat did 3 more jumps than Tami. How many jumps did Pat do? _____ jumps

6. [ ]

7. [ ]

8. [ ]

Use addition and subtraction within 20 to solve word problems.
Show situations with unknowns in all positions.

Name ______________________________

Read the Problem

Ed went to the park 15 times in May. He went 8 times with Dad. The other times he went with Mom.
How many times did Ed go to the park with Mom?

Think About It

1. You will find out how many times Ed went to the park _____.
   ○ with Dad   ○ with Mom   ○ in a car

2. Mark the number sentence that tells about the problem.
   ○ 8 – 15 = ?   ○ 15 + 8 = ?   ○ ? = 15 – 8

Solve the Problem

3. Use this work space.

4. Ed went to the park _____ times with Mom.

Check Your Work

5. Do your answers make sense?   ○ yes   ○ no

Use addition and subtraction within 20 to solve word problems.
Show situations with unknowns in all positions.

Operations and Number Relationships

Unit Contents

Math Process Skills in This Unit

Make sense of problems and persevere in solving them: *pages 41, 45, 50*

Reason abstractly and quantitatively: *pages 39, 40, 41, 42, 43, 44, 45, 47, 48, 49, 50*

Construct viable arguments and critique the reasoning of others: *pages 38, 42, 46*

Model with mathematics: *pages 38, 41, 42, 45, 50*

Attend to precision: *pages 41, 45, 50*

Look for and make use of structure: *pages 39, 40, 43, 44, 47, 48*

Math Models

Commutative property

You can change the order of addends.

If you know that 5 + 8 = 13, then you also know that 8 + 5 = 13.

This is one way to show how the order can be changed:

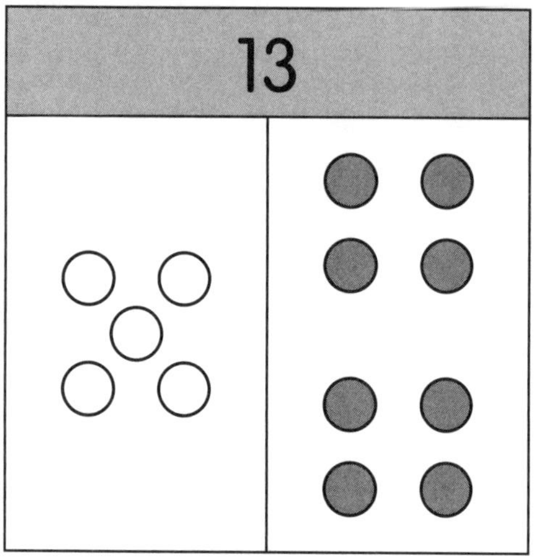

5 + 8 = 13

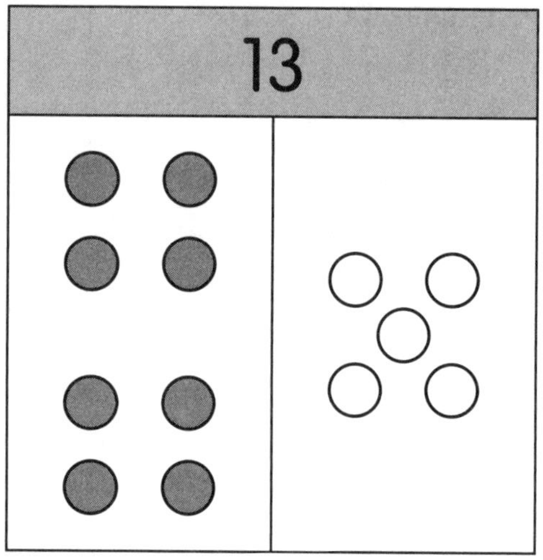

8 + 5 = 13

Explain another type of model you could use to show **5 + 8 = 13** and **8 + 5 = 13**.

Apply properties of operations to add (commutative property).

Name ______________________________

Add. Write a new number sentence by changing the order of the addends.

Example

Add.

7 + 3 = 10

Change the order.

3 + 7 = 10

Add	Change the Order
❶ 4 + 12 = ____	12 + 4 = 16
❷ 10 + 7 = ____	____ + ____ = ____
❸ 5 + 11 = ____	____ + ____ = ____
❹ 80 + 1 = ____	____ + ____ = ____

Name ____________________

Add. Then write a new number sentence by changing the order of the addends.

1. If 10 + 6 = ____, then 6 + 10 = 16.

____

2. If 7 + 8 = ____, then ____ + ____ = ____.

____

3. If 9 + 4 = ____, then ____ + ____ = ____.

____

4. If 17 + 3 = ____, then ____ + ____ = ____.

____

5. If 1 + 69 = ____, then ____ + ____ = ____.

____

6. If 100 + 10 = ____, then ____ + ____ = ____.

 Apply properties of operations to add (commutative property).

Name ______________________

Read the Problem

Carl has 8 blue socks and 4 white socks.
Ali has 4 blue socks and 8 white socks.
How many socks does Carl have?
How many socks does Ali have?

Think About It

1. You will find out how many socks Carl and Ali have ______.
   - ○ altogether ○ each ○ left over

2. Mark the **two** number sentences that have the same sum.
   - ○ 8 + 4 = ? ○ 8 + 8 = ? ○ 4 + 8 = ?

Solve the Problem

3. Use this work space.

4. Carl has ______ socks.

5. Ali has ______ socks.

Check Your Work

6. Do your answers make sense? ○ yes ○ no

When you add three or more numbers, you can change the grouping.

$$4 + 1 + 5 = 10$$

These are some ways to show how grouping can be changed:

a

$$(4 + 1) + 5 = 10$$

$$5 + 5 = 10$$

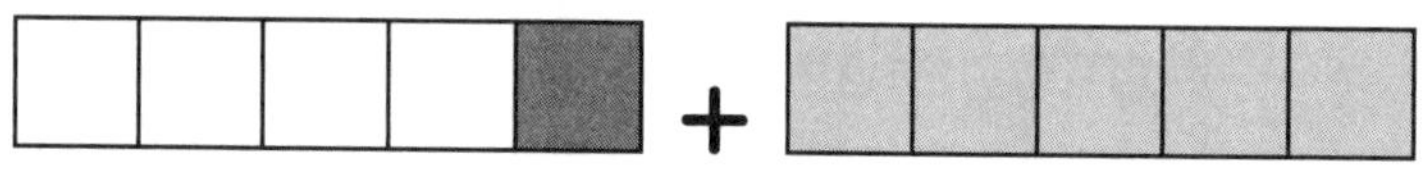

b

$$4 + (1 + 5) = 10$$

$$4 + 6 = 10$$

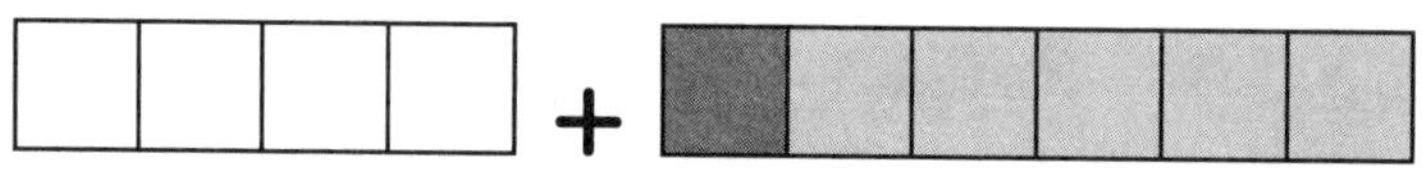

c

$$4 + 1 + 5 = 10$$

$$1 + 9 = 10$$

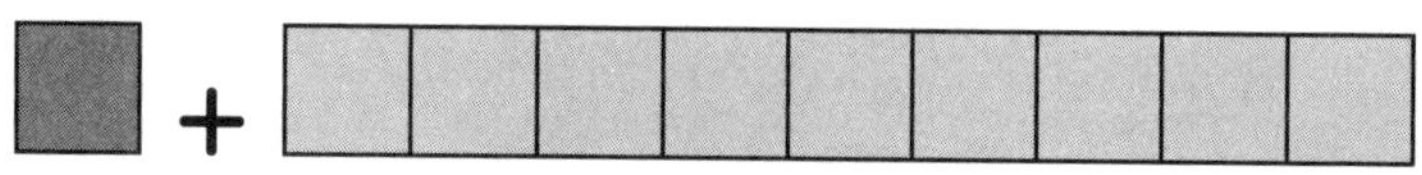

Look at **a**, **b**, **c**. Explain which grouping you would choose to solve this problem.

Name ______________________________

Add. Then add again in a different order.

Example

$(3 + 7) + 4 =$?
$10 + 4 =$ 14

$3 + (7 + 4) =$?
$3 + 11 =$ 14

❶ $5 + (10 + 2) =$ ____ $(5 + 10) + 2 =$ ____

❷ $(15 + 5) + 0 =$ ____ $15 + (5 + 0) =$ ____

❸ $20 + (5 + 5) =$ ____ $(20 + 5) + 5 =$ ____

❹ $(80 + 0) + 1 =$ ____ $80 + (0 + 1) =$ ____

Add. Draw a line around the numbers you chose to add first.

1. 10 + (4 + 5) = ____

2. 7 + 3 + 7 = ____

3. 8 + 3 + 6 = ____

4. 9 + 1 + 5 = ____

5. 2 + 8 + 10 = ____

6. 20 + 10 + 30 = ____

Name ______________________________

Read the Problem

The kids saw 6 tigers, 4 bears, and 8 zebras at the zoo.
How many animals did the kids see?

Think About It

1. You will find out how many _____ were seen.
   - ○ animals ○ zoos ○ lions
2. Mark the grouping you like best.
   - ○ $(6 + 4) + 8 = ?$ ○ $6 + (4 + 8) = ?$ ○ $(6 + 8) + 4 = ?$

Solve the Problem

3. Use this work space.

4. The kids saw _____ animals.

Check Your Work

5. Do your answers make sense? ○ yes ○ no

Math Models

Using the unknown addend

You can solve a subtraction problem by finding the unknown addend.

$10 - 6 = ?$ ← unknown addend

Related addition fact ⟶ $6 + ? = 10$

↑ unknown addend

These are two ways to find the **unknown addend**:

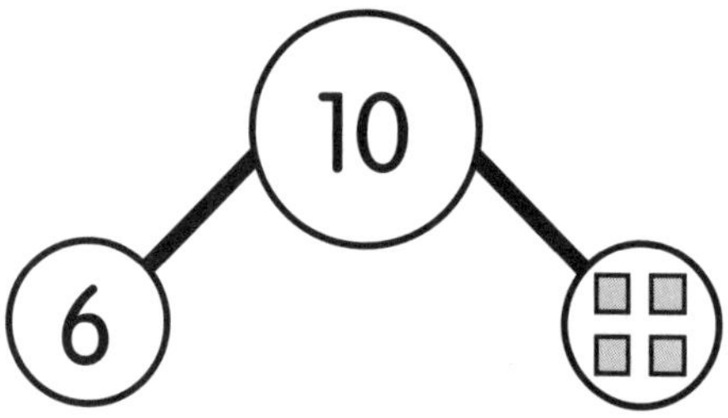

unknown addend

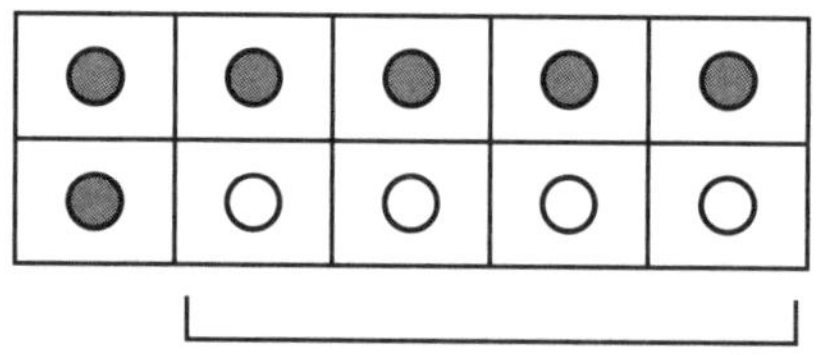

unknown addend

If $6 + \underline{4} = 10$, then $10 - 6 = \underline{4}$.

Maya says that the number sentence **7 + 8 = 15** can help her solve **15 – ? = 7**. Do you agree? Explain your thinking.

Name ______________________

Find the unknown addend first. Then use the unknown addend to help you find the difference.

Example

First, add. $3 + \underline{10} = 13$

Then subtract. $13 - 3 = \underline{10}$

1. First, add.

   $7 + \_\_\_\_ = 15$

   Then subtract.

   $15 - 7 = \_\_\_\_$

2. First, add.

   $\_\_\_\_ + 9 = 20$

   Then subtract.

   $20 - 9 = \_\_\_\_$

3. First, add.

   $\_\_\_\_ + 5 = 12$

   Then subtract.

   $12 - 5 = \_\_\_\_$

4. First, add.

   $10 + \_\_\_\_ = 40$

   Then subtract.

   $40 - 10 = \_\_\_\_$

Name ____________________

Find the unknown addend.
Use the unknown addend to help you find the difference.

1. Add. $7 + \_\_\_ = 17$ Subtract. $17 - 7 = \_\_\_$

2. Add. $\_\_\_ + 6 = 15$ Subtract. $15 - \_\_\_ = 6$

3. Add. $11 + \_\_\_ = 20$ Subtract. $20 - 11 = \_\_\_$

4. Add. $\_\_\_ + 20 = 30$ Subtract. $30 - \_\_\_ = 20$

5. Add. $20 + 80 = \_\_\_$ Subtract. $80 = 100 - \_\_\_$

Name ____________________

Mark the addition number sentence that can help you solve each subtraction number sentence. Then write the answer.

Example

$15 - 5 =$ 10

○ $15 + 5 = 20$
● $10 + 5 = 15$

❶ $21 - 1 =$ ____

○ $1 + 20 = 21$
○ $10 + 11 = 21$

❷ $18 - 9 =$ ____

○ $9 + 9 = 18$
○ $6 + 3 = 9$

❸ $14 - 8 =$ ____

○ $4 + 4 = 8$
○ $8 + 6 = 14$

❹ $50 - 10 =$ ____

○ $50 + 10 = 60$
○ $10 + 40 = 50$

Understand subtraction as an unknown-addend problem.

Name ________________________________

Read the Problem

Cam saw 13 books on the table. She put 6 of them away. How many books were left on the table?

Think About It

1. Mark the subtraction number sentence that tells about the problem.

   ○ $6 - 3 = ?$ ○ $13 - 6 = ?$ ○ $31 - 6 = ?$

2. Mark the addition number sentence that can help you.

   ○ $13 + 6 = 19$ ○ $13 + 7 = 20$ ○ $6 + 7 = 13$

Solve the Problem

3. Use this work space.

4. _____ books were left on the table.

Check Your Work

5. Do your answers make sense? ○ yes ○ no

Add and Subtract Within 20

Unit Contents

Math Process Skills in This Unit

Make sense of problems and persevere in solving them: *pages 55, 59, 63, 67, 72*

Reason abstractly and quantitatively: *pages 52, 53, 54, 55, 56, 57, 58, 59, 60, 61, 62, 63, 64, 65, 66, 67, 68, 69, 70, 71, 72*

Construct viable arguments and critique the reasoning of others: *pages 52, 56, 60, 64, 68*

Model with mathematics: *pages 52, 53, 54, 55, 56, 57, 58, 59, 60, 61, 62, 63, 64, 65, 66, 67, 68, 69, 70, 71, 72*

Attend to precision: *pages 52, 53, 54, 55, 56, 57, 58, 59, 60, 61, 62, 63, 64, 65, 66, 67, 68, 69, 70, 71, 72*

Look for and make use of structure: *pages 52, 53, 56, 57, 60, 61, 64, 65, 68, 69*

You can count on to add small numbers such as 1, 2, or 3.

$$11 + 3 = ?$$

These are some ways to **count on**:

You can use a diagram.

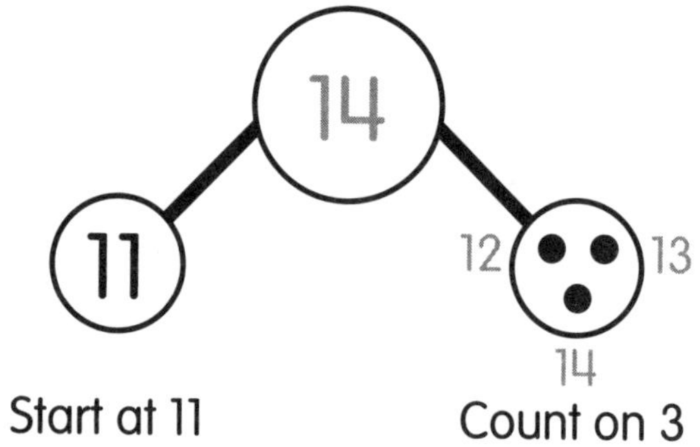

You can draw counters.

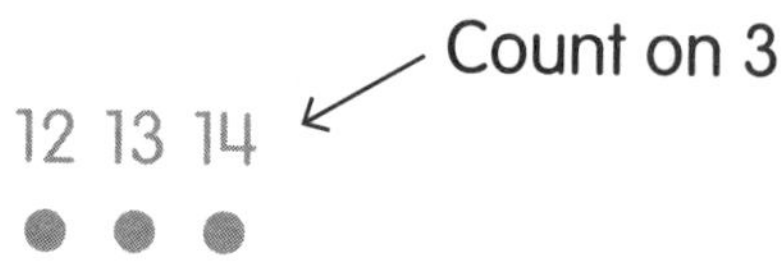

$11 + 3 =$ 14

Start at 11

You can use a number line.

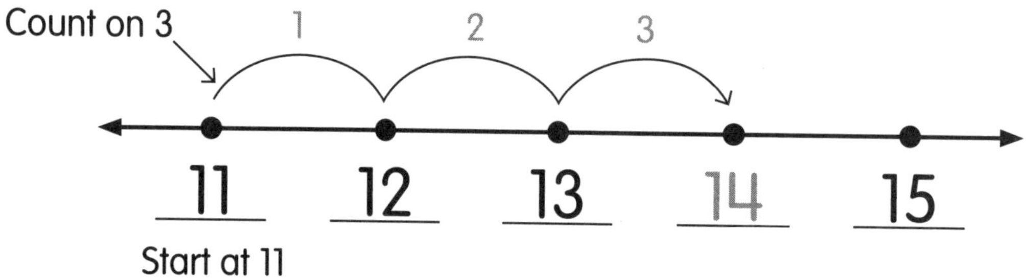

Kris wants to add **17 + 2 = ?** She made a number line that starts with **2**. Do you agree? Explain your thinking.

Name ____________________

Look at each number sentence. Show one way to solve with counting on.

Example

$9 + 2 = ?$

Use a diagram.	Draw counters.	Use a number line.
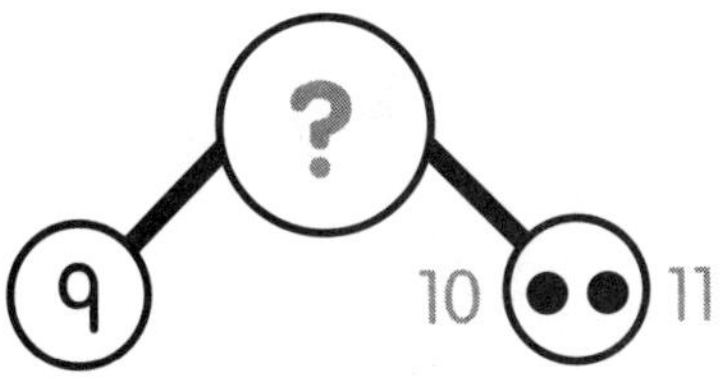	10 11 ● ● $9 + 2 =$ 11	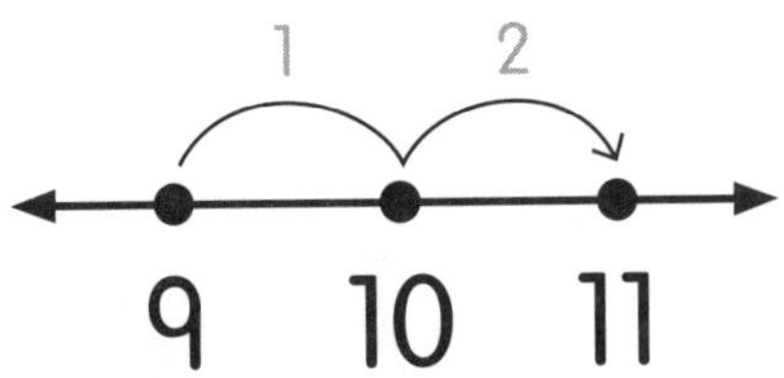

❶ $7 + 1 =$ ____

❸ $10 + 2 =$ ____

❷ $12 + 3 =$ ____

❹ $2 + 14 =$ ____

Relate counting to addition.
Use counting on to add.

Name ____________________

Look at each number sentence. Show one way to solve with counting on.

1. $8 + 3 =$ ____

4. $6 + 3 =$ ____

2. $2 + 17 =$ ____

5. $13 + 1 =$ ____

3. $15 + 1 =$ ____

6. $18 + 2 =$ ____

Relate counting to addition.
Use counting on to add.

Name ______________________________

Read the Problem

Dad ate 7 grapes.
Then he ate 2 more.
How many grapes did Dad eat?

Think About It

1. You will find out how many grapes Dad ____.
   ○ picked ○ gave away ○ ate

2. To solve the problem, you will ____.
   ○ count on from 7 ○ count on from 2

Solve the Problem

3. Use this work space.

4. Dad ate ____ grapes.

Check Your Work

5. Do your answers make sense? ○ yes ○ no

Relate counting to addition.
Use counting on to add.

Math Models

Counting back to subtract

You can count back to subtract small numbers such as 1, 2, or 3.

$$18 - 2 = ?$$

These are some ways to **count back**:

You can use a diagram.

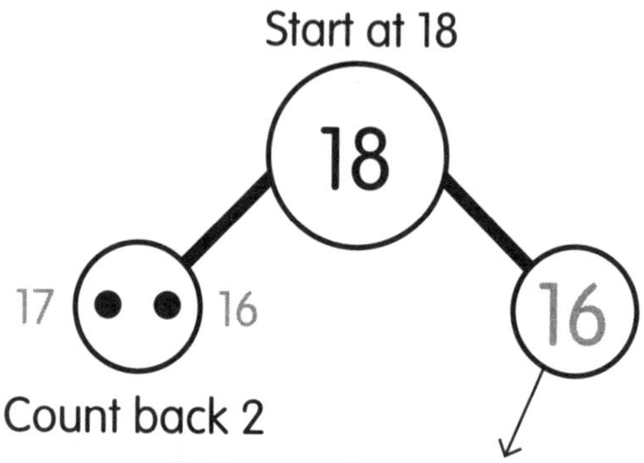

$18 - 2 = 16$

You can draw counters.

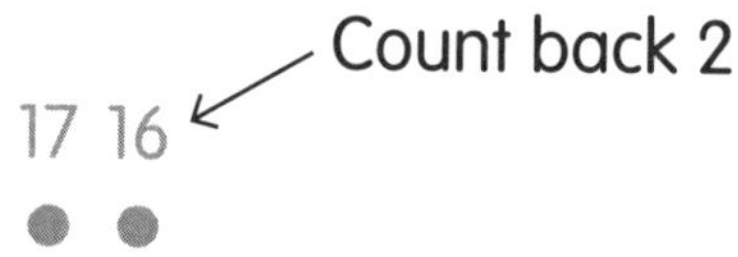

$18 - 2 =$ 16

Start at 18

You can use a number line.

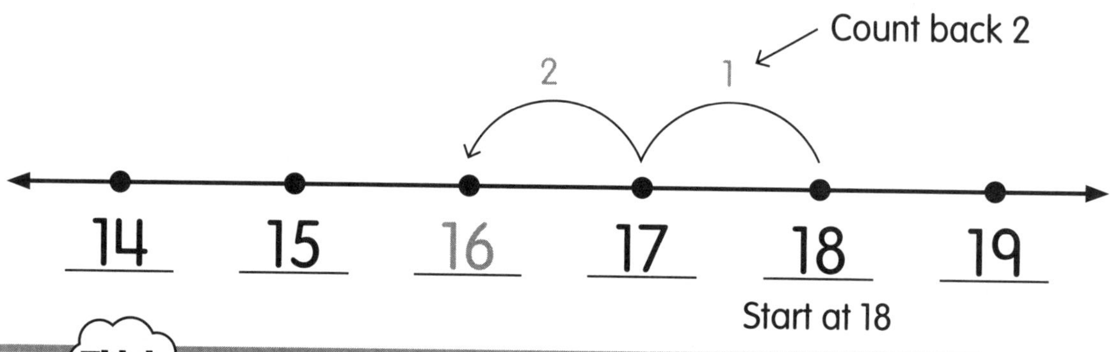

Maria wants to solve **20 – 3 = ?** She counts back, saying, "**19, 18, 17**." Then she says, "I know that **20 – 3 = 17**!" Do you agree? Explain your thinking.

Name ______________________________

Look at each number sentence. Show one way to solve with counting back.

Example

$8 - 3 = ?$

Use a diagram.

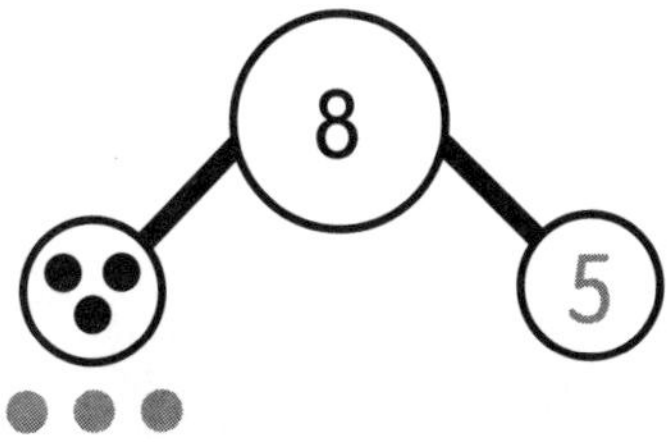

7 6 5 ← Count back 3

Draw counters.

Count back 3
7 6 5
● ● ●

$8 - 3 = \underline{5}$

Use a number line.

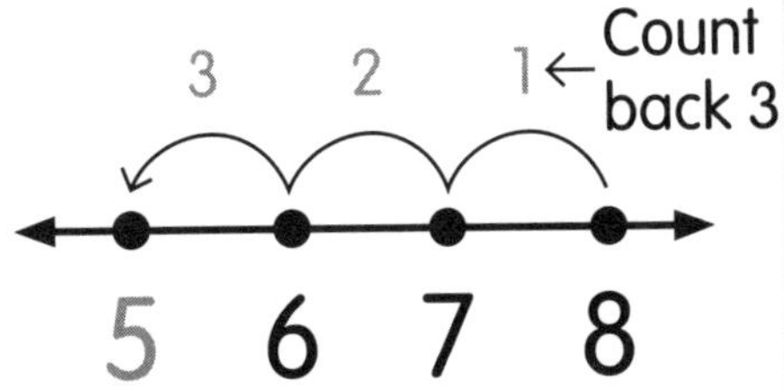

❶ $9 - 1 =$ ____

❸ $11 - 2 =$ ____

❷ $15 - 3 =$ ____

❹ $20 - 1 =$ ____

Name ____________________

Look at each number sentence. Show one way to solve with counting back.

1. $12 - 1 =$ ____
2. $18 - 3 =$ ____
3. $14 - 2 =$ ____
4. $13 - 2 =$ ____
5. $16 - 1 =$ ____
6. $17 - 3 =$ ____

Name ____________________

Read the Problem

Jan had 12 pencils.
She gave 2 pencils to Kai.
How many pencils did Jan have left?

Think About It

1. You will find out how many pencils Jan ____.
   - ○ gave to Kai
   - ○ had left
   - ○ will get

2. To solve the problem, you will ____.
   - ○ count back from 2
   - ○ count back from 12

Solve the Problem

3. Use this work space.

4. Jan had ____ pencils left.

Check Your Work

5. Do your answers make sense? ○ yes ○ no

Math Models

Making a ten

You can make a ten to help you add.

$$4 + 7 = ?$$

These are two ways to **make a ten**:

Use a ten frame.

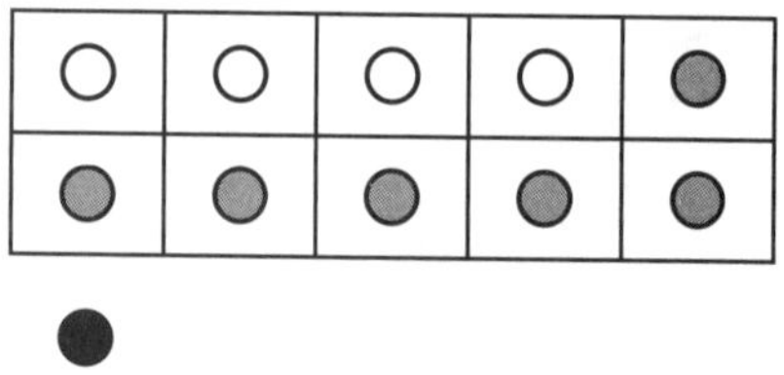

$$(4 + 6) + 1 = 11$$

$$4 + 7 = 11$$

Draw a chart.

$$4 + 7 = ?$$

$$1 + (3 + 7) = ?$$

10

$$1 + 10 = 11$$

How can you make a ten to solve **11 + 5**?
Explain your thinking. Draw your answer below.

Name ______________________________

Look at each number sentence. Show one way to solve by making a ten.

Example

$8 + 5 = ?$

Use a ten frame.

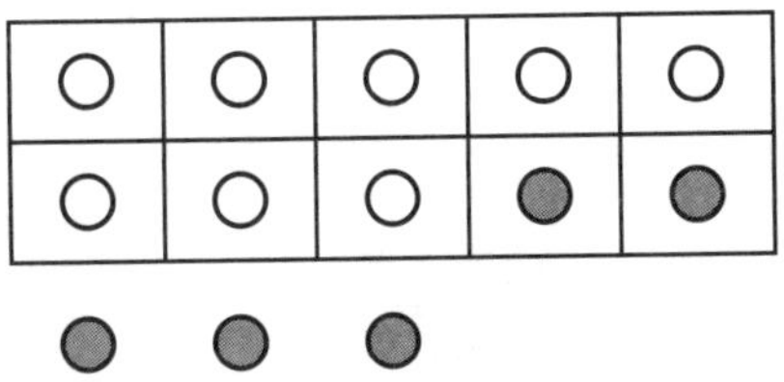

$8 + 5 = ?$

$(8 + 2) + 3 = 13$

Draw a chart.

$8 + 5 = ?$

$\underbrace{(8 + 2)}_{10} + 3 = 13$

❶ $6 + 7 =$ ____

❷ $9 + 4 =$ ____

❸ $7 + 8 =$ ____

❹ $5 + 11 =$ ____

Look at each number sentence. Show one way to solve by making a ten.

1. $5 + 9 =$ ____

2. $6 + 5 =$ ____

3. $11 + 3 =$ ____

4. $12 + 7 =$ ____

5. $8 + 9 =$ ____

6. $13 + 6 =$ ____

Name ______________________

Read the Problem

Ron likes hats.
He has 7 baseball caps.
He has 6 cowboy hats.
How many hats does Ron have?

Think About It

1. You will find out how many hats Ron ____.
   ○ lost ○ has ○ gave away

2. Mark the number sentence that makes a ten to add.
   ○ (7 + 3) + 3 ○ (7 + 4) + 2 ○ (7 + 5) + 1

Solve the Problem

3. Use this work space.

4. Ron has ____ hats.

Check Your Work

5. Do your answers make sense? ○ yes ○ no

Use making a ten as a strategy to add.

You can take a number apart, leading to a ten to help you subtract.

$$15 - 8 = ?$$

These are two ways to **lead to a ten**:

Use a ten frame.

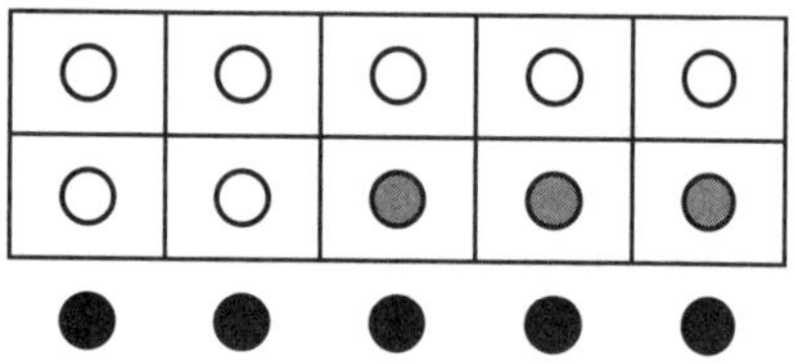

$$(15 - 5) - 3 = 7$$

$$15 - 8 = 7$$

Draw a chart.

$$15 - 8 = ?$$

$$(15 - 5) - 3 = ?$$

10

$$10 - 3 = 7$$

If you solve **13 – 5**, how can you lead to a ten? Explain your thinking.

Name ______________________

Look at each number sentence. Show one way to lead to a ten to subtract.

Example

$13 - 4 = ?$

Use a ten frame.

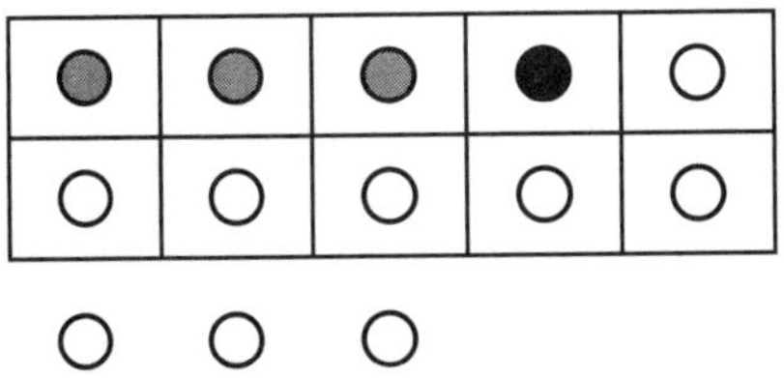

$(13 - 3) - 1 = 9$

$13 - 4 = 9$

Draw a chart.

$13 - 4 = ?$

$(13 - 3) - 1 = 9$

10

$10 - 1 = 9$

1. $12 - 5 =$ ____

3. $11 - 3 =$ ____

2. $15 - 6 =$ ____

4. $14 - 9 =$ ____

Name ____________________

Look at each number sentence. Show one way to subtract by leading to a ten.

1. $13 - 7 =$ ____

4. $16 - 7 =$ ____

2. $17 - 8 =$ ____

5. $11 - 4 =$ ____

3. $15 - 9 =$ ____

6. $12 - 4 =$ ____

 Use decomposing a number leading to a ten to subtract.

Name ______________________________

Read the Problem

16 children were painting.
Then 9 of them went out to play.
How many children were still painting?

Think About It

1. You will find out how many children were ____.
   - ○ still painting ○ still playing ○ painting outside

2. Mark the number sentence that leads to a ten.
   - ○ (16 – 4) – 5 = ? ○ (16 – 5) – 4 = ? ○ (16 – 6) – 3 = ?

Solve the Problem

3. Use this work space.

4. ____ children were still painting.

Check Your Work

5. Do your answers make sense? ○ yes ○ no

Math Models

Using equivalent or known sums

You can use a math fact you already know to help you add or subtract.

These are some examples:

Use doubles + 1.

7 + 8 = ?

I know 7 + 7 = 14.
So, 7 + (7 + 1) = 15.

7 + 8 = 15

Use an easier math fact.

7 + 9 = ?

I know 7 + 10 = 17.
So, 7 + (10 – 1)= 16.

7 + 9 = 16

Think addition.

13 – 6 = ?

I know 6 + 6 = 12.
So, 6 + (6 + 1) = 13.

13 – 6 = 7

Use an easier difference.

16 – 5 = ?

I know 15 – 5 = 10.
So, (15 + 1) – 5 = 11.

16 – 5 = 11

Think of a math fact you already know that can help you solve **17 – 8 = ?** Explain your thinking.

Name ____________________

Look at each number sentence. Use a math fact that you already know to help you solve it.

Example

$9 + 8 = ?$

I know $10 + 8 = 18$.
So, $(10 - 1) + 8 = 17$.

$9 + 8 = \underline{17}$

$14 - 8 = ?$

I know $14 - 7 = 7$.
So, $14 - (7 + 1) = 6$.

$14 - 8 = \underline{6}$

1. $6 + 7 = ?$

   I know
   So,

   $6 + 7 =$ ____

2. $15 - 9 = ?$

   I know
   So,

   $15 - 9 =$ ____

Name ____________________

Look at each number sentence. Use a math fact that you already know to help you solve it.

❶ $6 + 5 = ?$

I know $5 + 5 = 10$
So, $(5 + 1) + 5 = 11$

$6 + 5 =$ ____

❷ $9 + ? = 16$

I know
So,

$9 +$ ____ $= 16$

❸ $14 - 6 = ?$

I know
So,

$14 - 6 =$ ____

❹ $19 - 8 = ?$

I know
So,

$19 - 8 =$ ____

Name ____________________

Write the missing number to complete each number sentence.
Mark the number sentence that can help you solve it.

Example

6 + 7 = 13

● 6 + 6 = 12
○ 13 + 7 = 20

❶ 15 − ____ = 8

○ 7 + 8 = 15
○ 7 + 1 = 8

❷ ____ + 9 = 17

○ 9 + 3 = 12
○ 8 + 8 = 16

❸ 5 + 6 = ____

○ 5 + 5 = 10
○ 5 + 1 = 6

❹ 20 − ____ = 9

○ 4 + 5 = 9
○ 10 + 10 = 20

Name ______________________________

Read the Problem

Mom picked 12 apples.
She used 7 apples to make a pie.
How many apples were left?

Think About It

1. You will find out how many apples were _____.

   ○ used ○ left ○ picked

2. Mark **two** number sentences that can help you.

   ○ 12 + 7 = 19 ○ 6 + 6 = 12 ○ 12 − 6 = 6

Solve the Problem

3. Use this work space.

4. _____ apples were left.

Check Your Work

5. Do your answers make sense? ○ yes ○ no

Equivalency and Unknown Numbers

Unit Contents

Math Process Skills in This Unit

Make sense of problems and persevere in solving them: *pages 77, 82*

Reason abstractly and quantitatively: *pages 74, 75, 76, 77, 78, 79, 80, 81, 82*

Construct viable arguments and critique the reasoning of others: *pages 74, 78*

Model with mathematics: *pages 77, 82*

Attend to precision: *pages 74, 77, 78, 82*

Look for and make use of structure: *pages 74, 75, 76, 77, 78, 79, 80, 81, 82*

You can find out if addition or subtraction number sentences are true or false.

Numbers on both sides of = should have the same value.

These are some examples:

True

$3 = 3$

$6 = 7 - 1$

$6 = 6$

$5 + 3 = 4 + 4$

$8 = 8$

False

$3 = 4$

$6 = 7 + 1$

$6 = 8$

$5 + 3 = 4 + 6$

$8 = 10$

Is **7 + 2 = 6 + 3** true or false? Explain your thinking.

Name ____________________

Look at each number sentence.

Circle true ☺ or false ☹.

Example

$12 = 6 + 7$

$12 = 13$

true ☺ | false ☹ (circled)

❶ $15 = 15$

true ☺ | false ☹

---

❷ $5 + 8 = 4 + 10$

true ☺ | false ☹

---

❸ $18 - 9 = 6 + 3$

true ☺ | false ☹

Understand the meaning of the equal sign.
Determine if addition or subtraction equations are true or false.

Name ____________________

Look at each number sentence.
Circle true or false.

❶ 16 = 61 — true / false

❷ 2 + 11 = 11 + 2 — true / false

❸ 5 + 2 = 17 − 10 — true / false

❹ 8 + 6 = 7 + 7 — true / false

Understand the meaning of the equal sign.
Determine if addition or subtraction equations are true or false.

Name ______________________________

Read the Problem

Pat has 3 pink shirts and 4 white shirts.
Fran has 5 pink shirts and 2 white shirts.
Do Pat and Fran have the same number of shirts?

Think About It

1. You will find out if Pat and Fran have ______.

   ○ more pink than white shirts ○ the same number of shirts

2. Mark the number sentence that tells about the problem.

   ○ $3 + 4 = 5 - 2$ ○ $3 + 4 = 5 + 2$ ○ $4 - 3 = 5 - 2$

Solve the Problem

3. Use this work space.

4. Pat and Fran have the same number of shirts.

   ○ yes ○ no

Check Your Work

5. Do your answers make sense? ○ yes ○ no

Understand the meaning of the equal sign.
Determine if addition or subtraction equations are true or false.

You can find the unknown number to make a number sentence that is true.

$$? + 4 = 7$$

Both sides of = need the same value.

These are some ways to find an unknown number to make a true number sentence:

You can take apart the sum.

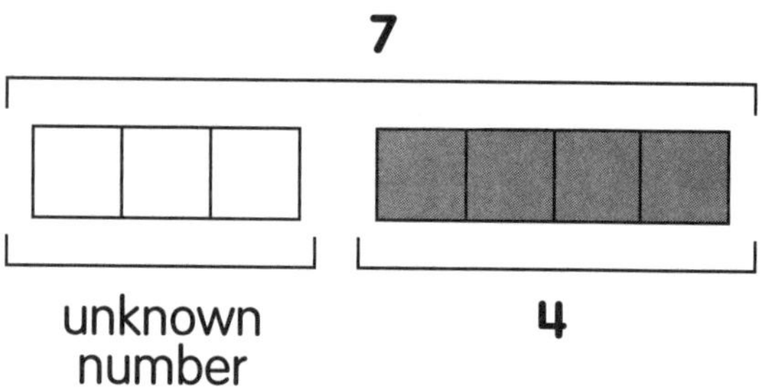

You can use a diagram.

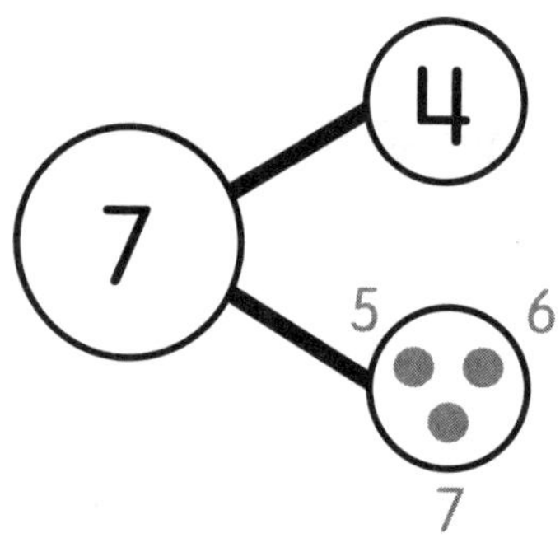

Count on from 4

3 is the unknown number

$$3 + 4 = 7$$

$7 = 7$ is true. ☺

Think of **11 + 9 = ?** Which is true: **11 + 9 = 19** or **11 + 9 = 20**? Explain your thinking.

Name ______________________________

Mark the number that makes each number sentence true.
Show your work.

Example

$6 + \underline{\ ?\ } = 14$

● 8 ○ 9

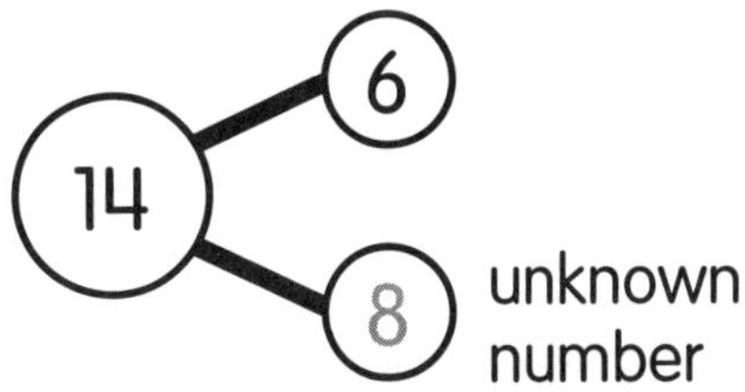

Work Space

❶ $\underline{\ ?\ } + 7 = 11$

○ 3 ○ 4

❷ $8 + 9 = \underline{\ ?\ }$

○ 17 ○ 18

❸ $10 = 15 - \underline{\ ?\ }$

○ 4 ○ 5

Determine the unknown whole number to make a true equation.

Name ______________________________

Mark the number that makes each number sentence true.
Show your work.

	Work Space
❶ 3 + __?__ = 15 ○ 11 ○ 12	
❷ 19 = __?__ + 8 ○ 10 ○ 11	
❸ __?__ + 7 = 12 ○ 5 ○ 6	
❹ 6 + 5 = __?__ ○ 10 ○ 11	

Name ____________________

Equivalency and Unknown Numbers
Finding unknown numbers

5

Write the unknown number that makes each number sentence true.
Mark the model that tells about the number sentence.

Example

6 + <u>4</u> = 10

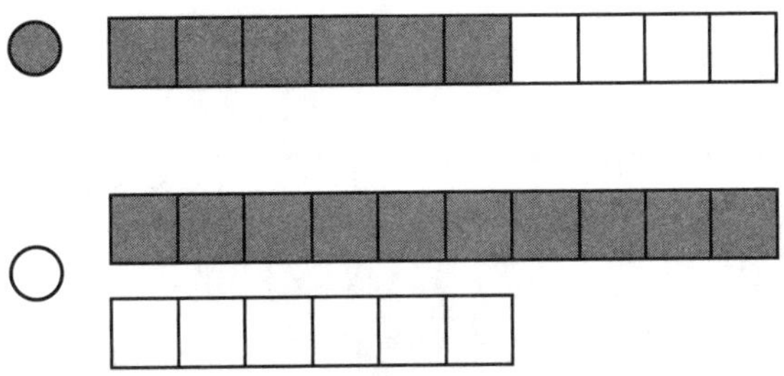

1. ____ + 11 = 16

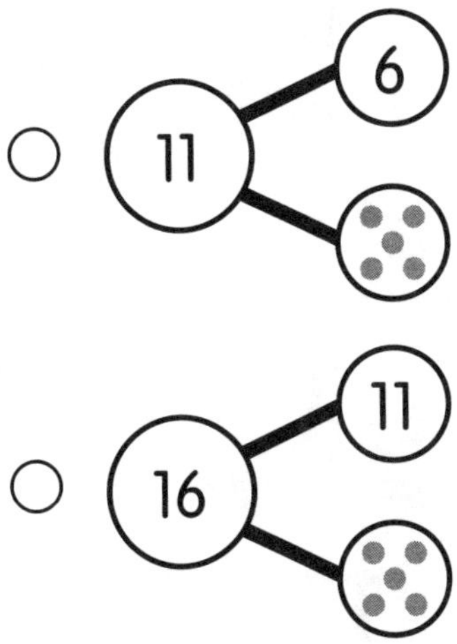

2. 15 – 9 = ____

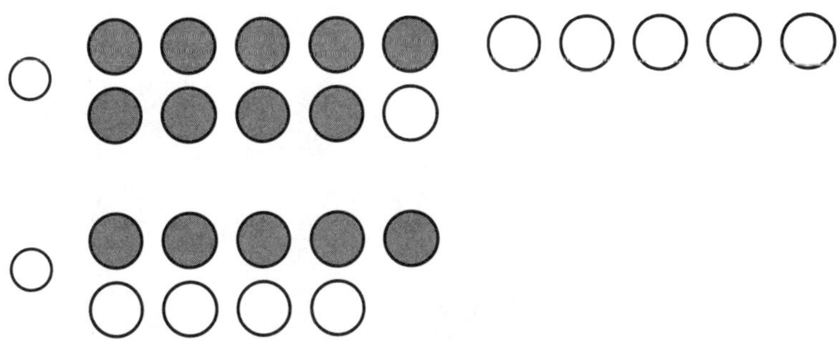

3. 20 = ____ + 8

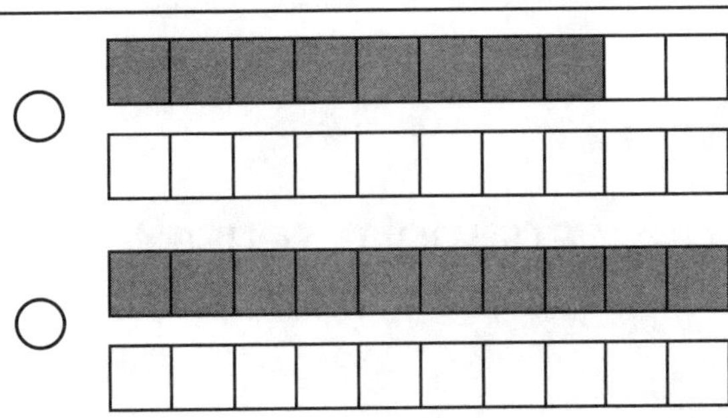

Determine the unknown whole number to make a true equation.

Name ______________________________

Read the Problem

Travis had 12 rocks in his pocket. Some rocks fell out. Travis had 7 rocks left. How many rocks fell out?

Think About It

1. You will find out how many rocks ____.

   ○ fell out ○ Travis had ○ in all

2. Mark **two** number sentences that are true.

   ○ 12 = 7 + 5 ○ 12 + 5 = 16 ○ 12 – 5 = 7

Solve the Problem

3. Use this work space.

4. ____ rocks fell out.

Check Your Work

5. Do your answers make sense? ○ yes ○ no

 Determine the unknown whole number to make a true equation.

Counting and Number Sequences

Unit Contents

Math Process Skills in This Unit

Make sense of problems and persevere in solving them: *pages 88, 92, 96, 100, 104*

Reason abstractly and quantitatively: *pages 84, 85, 86, 87, 88, 89, 90, 91, 92, 93, 94, 95, 96, 97, 98, 99, 100, 101, 102, 103, 104*

Construct viable arguments and critique the reasoning of others: *pages 84, 89, 93, 97, 101*

Model with mathematics: *pages 84, 85, 86, 87, 88, 89, 90, 91, 92, 93, 94, 95, 96, 97, 98, 99, 100, 101, 102, 103, 104*

Attend to precision: *pages 84, 85, 86, 87, 88, 89, 90, 91, 92, 93, 94, 95, 96, 97, 98, 99, 100, 101, 102, 103, 104*

Look for and make use of structure: *pages 84, 85, 86, 87, 88, 89, 90, 91, 92, 93, 94, 95, 96, 97, 98, 99, 100, 101, 102, 103, 104*

Look for and express regularity in repeated reasoning: *pages 84, 85, 86, 87, 89, 90, 91, 92, 93, 94, 95, 96, 97, 98, 99, 100, 101, 102, 103, 104*

You can count to tell how many.

These are some ways you can count things that are real:

You can draw a picture.

You can use a chart.

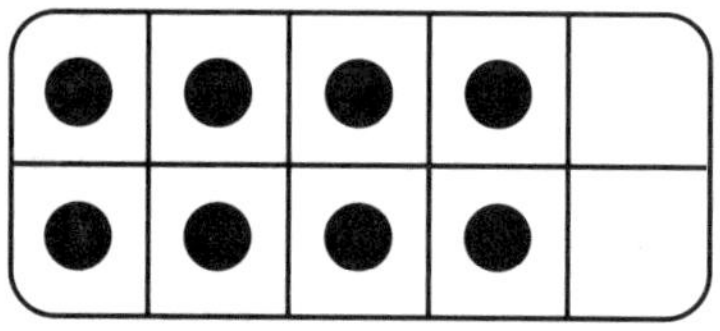

You can use a number line.

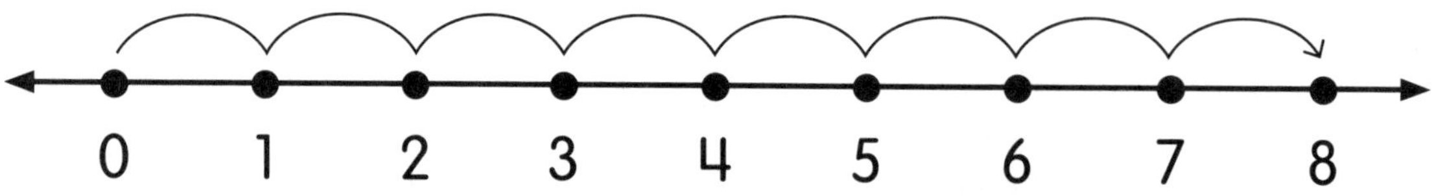

Ben says it is easier to draw ● than  to show **8**.
Do you agree? Explain your thinking.

Name ___________________________

Show some ways to count things.

Examples

Count to 13.

Draw a picture.

Draw a chart.

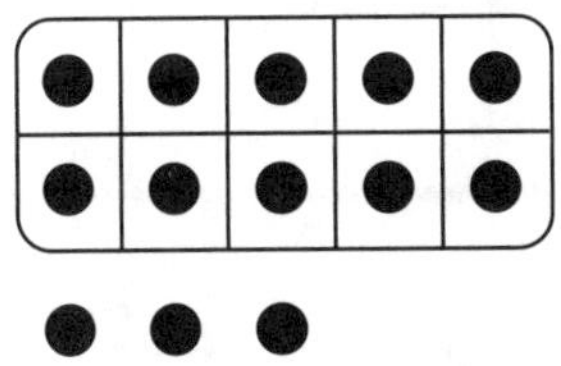

Draw a number line.

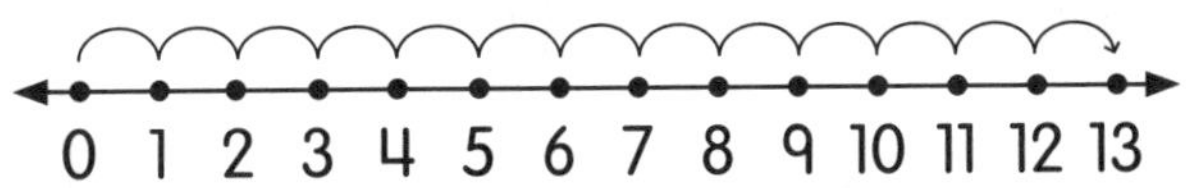

Count to 20.

1. Draw a picture.

2. Draw a chart.

3. Draw a number line.

Name ____________________

Count how many. Write the number.

1 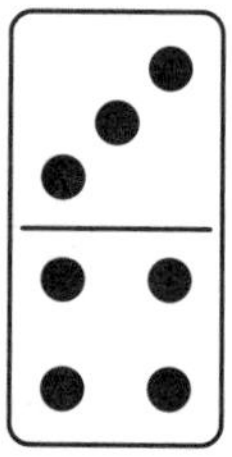

____ dots

2 

____ butterflies

3 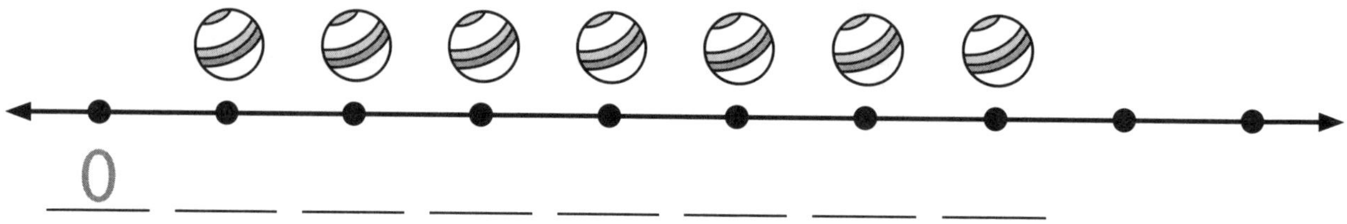

____ balls

4 

____ hearts

5 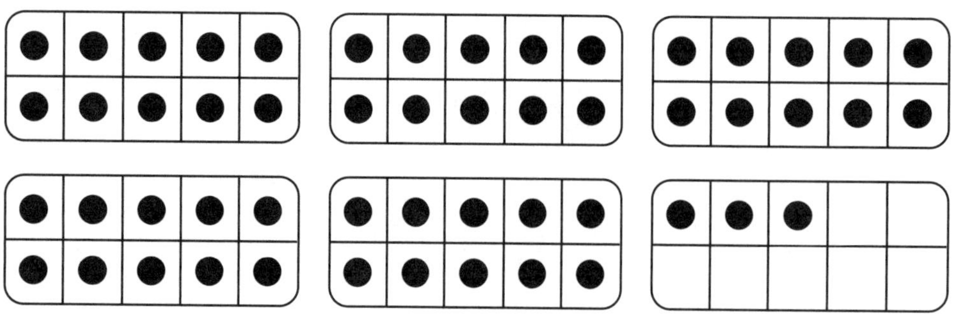

____ dots

Count objects.
Read and write numerals that represent a number of objects.

Name ______________________

Look at the picture next to each item. Count how many in the picture above. Color or mark each item you count. Write the number on the line.

1.  ______

4. 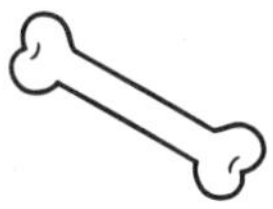 ______

2.  ______

5. 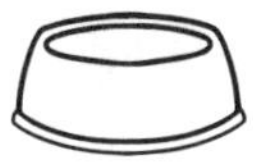 ______

3.  ______

6.  ______

Count objects.
Read and write numerals that represent a number of objects.

Name ______________________________

Read the Problem

Count the chairs in your classroom.
Draw a model in the work space below.
Write the number that tells how many.

Think About It

❶ The problem says to _____.
○ sit on the chairs ○ count the chairs

❷ What kind of model will you draw?
○ picture ○ chart ○ number line ○ other

Solve the Problem

❸ Use this work space.

❹ There are _____ chairs.

Check Your Work

❺ Do your answers make sense? ○ yes ○ no

Count objects.
Read and write numerals that represent a number of objects.

Math Models

Counting on: 1 to 50

You can count on from any number.

You know that 20 cars are in the box. You can count on from 20 to find out how many cars there are.

These are some ways to **count on**:

You can use cubes.

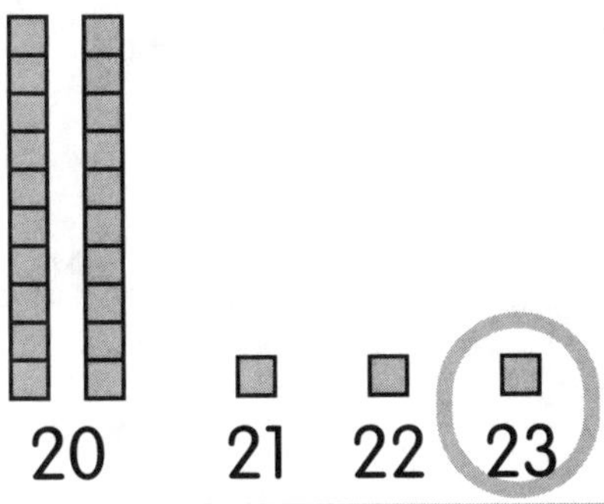

You can use a chart.

1	2	3	4	5	6	7	8	9	10
11	12	13	14	15	16	17	18	19	20
21	22	23	24	25	26	27	28	29	30
31	32	33	34	35	36	37	38	39	40
	42			45			48		50

You can use a number line.

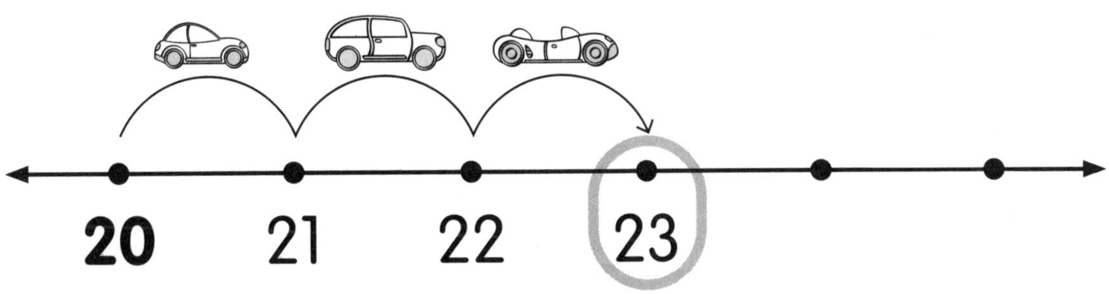

Think about a time you can use **counting on**.

Count, starting with any number.
Represent a number of objects with a numeral.

Name ______________________

Count on to tell how many. Write the numbers.

Examples

10 11 12 13

13 marbles

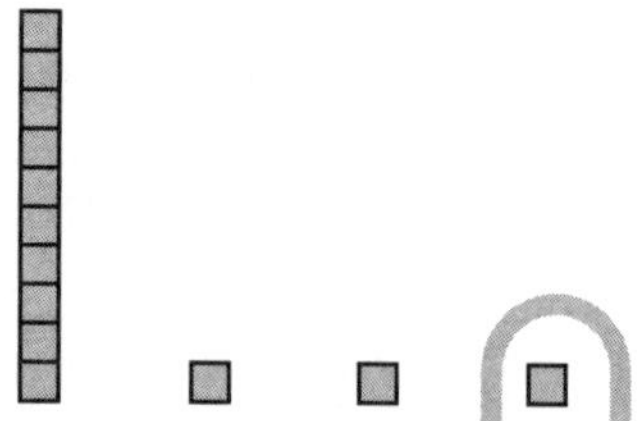

10 11 12 13

13 marbles

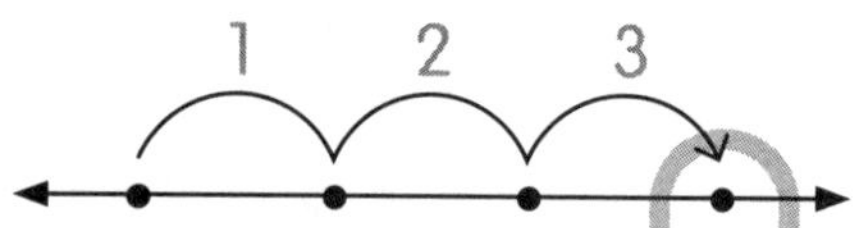

10 11 12 13

13 marbles

1

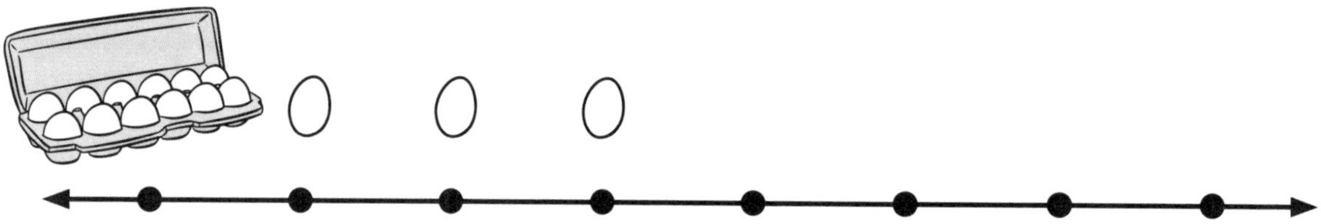

12 ____ ____ ____

____ eggs

2

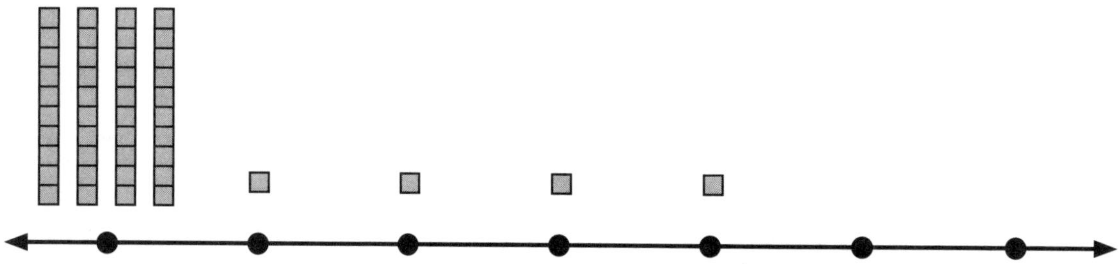

40 ____ ____ ____ ____

____ cubes

3

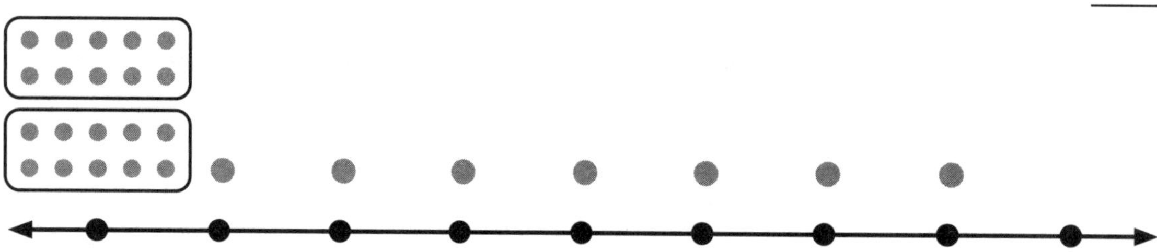

20 ____ ____ ____ ____ ____ ____ ____

____ dots

Count, starting with any number.
Represent a number of objects with a numeral.

Name ______________________________

Count on to tell how many. Write the numbers.

1

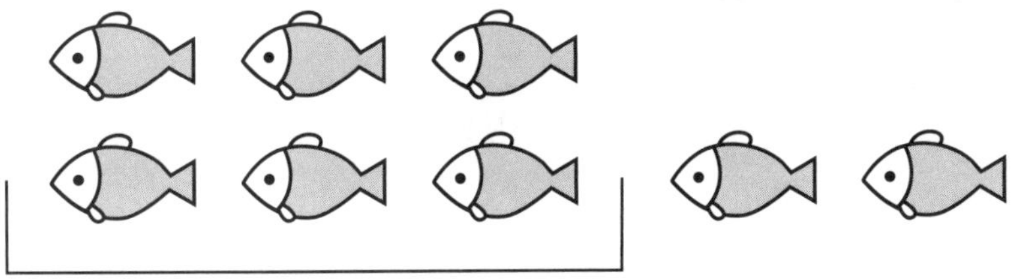

6 ____ ____ ____ fish

2

10 ____ ____ ____ ____ ____ cups

3

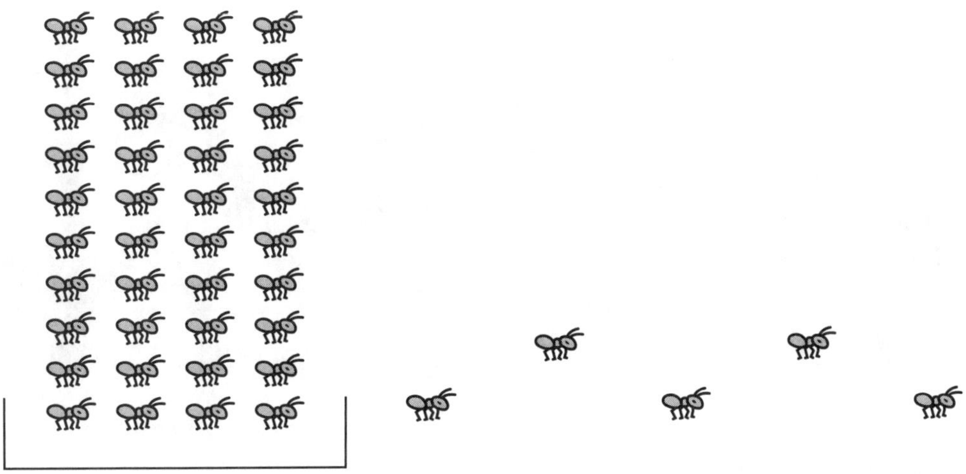

40 ____ ____ ____ ____ ____ ____ ants

Count, starting with any number.
Represent a number of objects with a numeral.

Name ______________________

Read the Problem

A frog needs help finding its pond. Count on from 4.
Write the missing numbers from 1 to 50.

Think About It

1. The problem says to ______.
   ○ count on from 1 ○ count on from 4

2. You will write the missing numbers. ○ yes ○ no

Solve the Problem

3.

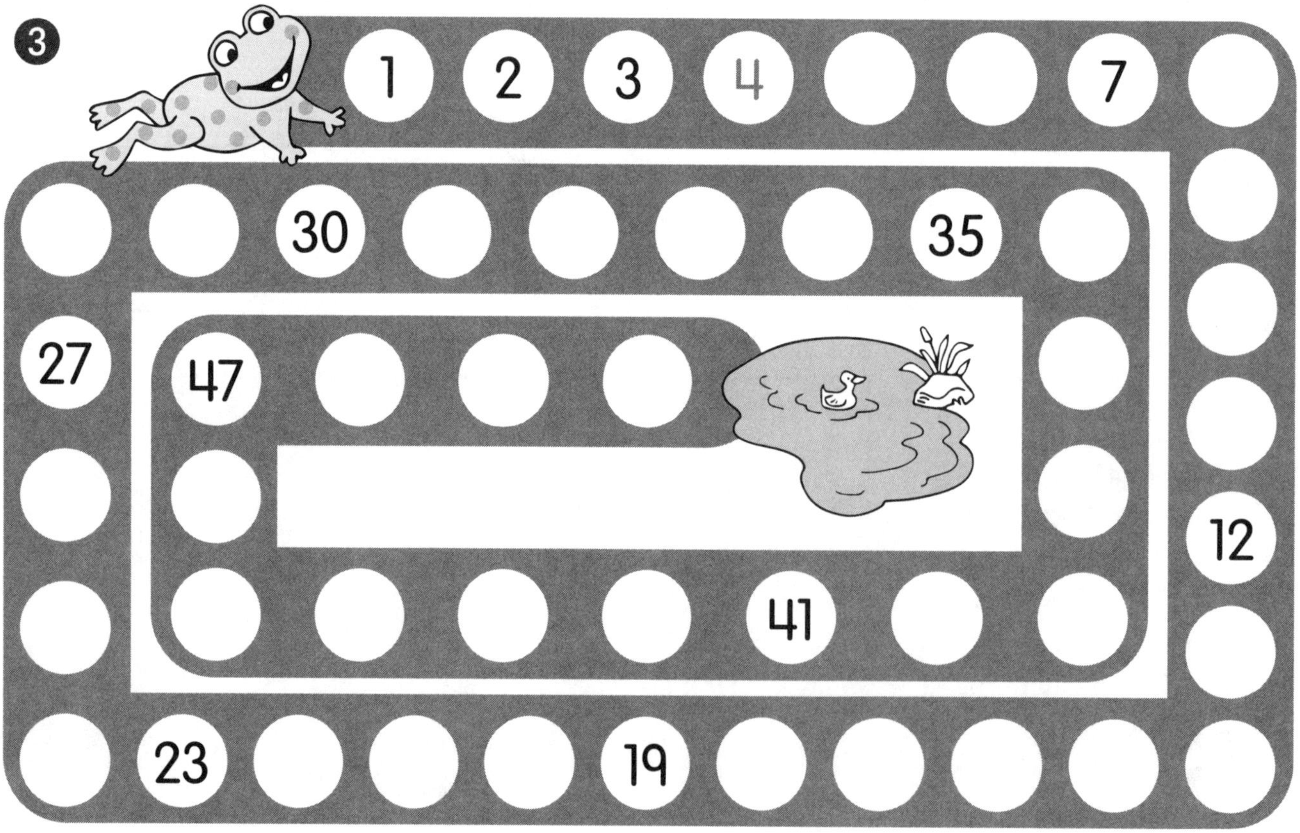

Check Your Work

4. Do your answers make sense? ○ yes ○ no

Count, starting with any number.
Represent a number of objects with a numeral.

Math Models

Counting on: 51 to 120

You can count on from a large number.

You know there are 60 apples. You can count on from 60 to find out how many apples there are.

These are some ways to **count on**:

You can use cubes.

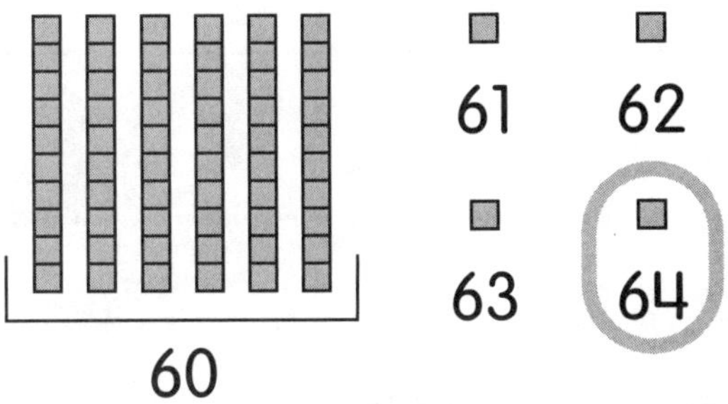

You can use a chart.

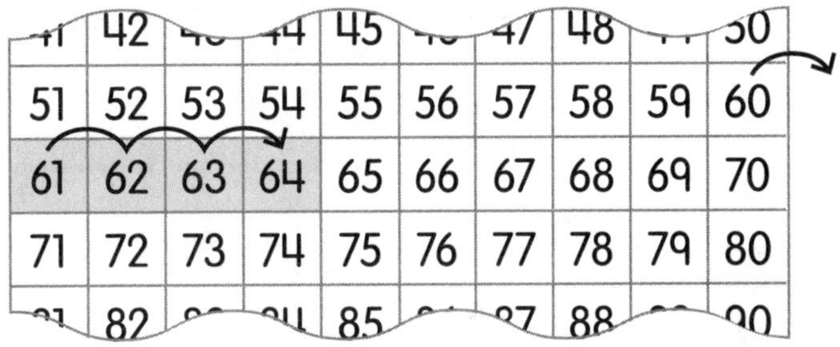

You can use a number line.

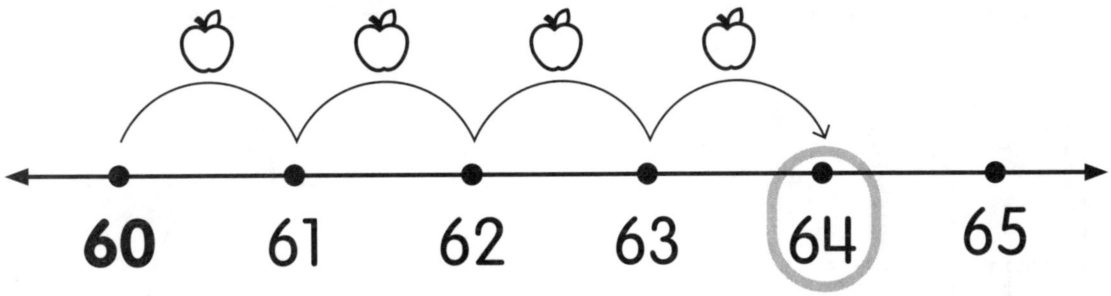

Explain how you can count on  from **99** apples.

Count to 120, starting at any number.
Represent a number of objects with a numeral.

Name ________________________________

Count on from each number. Write the numbers.

Examples

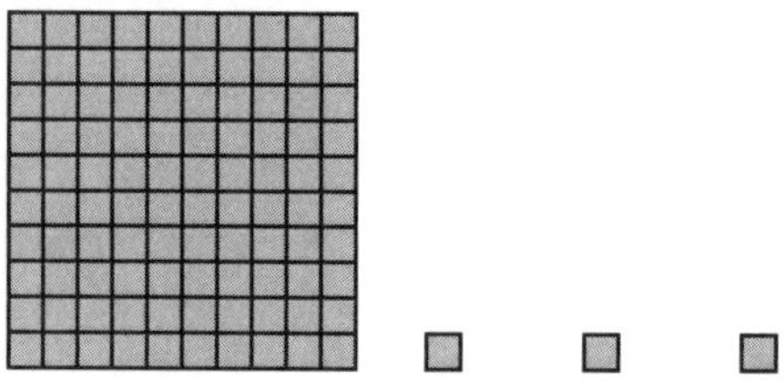

100 101 102 103

1 2 3

100	101	102	103

1 2 3

100 101 102 103

❶

81									

❷

105 ______ ______ ______ ______ ______

❸

111 ______ ______ ______ ______ ______

Count to 120, starting at any number.
Represent a number of objects with a numeral.

Name ______________________________

Count on from each number. Write the numbers.

1. 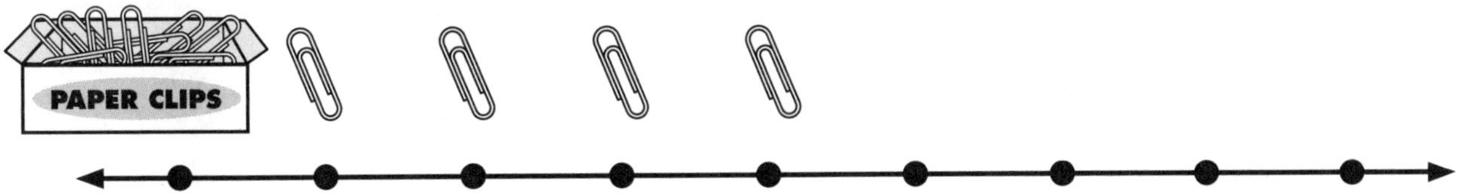

50 ____ ____ ____ ____

____ paper clips

2.

74						

3. 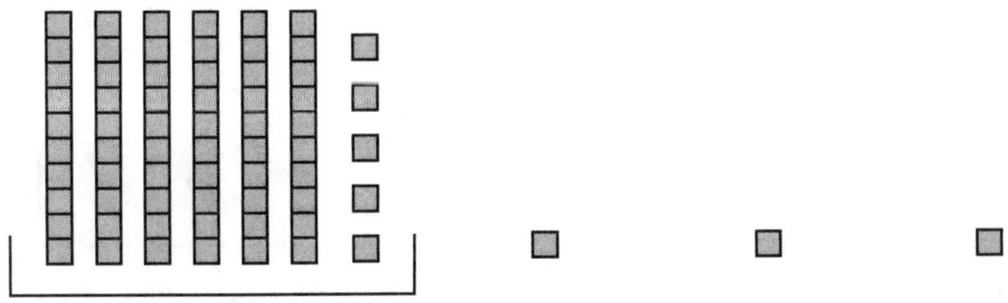

65 ____ ____ ____

4. 

99 ____ ____ ____ ____ ____ ____

Count to 120, starting at any number.
Represent a number of objects with a numeral.

Name ______________________________

Read the Problem

A bird needs help finding the way to its nest.
Color the boxes that count in order from 90 to 120.

Think About It

❶ I need to find numbers that _____.

○ count from 90 to 120 ○ count from 19 to 100

Solve the Problem

❷

90	91	92	93	60	43	29	74	52	80
44	19	40	94	95	96	97	98	99	61
30	98	36	79	63	68	51	43	100	39
109	108	107	106	105	104	103	102	101	37
110	77	64	65	54	42	84	50	25	79
111	112	113	114	115	116	117	118	119	120

Check Your Work

❸ Do your answers make sense? ○ yes ○ no

Count to 120, starting at any number.
Represent a number of objects with a numeral.

Math Models

Skip counting

You can skip count groups of things.

You can skip count by **tens**.

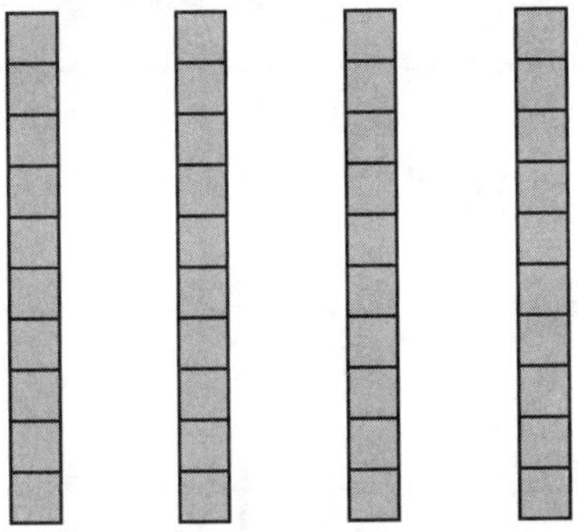

10 20 30 40

You can skip count by **fives**.

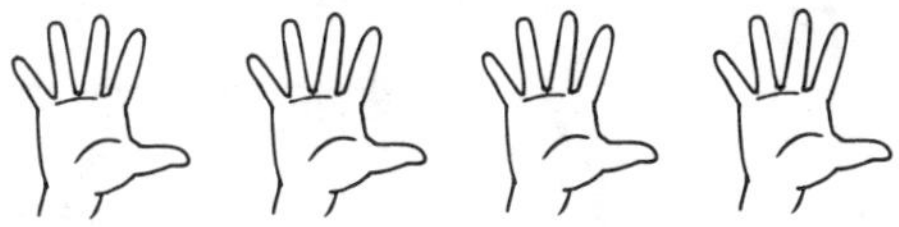

5 10 15 20

You can skip count by **twos**.

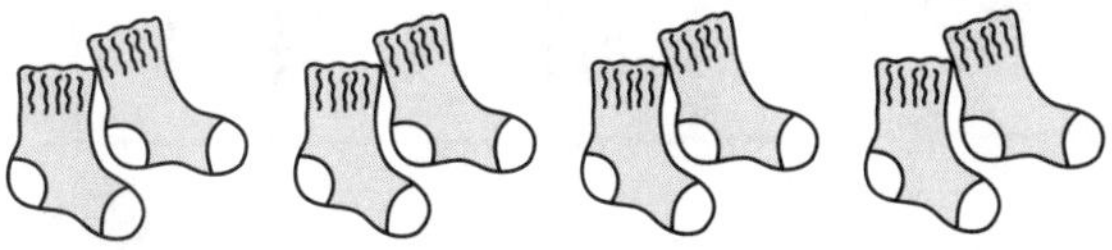

2 4 6 8

These are some ways to **skip count**:

You can use a number line.

tens

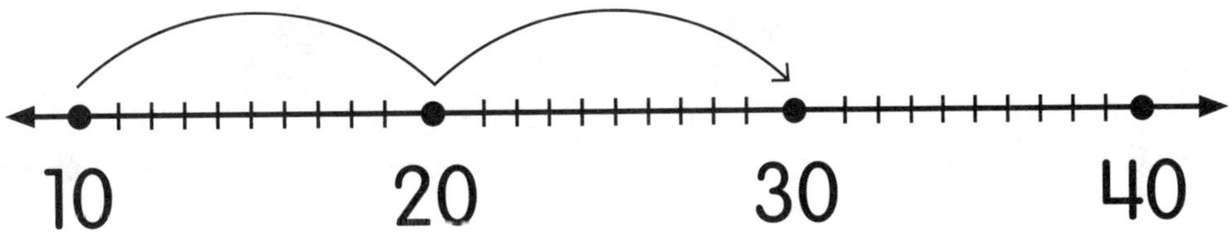

fives

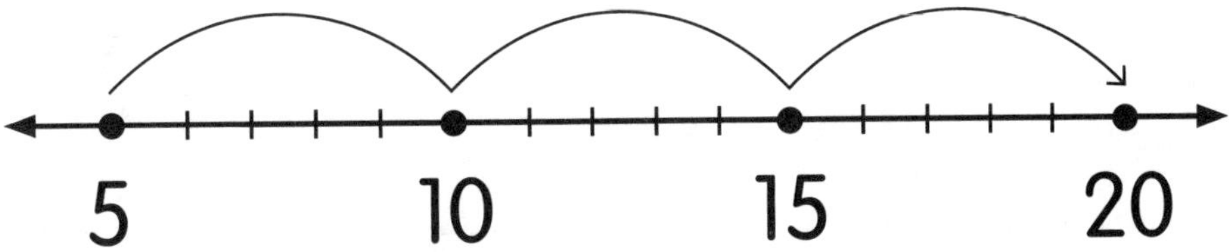

twos

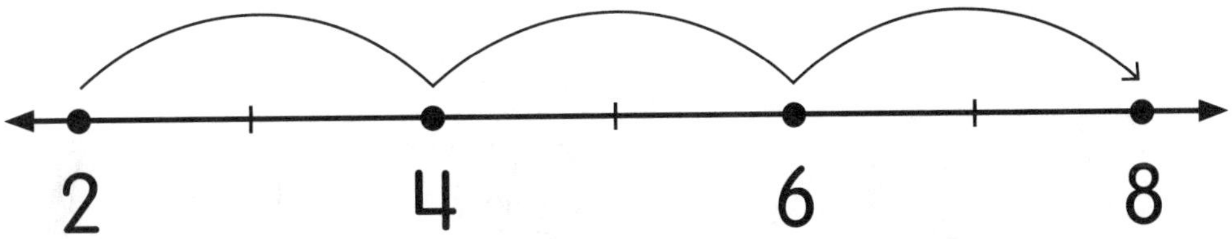

Skip count by tens, fives, and twos up to **100**.
You can use a **100** chart.

Count, starting at any number.
Represent a number of objects with a numeral.

Name ______________________

Skip count by tens, fives, or twos. Write the missing numbers.

Examples

I see groups of two eyes. I can count by twos.

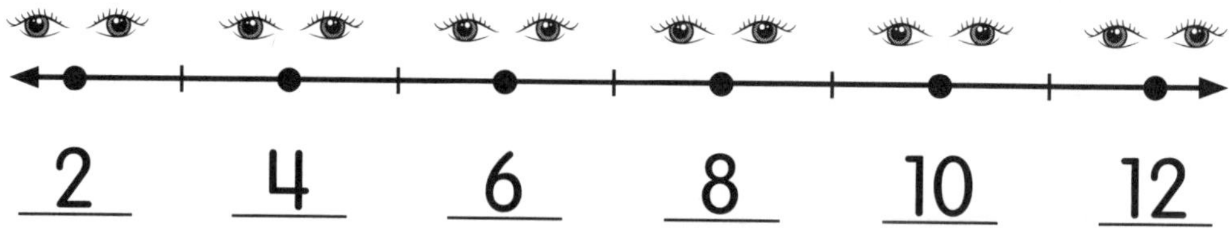

❶

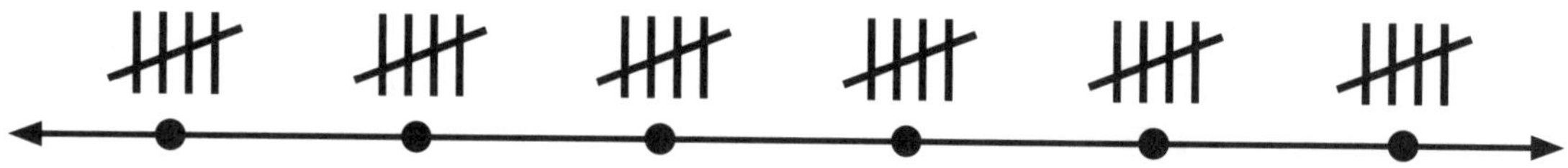

____ ____ ____ ____ ____ ____

❷

____ ____ ____ ____ ____ ____

❸

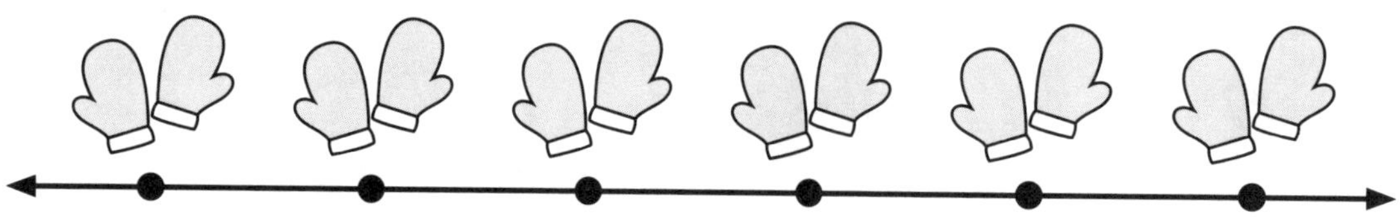

____ ____ ____ ____ ____ ____

Count, starting at any number.
Represent a number of objects with a numeral.

Name ______________________________

Skip count.

1. Count by tens. Color each number you counted **yellow**.
2. Count by fives. Draw a circle around each number you counted.
3. Count by twos. Draw an **X** on each number you counted.

1	2	3	4	5	6	7	8	9	10
11	12	13	14	15	16	17	18	19	20
21	22	23	24	25	26	27	28	29	30
31	32	33	34	35	36	37	38	39	40
41	42	43	44	45	46	47	48	49	50
51	52	53	54	55	56	57	58	59	60
61	62	63	64	65	66	67	68	69	70
71	72	73	74	75	76	77	78	79	80
81	82	83	84	85	86	87	88	89	90
91	92	93	94	95	96	97	98	99	100
101	102	103	104	105	106	107	108	109	110
111	112	113	114	115	116	117	118	119	120

Count, starting at any number.
Represent a number of objects with a numeral.

Name ______________________________

Read the Problem

Dan counted how many people were at the beach.
He counted 𝍸 𝍸 𝍸 𝍸 𝍸 𝍸 people.
Write the number in the work space.

Think About It

1. Dan _____ the people.
   ○ played with ○ counted ○ lost

2. You can count Dan's marks by _____.
   ○ fives ○ twos

Solve the Problem

3. Use this work space.

4. There were _____ people at the beach.

Check Your Work

5. Do your answers make sense? ○ yes ○ no

Math Models

Counting back

You can count back from any number.

Sometimes you need to count back.

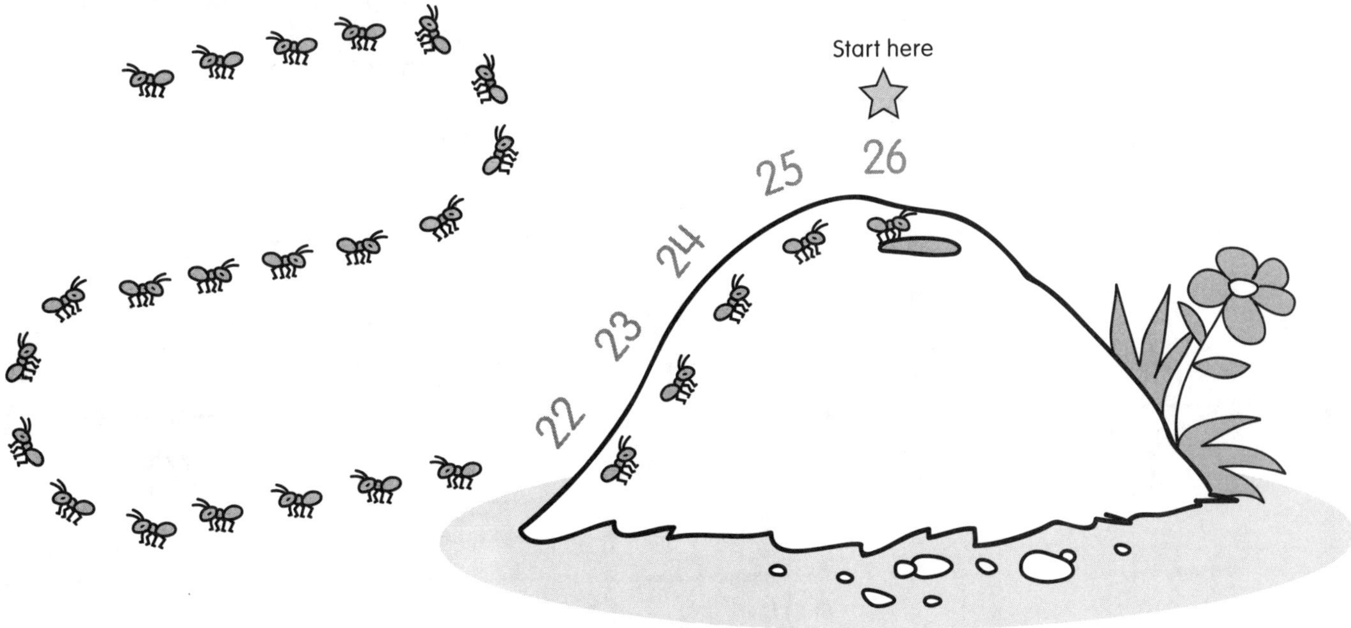

These are some ways to **count back**:

You can use a number line.

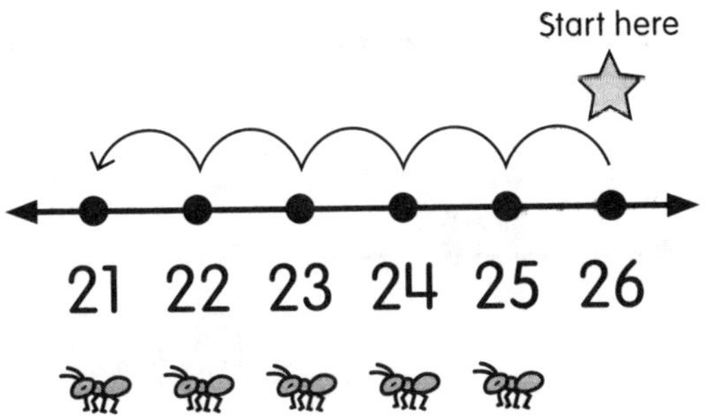

You can use a chart.

1	2	3	4	5	6	7	8	9	10
11	12	13	14	15	16	17	18	19	20
21	22	23	24	25	26	27	28	29	30
31	32	33	34	35	36	37	38	39	40
[illegible]	42	[illegible]	[illegible]	45	[illegible]	47	48	[illegible]	50

Try counting back from **50** to **1** without looking at a chart or a number line.

Name ______________________

Count back. Write the missing numbers.

Examples

Start here

18 19 20

Start here

18	19	20

1 Start here

39 ___ 41

2 Start here

68 ___ 70

3 Start here

55					60

4 Start here

95		97			100

5 Start here

___ 88 ___ ___ ___ ___ 93

6 Start here

111									120

Name ____________________

Count back. Write the missing numbers.

❶ 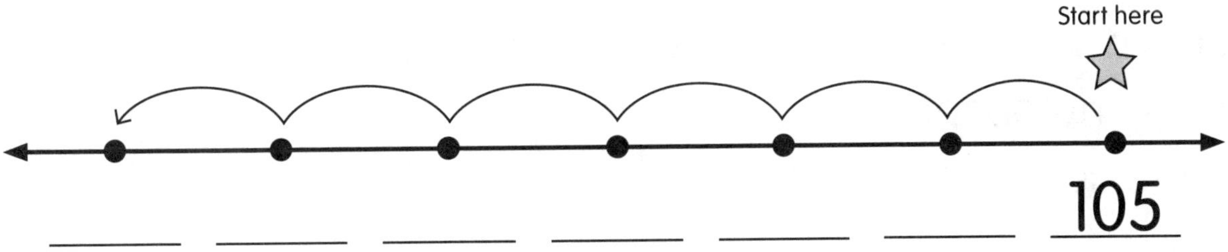

❷ 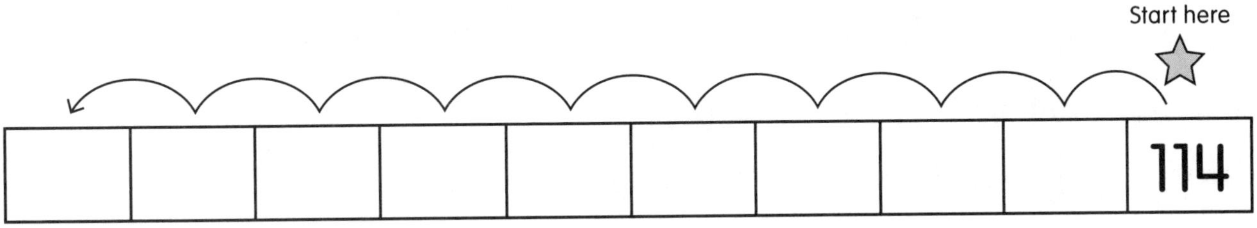

❸ 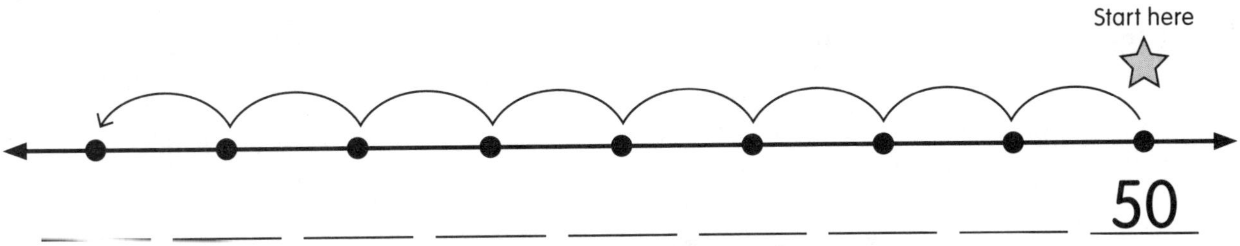

❹ 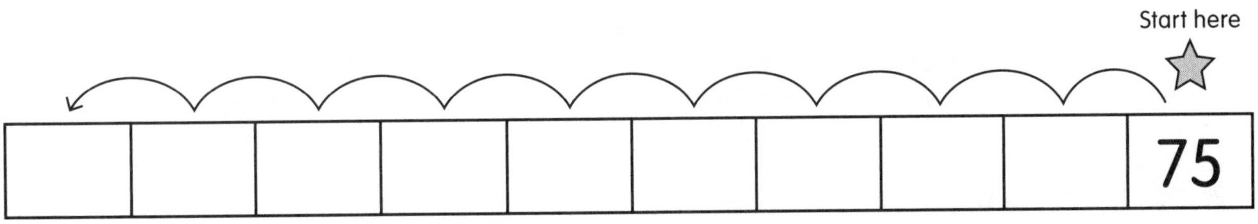

Name ____________________

Read the Problem

Mrs. Beck said to count back from 103 to 98.
Finish the number line.
Write the numbers.

Think About It

❶ You will ____.

○ skip count ○ count on ○ count back

❷ You will write numbers on a ____.

○ number line ○ chart

Solve the Problem

❸ Use this work space.

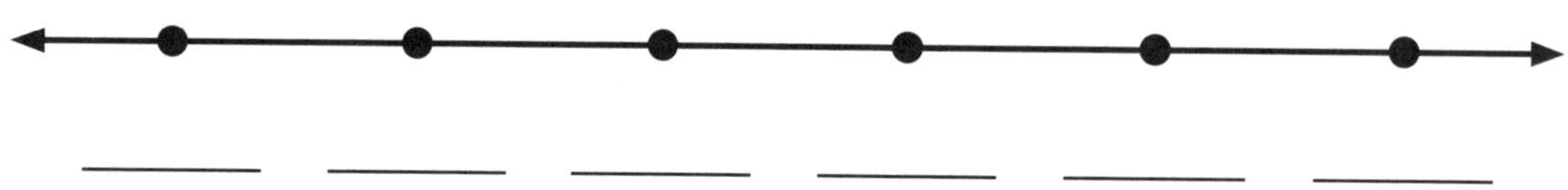

Check Your Work

❹ Do your answers make sense? ○ yes ○ no

Place Value: Two-Digit Numbers

Unit Contents

Math Process Skills in This Unit

Make sense of problems and persevere in solving them: *pages 109, 113, 118*

Reason abstractly and quantitatively: *pages 106, 107, 108, 109, 110, 111, 112, 113, 114, 115, 116, 117, 118*

Construct viable arguments and critique the reasoning of others: *pages 106, 109, 110, 114*

Model with mathematics: *pages 106, 107, 108, 109, 110, 111, 112, 113, 114, 115, 116, 117, 118*

Attend to precision: *pages 106, 109, 110, 113, 114, 118*

Look for and make use of structure: *pages 106, 107, 108, 110, 111, 112, 114, 115, 116, 117*

Look for and express regularity in repeated reasoning: *pages 106, 107, 108, 111, 112, 114, 116, 117*

You can tell how many groups of ten are in a two-digit number.

These are two examples:

Number	Model	Tens	Ones
10 ↙ ↘ tens ones		1	0
20 ↙ ↘ tens ones	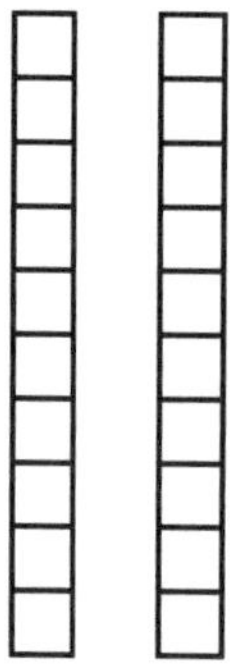	2	0

How many tens are in the numbers **30**, **50**, and **80**? Explain your thinking.

Name ______________________________

Look at each number. Draw a line to the tens for each number.

Example

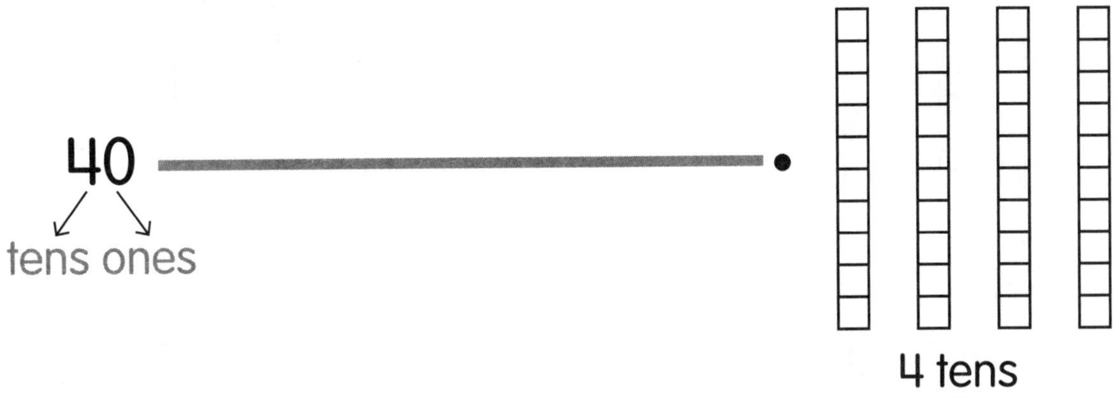

❶ 20

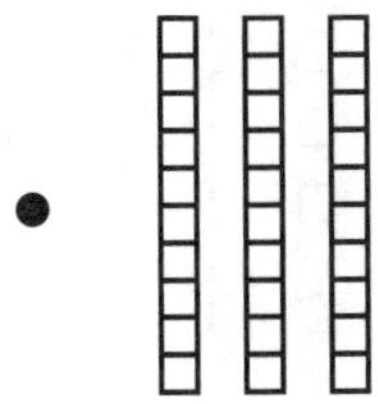

❷ 80

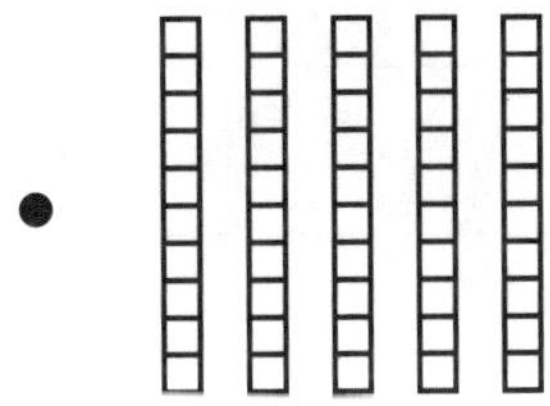

❸ 30

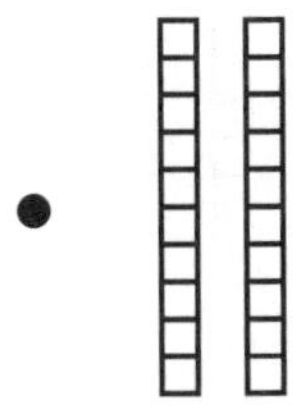

❹ 50

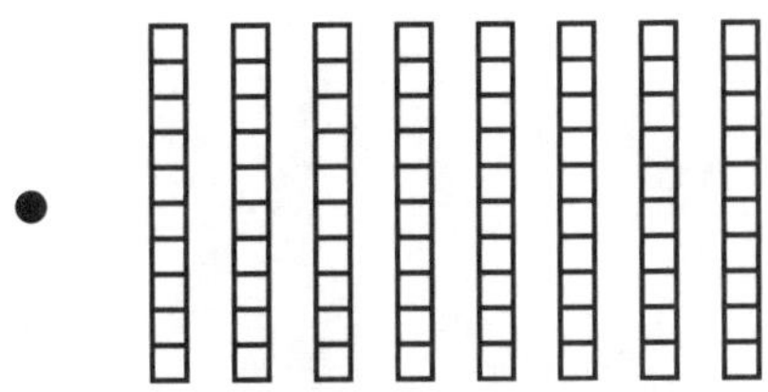

Name ____________________

Look at each group of cubes. Write the number that tells how many.

1. 

   30

2. 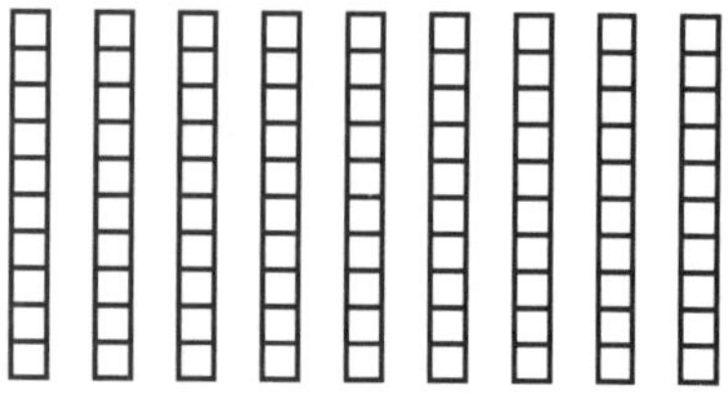

   ______

3. 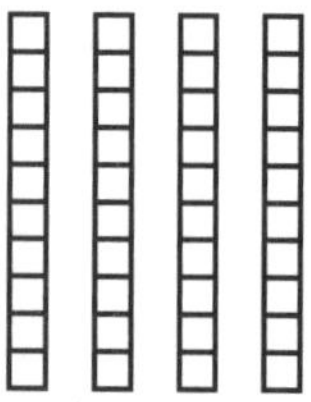

   ______

4. 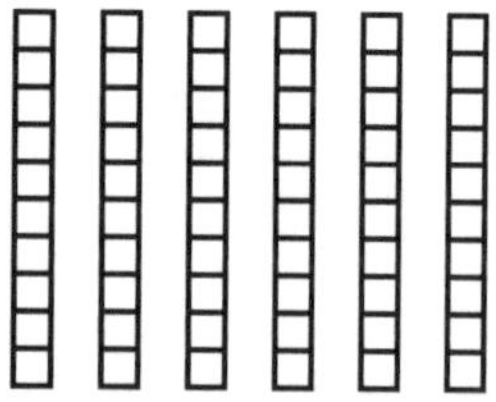

   ______

5. 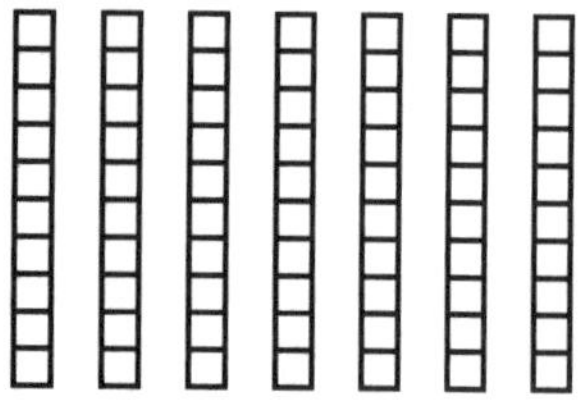

   ______

6. 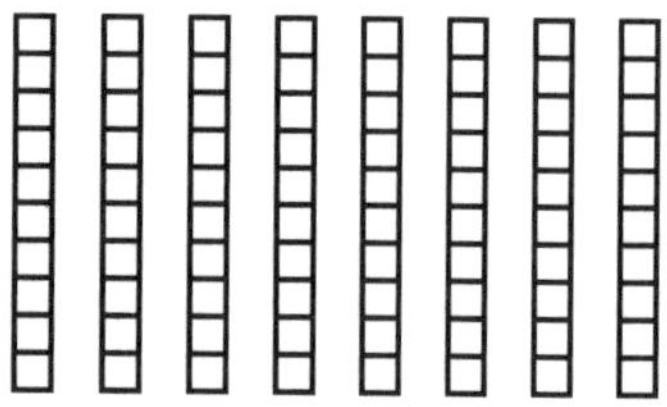

   ______

 Understand two-digit numbers as tens and ones.

Name ______________________

Read the Problem

Mrs. Beck has 3 boxes of pencils.
Each box has 10 pencils.
Tyson says Mrs. Beck has 30 pencils.
Do you agree?

Think About It

1. You will find out if Mrs. Beck has ______.
   ○ 3 boxes ○ 10 pencils ○ 30 pencils

2. How many tens are in **30**?
   ○ 30 tens ○ 3 tens ○ 0 tens

Solve the Problem

3. Use this work space.

4. Mrs. Beck has 30 pencils. ○ yes ○ no

Check Your Work

5. Do your answers make sense? ○ yes ○ no

Math Models

Tens and ones

Place Value: Two-Digit Numbers

You can show how two-digit numbers are made up of tens and ones.

These are some examples:

Number	Model	Tens	Ones
11 tens ones		1	1
22 tens ones	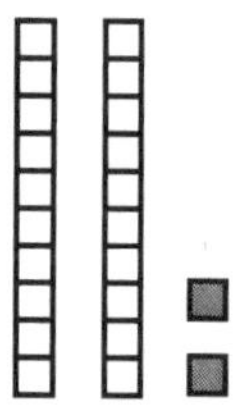	2	2
45 tens ones	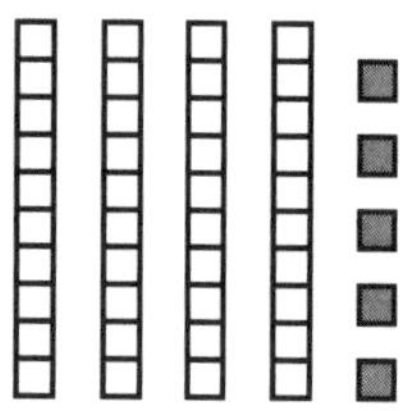	4	5

For each number **13** through **19**, tell the number of tens and ones. Do you notice a pattern? Explain your thinking.

Name ______________________________

Draw a model. Then write how many tens and ones.

Example

Number	Model	Tens	Ones
25 (tens ones)		2	5

Number	Model	Tens	Ones
1 16			
2 31			
3 52			

Understand two-digit numbers as tens and ones.

Name ______________________________

Mark the value of each underlined digit.

1. 19 (underlined: 9)
   - ○ 9 ones
   - ○ 9 tens

2. 58 (underlined: 5)
   - ○ 5 ones
   - ○ 5 tens

3. 90 (underlined: 0)
   - ○ 0 ones
   - ○ 9 tens

4. 83 (underlined: 8)
   - ○ 3 ones
   - ○ 8 tens

5. 30 (underlined: 3)
   - ○ 3 ones
   - ○ 3 tens

6. 62 (underlined: 2)
   - ○ 2 ones
   - ○ 2 tens

7. 75 (underlined: 5)
   - ○ 5 ones
   - ○ 7 tens

8. 49 (underlined: 4)
   - ○ 9 ones
   - ○ 4 tens

Name ____________________

Read the Problem

Mr. Lau said, "Guess my number!
It has 5 tens and 9 ones.
What number is it?"

Think About It

1. You will find out what number ____.
   - ○ has 5 tens and 9 ones
   - ○ has 5 ones and 9 tens

2. Mr. Lau's number has ____.
   - ○ one digit
   - ○ two digits
   - ○ three digits

Solve the Problem

3. Use this work space.

4. The number is ____.

Check Your Work

5. Do your answers make sense? ○ yes ○ no

Understand two-digit numbers as tens and ones.

Math Models

Comparing two-digit numbers

You can use (>), (=), and (<) to compare two-digit numbers.

These are some examples:

(>) greater than	(=) equal to	(<) less than
20 (>) 10	11 (=) 11	23 (<) 32

Steps to compare **two-digit numbers**:

1. Look at the tens digits.

Example:

12 (<) 31

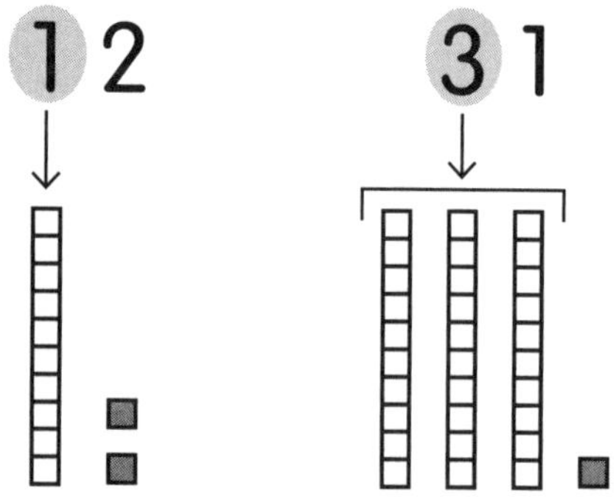

2. If the tens digits are the same, look at the ones digits, too.

Example:

14 (>) 11

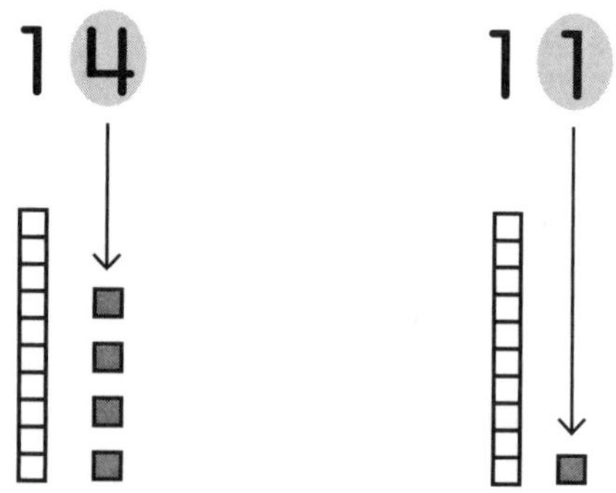

Is **72 < 27** true? Explain your thinking.

Name ____________________

Write **>**, **=**, or **<** to make a true number sentence. Then draw a model.

Examples

23 (<) 32

❶ 15 ◯ 15

❷ 27 ◯ 32

❸ 31 ◯ 21

Name ______________________________

Write **>**, **=**, or **<** to make a true number sentence. Then draw a model.

1. 32 ◯ 23

2. 16 ◯ 61

3. 40 ◯ 39

4. 52 ◯ 52

 Compare two two-digit numbers based on meanings of the tens and ones digits.

Name ____________________

Write a **two-digit** number to complete each number sentence. Then draw a model.

1. ___ = 12
2. 43 > ___
3. 50 = ___
4. ___ > 12
5. 43 < ___
6. ___ < 50

Name ______________________________

Read the Problem

Chris read 59 books. Dan read 61 books.

Use **>**, **=**, or **<**.

Write a number sentence to compare **59** and **61**.

Think About It

1. You will write a ______.

   ○ word problem ○ number sentence ○ math book

2. Mark the symbol that you can **not** use.

   ○ **>** greater than ○ **=** equal to ○ **<** less than

Solve the Problem

3. Use this work space.

4. Number sentence: ______ ◯ ______

Check Your Work

5. Do your answers make sense? ○ yes ○ no

 Compare two two-digit numbers based on meanings of the tens and ones digits.

Place Value: Addition and Subtraction

Unit Contents

Math Process Skills in This Unit

Make sense of problems and persevere in solving them: *pages 123, 127, 131, 132*

Reason abstractly and quantitatively: *pages 120, 121, 122, 123, 124, 125, 126, 127, 128, 129, 130, 131*

Construct viable arguments and critique the reasoning of others: *pages 120, 124, 128*

Model with mathematics: *pages 120, 121, 122, 123, 124, 125, 126, 127, 128, 129, 130, 131*

Attend to precision: *pages 120, 121, 122, 123, 124, 125, 126, 127, 128, 129, 130, 131*

Look for and make use of structure: *pages 120, 121, 122, 124, 125, 126, 128, 129, 130, 131*

Math Models

Adding two-digit numbers within 100

Sometimes you need to compose a ten when you add two-digit numbers.

Add tens and tens.
Add ones and ones.

These are some examples:

18 + 13 = 31

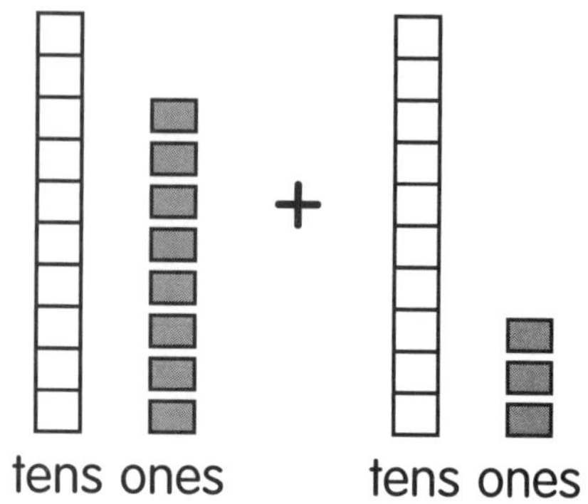

tens digits = 20
ones digits = 11

I need to compose a ten.

20 + 10 + 1
30 + 1 = 31

12 + 34 = 46

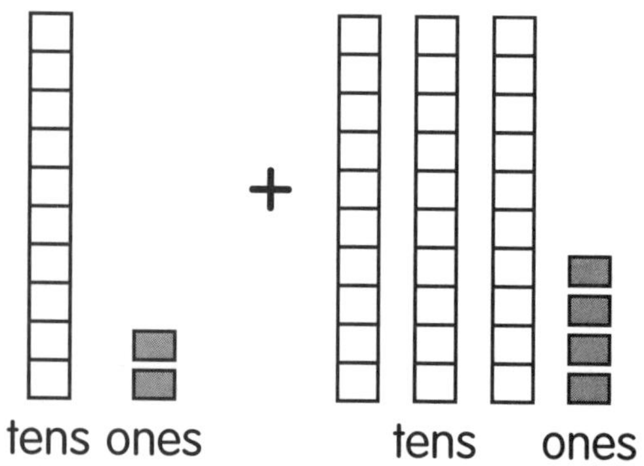

tens digits = 40
ones digits = 6

I do **not** need to compose a ten.

40 + 6 = 46

Explain how you can solve **48 + 9** and **32 + 10**.

In adding two-digit numbers, it is sometimes necessary to compose a ten.

Name ________________________

Add. Compose a ten if you need to.

Example

36 + 17 = 53

40 + 13 — I need to compose a ten.

40 + 10 + 3

50 + 3 = 53

Work Space

1. 42 + 20 = ____

2. 61 + 17 = ____

3. 57 + 15 = ____

In adding two-digit numbers, it is sometimes necessary to compose a ten.

Name ______________________

Add. Compose a ten if you need to.

	Work Space
❶ $60 + 27 =$ ____	
❷ $28 + 36 =$ ____	
❸ $91 + 6 =$ ____	
❹ $59 + 23 =$ ____	

In adding two-digit numbers, it is sometimes necessary to compose a ten.

Name ______________________________

Read the Problem

26 girls and 25 boys rode on the bus.
How many children rode on the bus altogether?

Think About It

1. You will find out how many children _____.
   - ○ were girls
   - ○ got off the bus
   - ○ rode on the bus

2. Will you need to compose a ten?
   - ○ yes
   - ○ no

Solve the Problem

3. Use this work space.

4. _____ children rode on the bus altogether.

Check Your Work

5. Do your answers make sense? ○ yes ○ no

In adding two-digit numbers, it is sometimes necessary to compose a ten.

You can find ten more or ten less than a number without counting.

Let's find 10 more and 10 less than **15**.

One way is to think of a number chart.

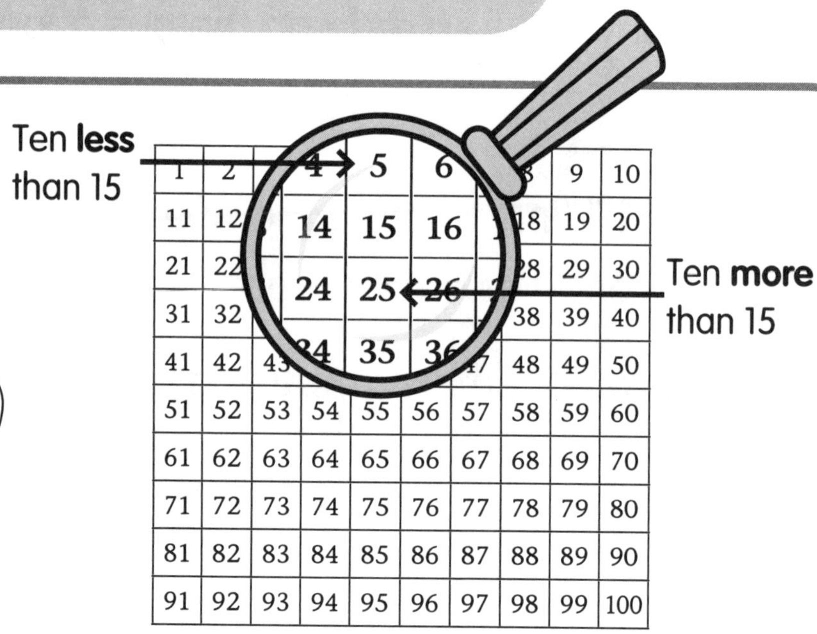

Another way is to think of skipping back or forward by ten from any number.

Ten less 12 ↑ Skip **back** by ten

22

Ten more 32 ↑ Skip **forward** by ten

Try mental math. What number is **ten more** than **89**? What number is **ten less** than **89**? Explain your thinking.

Name ____________________

Look at each number. Write ten more or ten less.

Examples

Ten More
27
37

Ten Less
13
23

Ten More

1.

60

2.

31

3.

76

4.

58

Ten Less

5.

19

6.

24

7.

47

8.

82

Given a two-digit number, mentally find 10 more or 10 less than the number.

Name ____________________

Look at each number. Write ten more or ten less.

Ten More

1. 11 ____
2. 27 ____
3. 63 ____
4. 75 ____

Ten Less

5. ____ 12
6. ____ 53
7. ____ 36
8. ____ 99

 Given a two-digit number, mentally find 10 more or 10 less than the number.

Name ______________________________

Read the Problem

I planted 25 seeds in the garden.
Mom planted 10 more seeds than I did.
How many seeds did Mom plant?

Think About It

1. You will find out how many seeds _____.
   - ○ Mom planted ○ I planted
2. Mark the number sentence that tells about the problem.
   - ○ 25 – 10 = ? ○ ? + 10 = 25 ○ 25 + 10 = ?

Solve the Problem

3. Use this work space.

4. Mom planted _____ seeds.

Check Your Work

5. Do your answers make sense? ○ yes ○ no

Given a two-digit number, mentally find 10 more or 10 less than the number.

You can subtract a multiple of ten from another multiple of ten.

These are some multiples of ten:

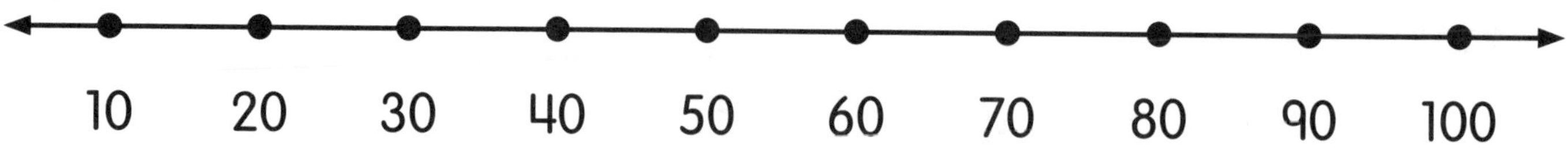

Let's subtract $50 - 20 = ?$

These are two ways to show it:

You can use cubes.

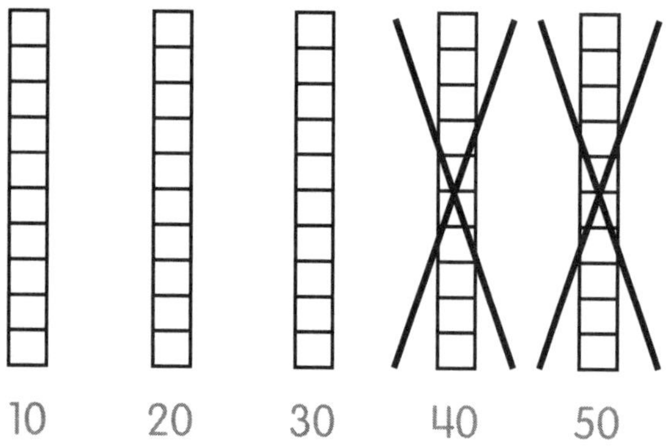

$50 - 20 = 30$

↑ ↑ ↑

You can use a diagram.

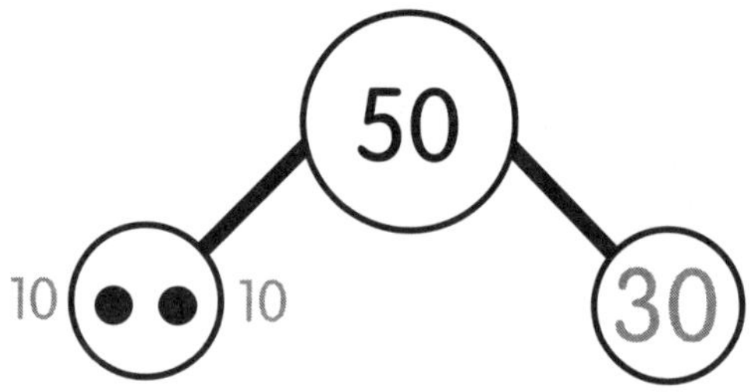

$50 - 20 = 30$

↑ ↑ ↑

Choose a way to solve **70 – 30 = ?** Explain your thinking.

Name ____________________

Subtract. Show your work.

Example

70 – 30 = 40

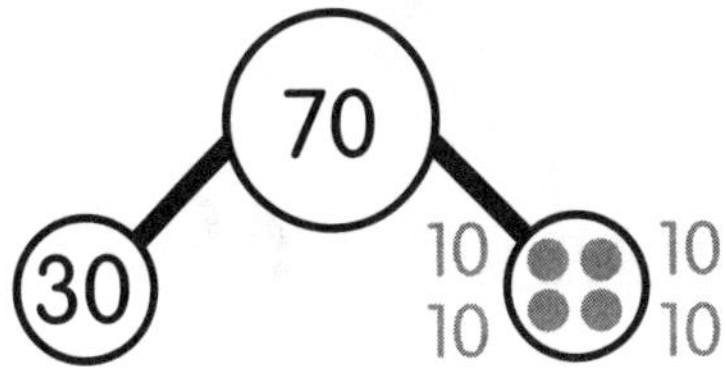

Work Space

1. 50 – 40 = ____	
2. 60 – 20 = ____	
3. 90 – 80 = ____	

Name ______________________________

Complete each number sentence. Show your work.

	Work Space
1. $80 - \_\_\_ = 60$	
2. $\_\_\_ - 10 = 30$	
3. $30 = 90 - \_\_\_$	
4. $70 - \_\_\_ = 20$	

Subtract multiples of ten from multiples of ten.
Show a model or strategy and explain the reasoning.

Name ____________________

Draw a line from each number sentence to the model that can help you solve the problem. Write the answer.

1. 90 – 70 = ____ •

• 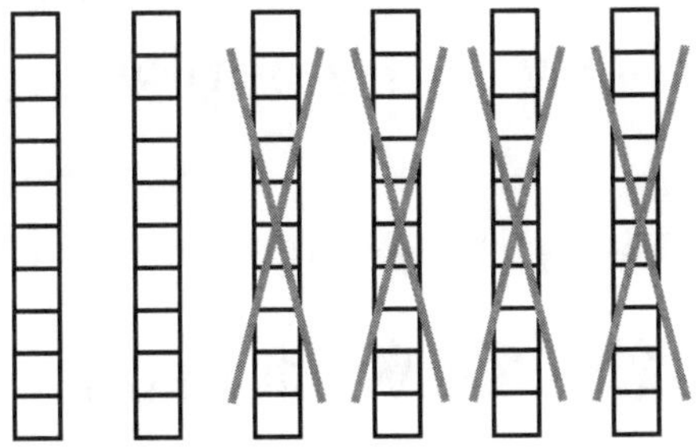

2. 40 – ____ = 20 •

• 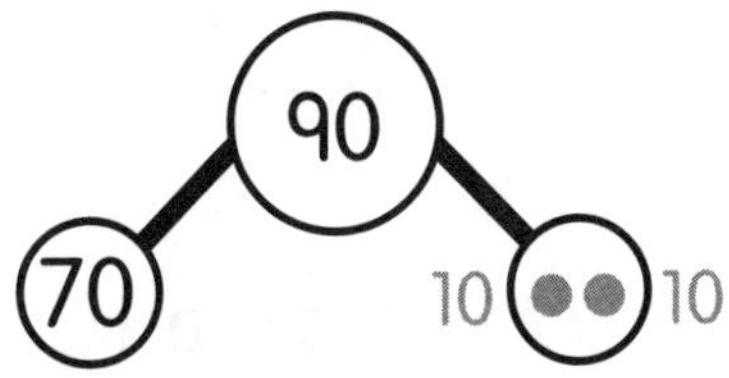

3. 60 – 40 = ____ •

• 20 + 20 = 40

4. ____ – 10 = 40 •

• 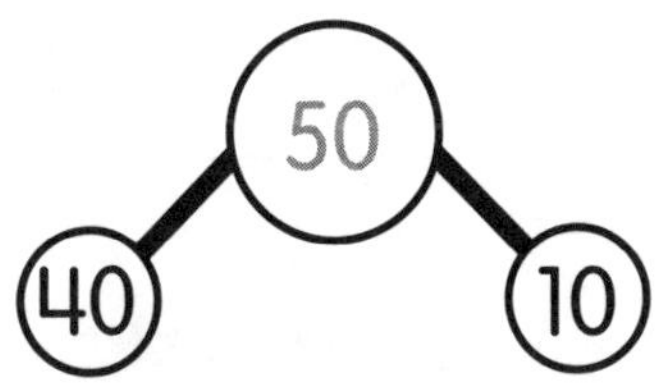

Name ______________________

Read the Problem

The store had 60 apples.
20 apples were sold.
How many apples were left?

Think About It

1. You will find out how many apples were ____.

   ○ sold ○ left ○ big

2. Mark the number sentence that tells about the problem.

   ○ ? = 60 – 20 ○ ? = 60 + 20 ○ ? = 80 – 20

Solve the Problem

3. Use this work space.

4. ____ apples were left.

Check Your Work

5. Do your answers make sense? ○ yes ○ no

Subtract multiples of ten from multiples of ten.
Show a model or strategy and explain the reasoning.

Measuring Length

Unit Contents

Ordering objects by length

Measuring and writing the length of objects

Math Process Skills in This Unit

Make sense of problems and persevere in solving them: *pages 137, 142*

Reason abstractly and quantitatively: *pages 134, 135, 136, 137, 138, 139, 140, 141, 142*

Construct viable arguments and critique the reasoning of others: *pages 134, 138*

Model with mathematics: *pages 135, 136, 137, 139, 140, 141, 142*

Attend to precision: *pages 134, 137, 138, 142*

Look for and make use of structure: *pages 134, 135, 136, 138, 139, 140, 141*

You can compare the length of objects and put them in order.

This is one way to compare and put things in order:

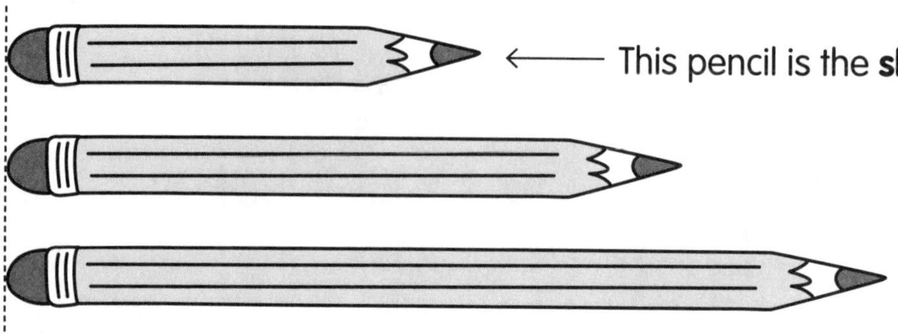

← This pencil is the **shortest**.

← This pencil is the **longest**.

This is another way to compare and put things in order:

This flower is the **tallest**.

This flower is the **shortest**.

Why is it important to line up the pencils to compare their lengths? Explain your answer.

Name ______________________________

Measuring Length
Ordering objects by length

1

Follow the directions to number each group of things in order by length.

Example

Number the worms from **longest** to **shortest**.

2 3 1

1. Number the dogs from **tallest** to **shortest**.

___ ___ ___

2. Number the bones from **shortest** to **longest**.

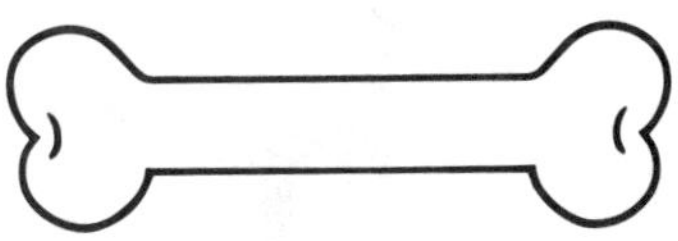 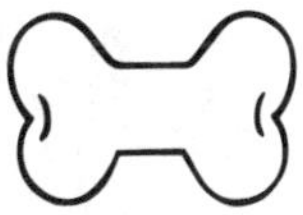 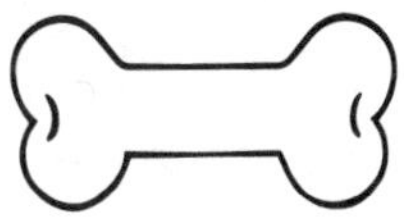

___ ___ ___

Name ______________________________

Measuring Length
Ordering objects by length

2

Follow the directions to number each group of things in order by length.

❶ Number the crayons from **longest** to **shortest**.

_____ _____ _____

❷ Number the sticks from **shortest** to **longest**.

_____ _____ _____

❸ Number the trees from **tallest** to **shortest**.

_____ _____ _____

Name ____________________

Read the Problem

Mike has 3 leaves.
He wants to put them in order from **shortest** to **tallest**.
Mark the group that shows how he put the leaves in that order.

Think About It

1. You will mark three leaves that are in order from ____.
   ○ tallest to shortest ○ shortest to tallest

2. The tallest leaf will be ____.
   ○ first ○ in the middle ○ last

Solve the Problem

3. Mark the group that is in order from **shortest** to **tallest**.

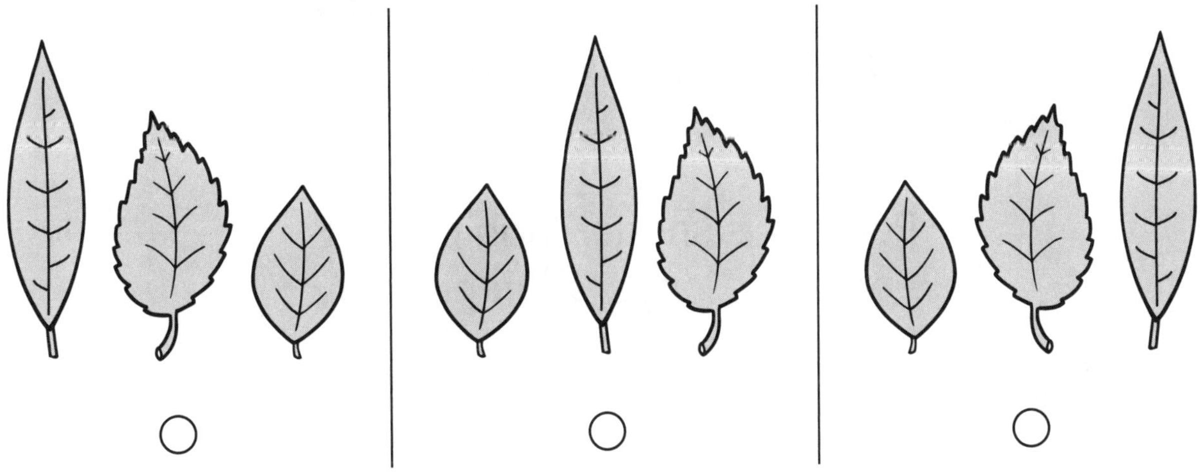

Check Your Work

4. Do your answers make sense? ○ yes ○ no

Math Models

Measuring and writing the length of objects

You can measure the length of objects.

One measuring tool you can use is cubes:

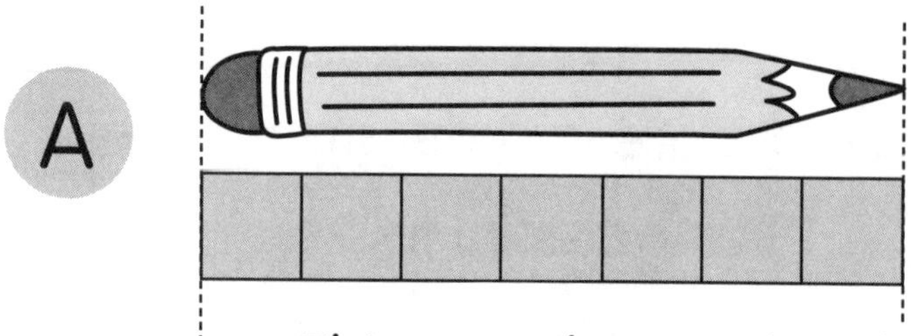

This pencil is **7** cubes long.

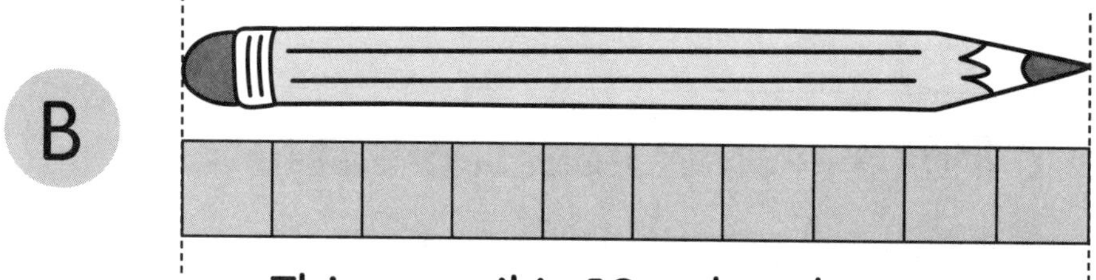

This pencil is **10** cubes long.

Pencil A is shorter than pencil B.
Pencil B is longer than pencil A.

Explain what you can do if an object is lined up with the **second** cube.

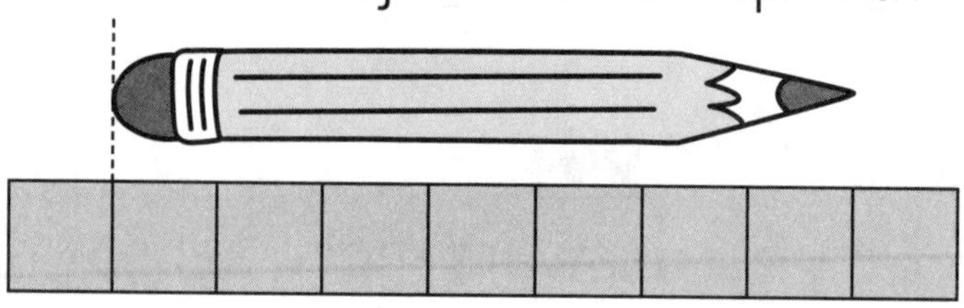

Compare the length of two objects by using a third object.
Use a short object to measure another object. Express the length as a whole number of length units.

Name ____________________

Measuring Length

Measuring and writing the length of objects

3

Look at the paper clips to measure each item. Write the length.

Example

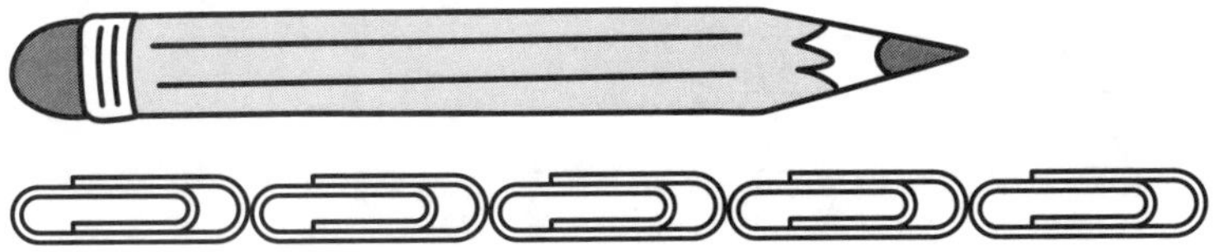

4 paper clips

❶

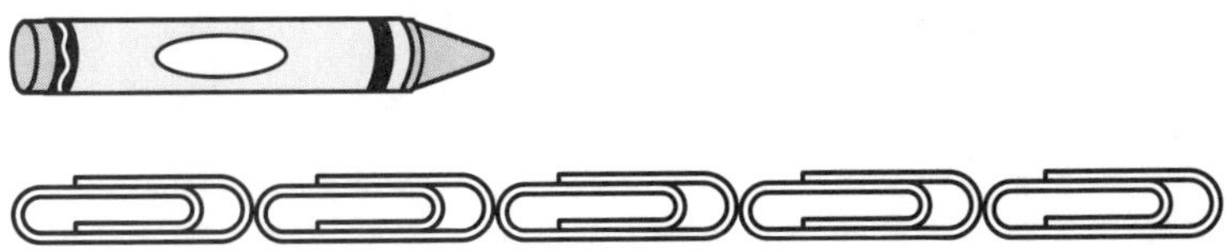

____ paper clips

❷

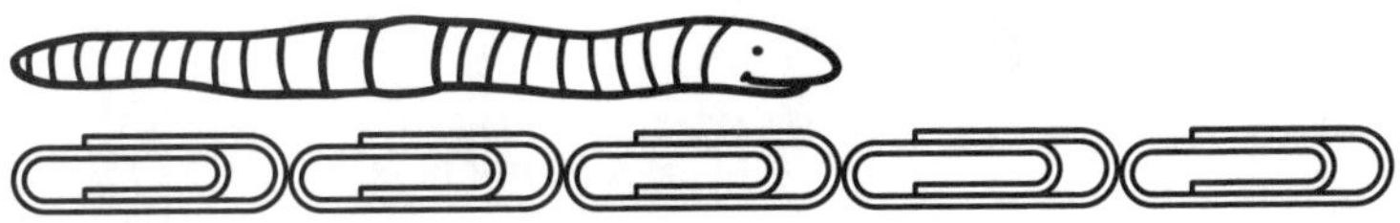

____ paper clips

❸

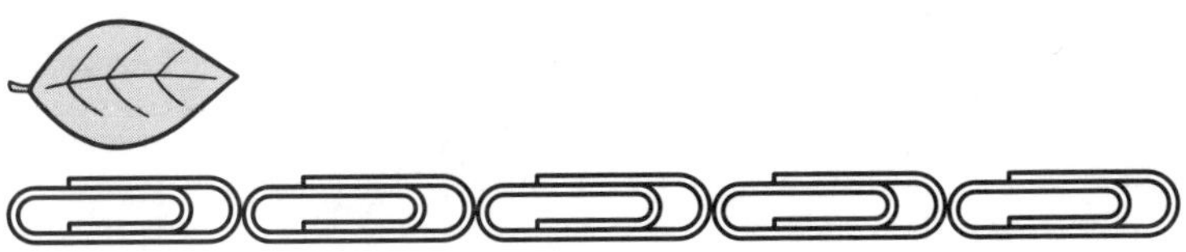

____ paper clips

Compare the length of two objects by using a third object.
Use a short object to measure another object. Express the length as a whole number of length units.

Name ______________________________

Measuring Length

Measuring and writing the length of objects

4

Look at the cubes to measure each item. Write the length.

❶

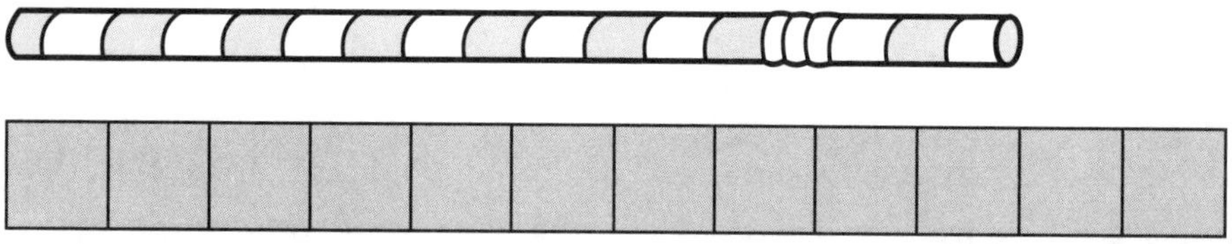

____ cubes

❷

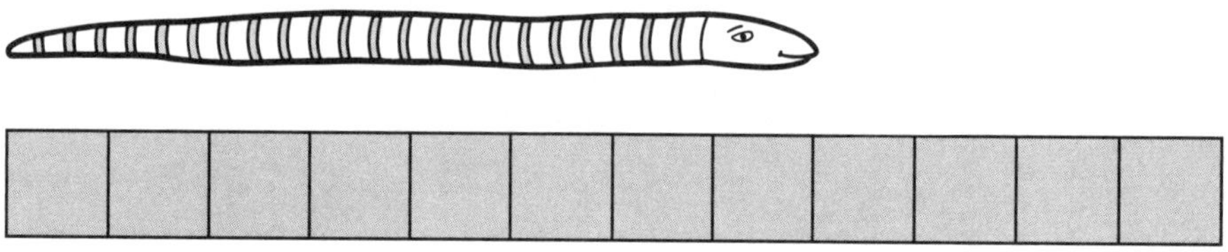

____ cubes

❸

____ cubes

❹

____ cubes

Compare the length of two objects by using a third object.
Use a short object to measure another object. Express the length as a whole number of length units.

Name ______________________________

Measuring Length

Measuring and writing the length of objects

5

Cut out the sticks. Use the sticks to measure the trees.

1. About how tall is the **tallest** tree?

   _____ sticks tall

2. About how tall is the apple tree?

   _____ sticks tall

3. About how tall is the **shortest** tree?

   _____ sticks tall

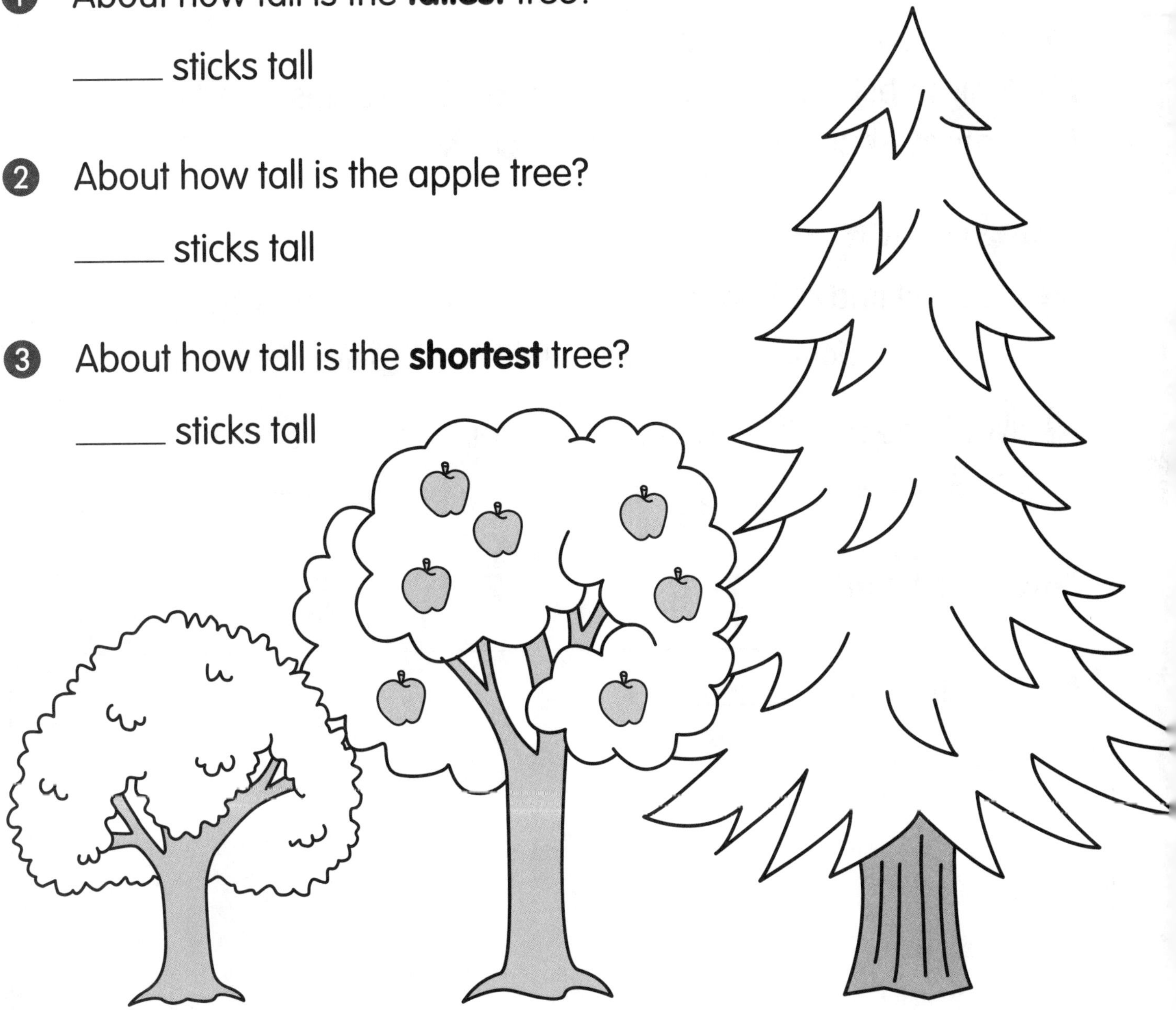

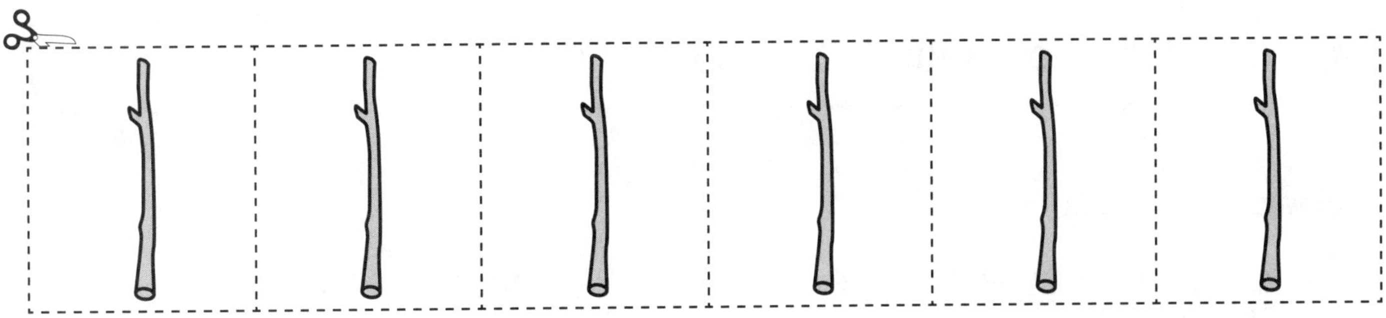

Compare the length of two objects by using a third object.
Use a short object to measure another object. Express the length as a whole number of length units.

Name ______________________________

Read the Problem

Sara used her shoe to measure desks.
Her desk was 5 shoes tall.
Mr. Hall's desk was 4 shoes taller than Sara's desk.
How many shoes tall was Mr. Hall's desk?

Think About It

1. You will find out how many shoes tall _____ was.
   - ○ Sara's desk ○ Mr. Hall ○ Mr. Hall's desk
2. Mark the number sentence that tells about the problem.
   - ○ $5 - 4 = ?$ ○ $5 + 4 = ?$ ○ $5 + 5 = ?$

Solve the Problem

3. Use this work space.

4. Mr. Hall's desk was _____ shoes tall.

Check Your Work

5. Do your answers make sense? ○ yes ○ no

Compare the length of two objects by using a third object.
Use a short object to measure another object. Express the length as a whole number of length units.

Time

Unit Contents

Math Process Skills in This Unit

Make sense of problems and persevere in solving them: *pages 147, 152*

Reason abstractly and quantitatively: *pages 147, 152*

Construct viable arguments and critique the reasoning of others: *pages 144, 148*

Model with mathematics: *pages 147, 152*

Attend to precision: *pages 147, 152*

Look for and make use of structure: *pages 144, 145, 146, 149, 150, 151*

Math Models

Telling time by the hour

You can measure time using clocks. You can tell and write time in hours.

Analog Clock

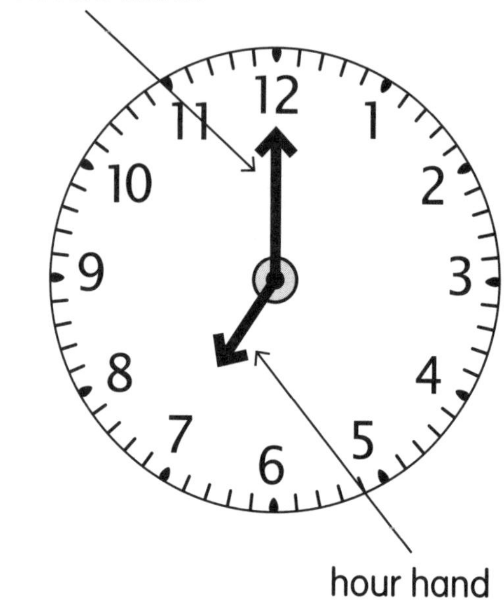

Digital Clock

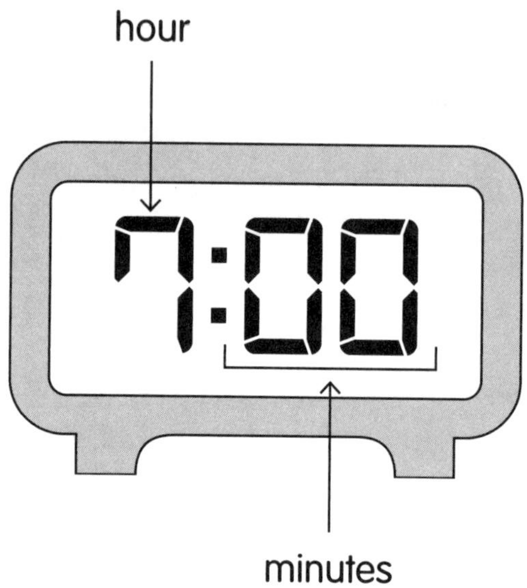

We say the time is **seven o'clock**. We write **7:00**.

One hour = 60 minutes. What time will it be **one hour** after **7:00**?

Name ________________________________

Look at the time on the analog clock. Draw a line to the digital clock with the same time.

Example

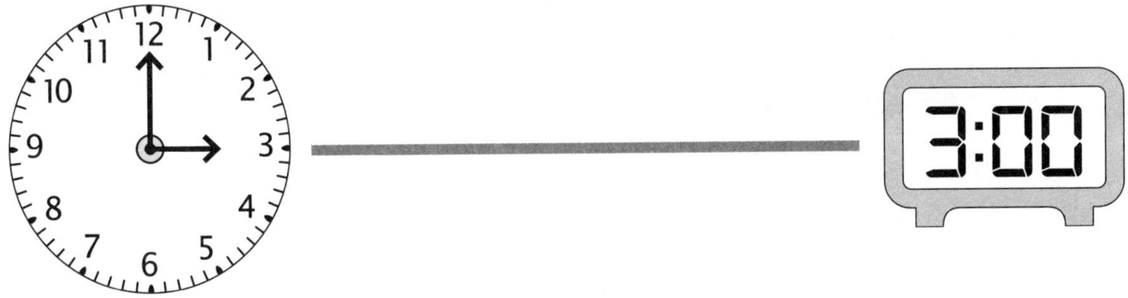

1. 

2. 

3. 

4. 

5. 

6. 

Name ____________________

Look at the time on the analog clock. Write the time on the digital clock.

1

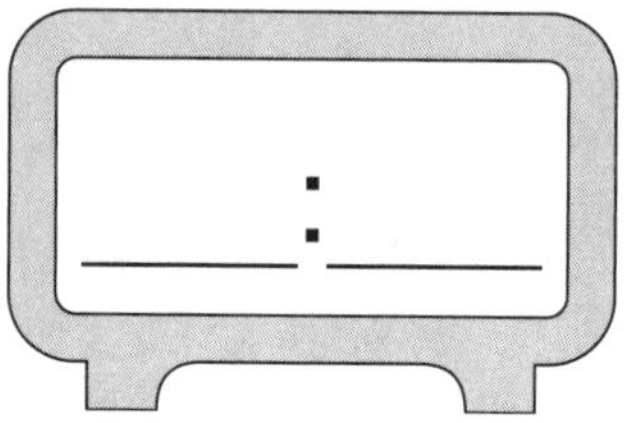

2

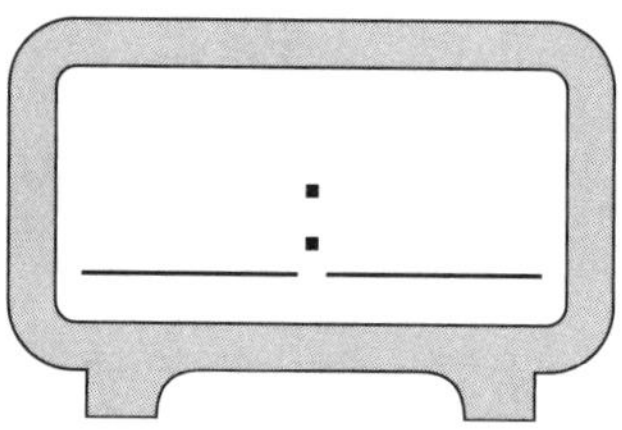

3

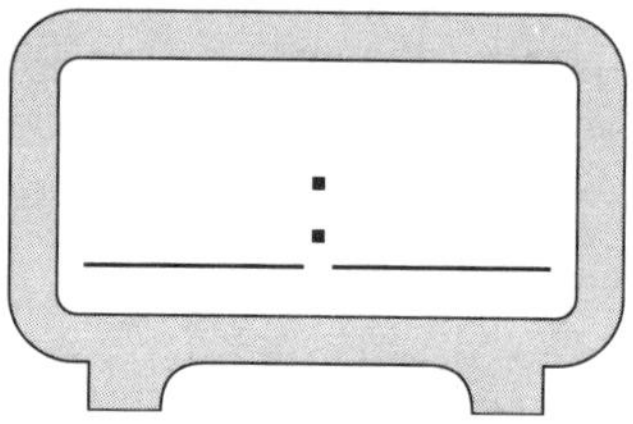

4

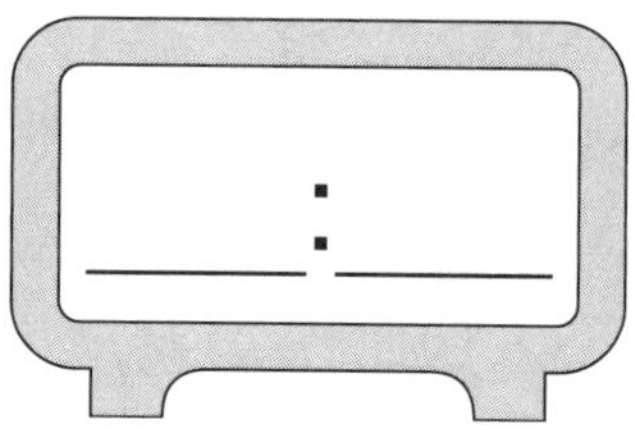

Name ______________________________

Read the Problem

The school day ends at 3:00.
A baseball game begins an hour later.
At what time does the game begin?

Think About It

1. You will find out what time ____.
   - ○ the school day ends
   - ○ the game begins

2. To find out the answer, you will ____.
   - ○ go ahead one hour
   - ○ go back one hour

Solve the Problem

3. Use this work space.

4. The game begins at ____:____.

Check Your Work

5. Do your answers make sense? ○ yes ○ no

Math Models

Telling time by the half-hour

Time

You can tell and write time in half-hours.

Analog Clock

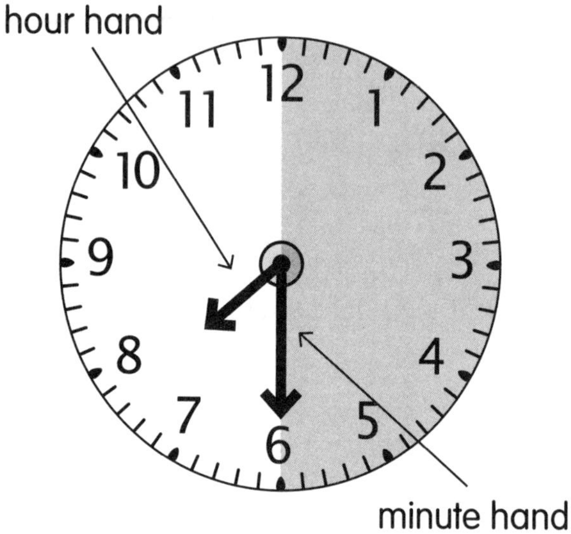

The hour hand is past 7.

The minute hand is 30 minutes past the hour.

Digital Clock

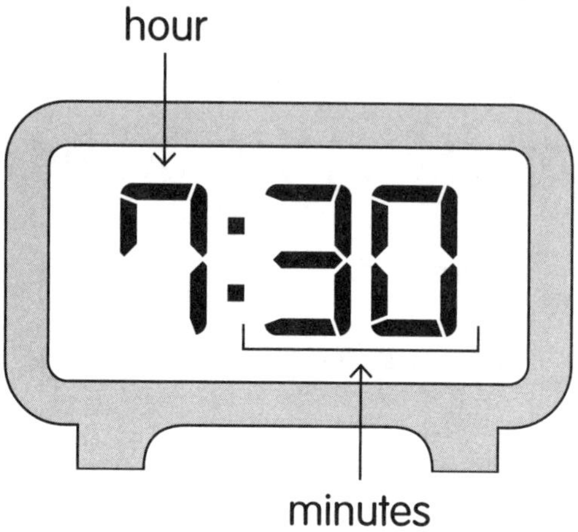

The hour shows 7.

The minutes show 30 minutes after the hour.

We say the time is **seven thirty** or **half past seven**. We write **7:30**.

What time will it be **30 minutes** after **7:30**?

Name ____________________

Look at the time on the analog clock. Draw a line to the digital clock with the same time.

Example

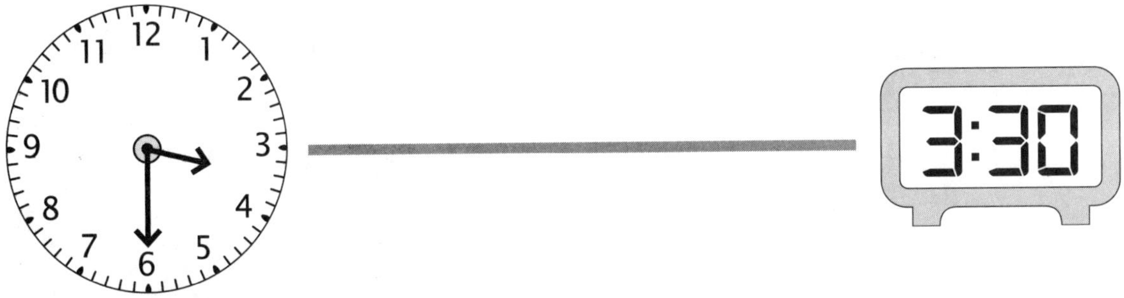

❶ 

❹ 

❷ 

❺ 

❸ 

❻ 

Tell and write time in half-hours using analog and digital clocks.

Name ____________________

Look at the time on the analog clock. Write the time on the digital clock.

1. 

3. 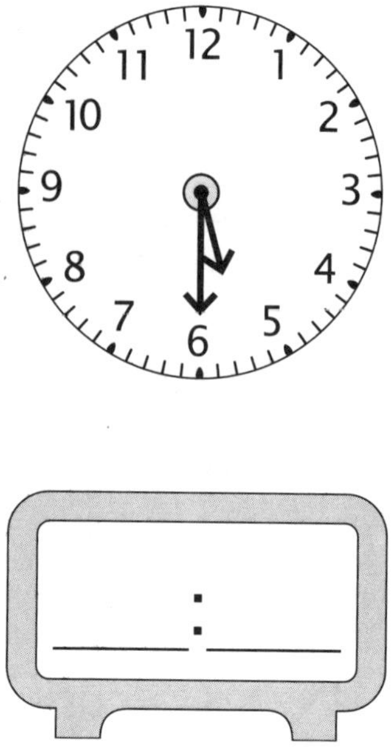

2. 

4. 

Name ______________________________

Fill in the circle below the digital clock that shows the same time as the analog clock.

1

○

○

2

○

○

3

○

○

4

○

○

Tell and write time in half-hours using analog and digital clocks.

Name ____________________

Read the Problem

Jason reads every night at 8:00.
He reads a half-hour before he goes to bed.
At what time does Jason go to bed?

Think About It

1. You will find out what time Jason ____.
   - ○ reads
   - ○ goes to bed

2. To find the answer, you will ____.
   - ○ go ahead a half-hour
   - ○ go back a half-hour

Solve the Problem

3. Use this work space.

4. Jason goes to bed at ____:____.

Check Your Work

5. Do your answers make sense? ○ yes ○ no

 Tell and write time in half-hours using analog and digital clocks.

Charts and Graphs

Unit Contents

Math Process Skills in This Unit

Make sense of problems and persevere in solving them: *pages 158, 162, 166, 170*

Reason abstractly and quantitatively: *pages 154, 155, 156, 157, 158, 159, 160, 161, 162, 163, 164, 165, 166, 167, 168, 169, 170*

Construct viable arguments and critique the reasoning of others: *pages 154, 159, 163, 167*

Model with mathematics: *pages 160, 161, 162, 164, 165, 166, 168, 169, 170*

Attend to precision: *pages 154, 155, 156, 157, 158, 159, 163, 167*

Look for and make use of structure: *pages 154, 155, 156, 157, 158, 159, 163, 167*

You can use charts and graphs to get meaning from data and answer questions.

Kim and her friends have pets. What kinds of pets do they have? These charts and graphs can show you.

Tally Chart

Our Pets

cats	𝍸
dogs	𝍸 |
birds	||

Picture Graph

Our Pets

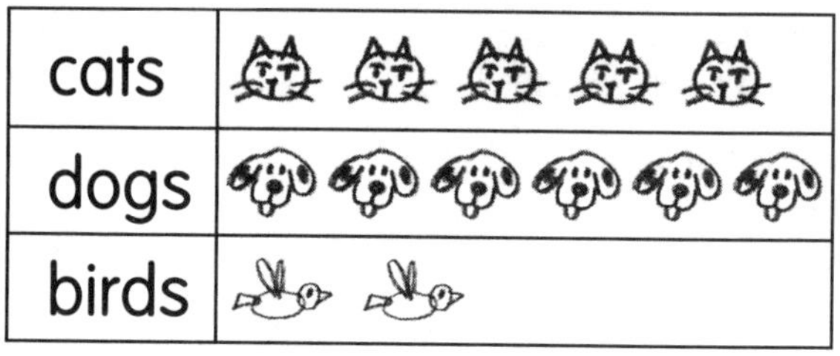

Bar Graph →

Our Pets

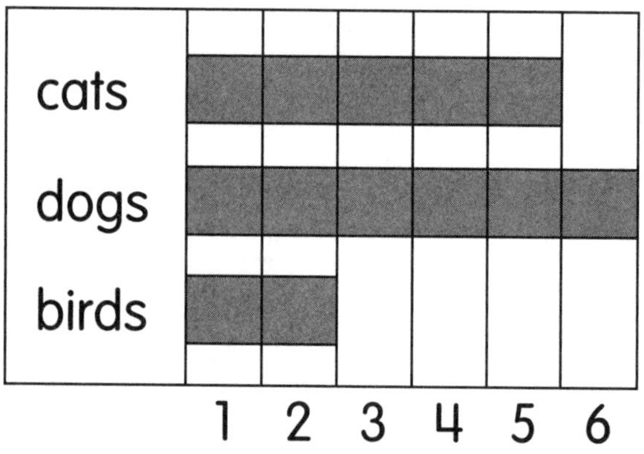

Bar Graph ↑

Our Pets

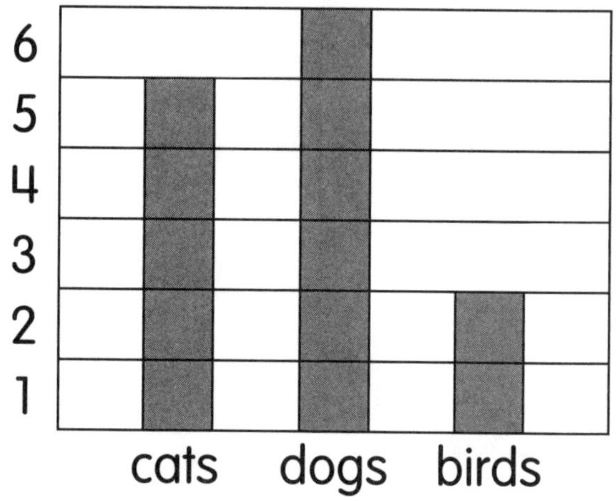

Which type of pet do Kim and her friends have the most of? Explain how each chart and graph shows you.

Name ______________________

Look at the tally chart. Answer the questions.

𝍸 = 5

Our Favorite Lunch	
 sandwiches	𝍸 |
 pizza	𝍸 ||
 tacos	𝍸 𝍸 |

1. What is this chart about? ______________________________

____

2. Which food was picked by the most people?

○ sandwiches ○ pizza ○ tacos

3. How many people like sandwiches the best?

_____ people

4. How many more people picked tacos than pizza?

_____ more people picked tacos

Interpret data with up to three categories.

Name ____________________

Look at the picture graph. Answer the questions.

1. What is this picture graph about? ____________________

____

2. How many people do **not** want to go?
   - ○ 5 people
   - ○ 3 people
   - ○ 2 people

3. How many people answered the question?

   _____ people

Name ______________________________

Look at the bar graph. Answer the questions.

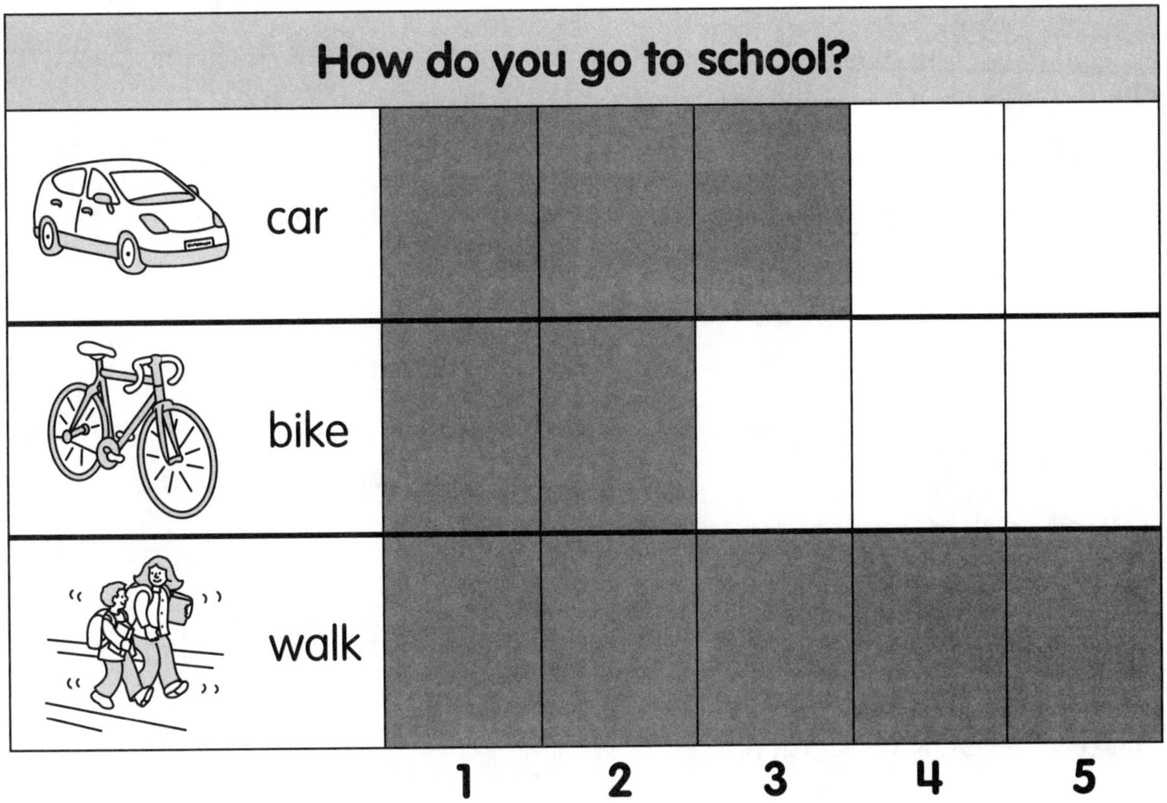

1. What is this bar graph about? ______________________________

____

2. How many more children walk than ride a bike?

    _____ more children

3. How do the most children go to school?

    ○ car ○ bike ○ walk

4. How many children answered the question? _____ children

Read the Problem and Complete the Graph

Last summer, Kate and her friends made a graph to show when each of them lost a tooth. Look at the graph. Answer the questions.

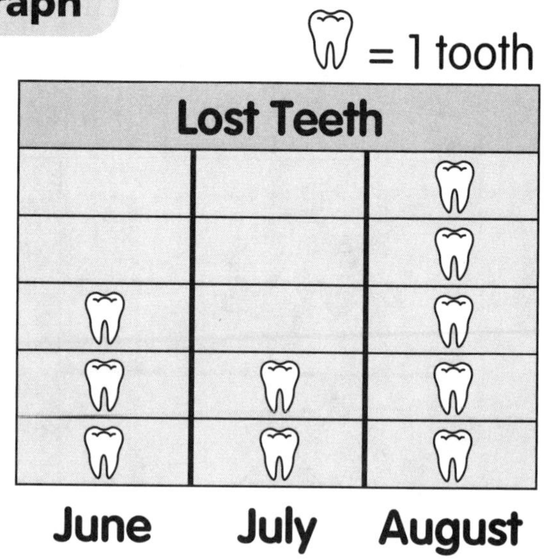

Think About It

❶ What is this graph about?

____

❷ You will look at each _____.

○ tally ○ picture ○ bar

Interpret the Graph

❸ The children lost the most teeth in the month of ____________.

❹ How many more teeth were lost in August than in June?

_____ more teeth

❺ How many teeth were lost in all? _____ teeth lost in all

Check Your Work

❻ Do your answers make sense? ○ yes ○ no

You can make a tally chart to show data and answer questions.

Jamie saw 10 blue jays, 2 crows, and 7 robins.
How many of each type of bird did he see?

I wrote one tally mark for each type of bird Jamie saw.

Birds

blue jays	𝍸 𝍸
crows	||
robins	𝍸 ||

Jamie saw the most blue jays.

Jamie saw the fewest crows.

Jamie saw 19 birds in all.

How many more blue jays than crows did Jamie see? Explain your thinking.

Name ____________________

Read the word problem. Use the data to complete the tally chart. Then answer the questions.

➤ Tim asked some children, "Have you ever been on an airplane?" 6 children said "Yes." 9 children said "No."

𝍸 = 5

1

Have you ever been on an airplane?	
Yes	
No	

2 What is this tally chart about? ____________________

____

3 Have most of the children been on a plane?
○ yes ○ no

4 How many children answered the question? _____ children

Name ____________________

Read the word problem. Use the data to complete the tally chart. Then answer the questions.

▷ Mrs. Soto's class voted for the game they like best. The data shows how the children voted.

𝍸 = 5

❶

Use this data:	
soccer	8
baseball	7
4-square	3

Our Favorite Game	
soccer	
baseball	
4-square	

❷ Which game got the most votes? ____________

❸ How many more children chose soccer than 4-square?

_____ more children

❹ How many children voted? _____ children

Name ______________________________

Read the Problem and Complete the Chart

1. Read the chart. Look at the total votes for each apple. Write the tally marks to complete the chart. Then answer the questions.

Apples We Like		
Color	Tallies	Total
red		11
green		5
yellow		4

Think About It

2. This chart is about which color apples children like.
   ○ yes ○ no

3. You completed the chart with _____.
   ○ tally marks ○ pictures ○ bars

Interpret the Chart

4. The least favorite apple is ______________.

5. How many more children voted for red apples than yellow?

   _____ more children

6. How many children voted in all? _____ children

Check Your Work

7. Do your answers make sense? ○ yes ○ no

You can make a picture graph to show data and answer questions.

Dad has a garden. He picked 3 carrots, 12 beans, and 2 radishes.

I drew one picture for each item Dad picked.

What did Dad pick?

carrots	
beans	
radishes	

Dad picked more beans than carrots or radishes.

Dad picked 17 vegetables altogether.

How many fewer carrots than beans did Dad pick? Explain your thinking.

Name ______________________________

Read the word problem. Draw to complete the picture graph. Then answer the questions.

➤ Keli asked some friends if they like funny or scary movies. 7 friends like funny movies. 3 friends like scary movies.

1. Write ☺ for what each friend likes.

☺ = 1 friend

Do you like funny or scary movies?	
funny	
scary	

2. What is this picture graph about? ______________________________

____

3. Most of the friends like _____ movies.

○ funny ○ scary

4. How many friends answered the question? _____ friends

Name ______________________________

Read the word problem. Draw to complete the picture graph. Then answer the questions.

Each sports team has a different color flag. Players on one team voted for a new flag color. 4 voted for yellow. 6 voted for green. 3 voted for red.

1. Draw one  for each vote.

New Flag Colors

yellow	**green**	**red**

2. What is this picture graph about? ______________________________

____

3. Which flag color got the most votes? ______________

Name ____________________

Read the Problem and Complete the Graph

A family voted for their favorite fruit.

Use this data:

5 voted for bananas

4 voted for plums

3 voted for grapes

Fruit		
bananas	**plums**	**grapes**

❶ Draw , , and  to complete the picture graph.

Think About It

❷ What is this picture graph about? ____________________

____

Interpret the Graph

❸ Which fruit was the favorite of most family members?

____

❹ How many family members voted? ______ family members

Check Your Work

❺ Do your answers make sense? ◯ yes ◯ no

Math Models

Bar graphs

You can make a bar graph to show data and answer questions.

Marie asked some friends to name their favorite weather.

This is what they said: **sunny 7**

rainy 2

snowy 6

A bar graph uses a shaded bar to show information.

I colored one ▮ for each friend's vote.

Our Favorite Weather

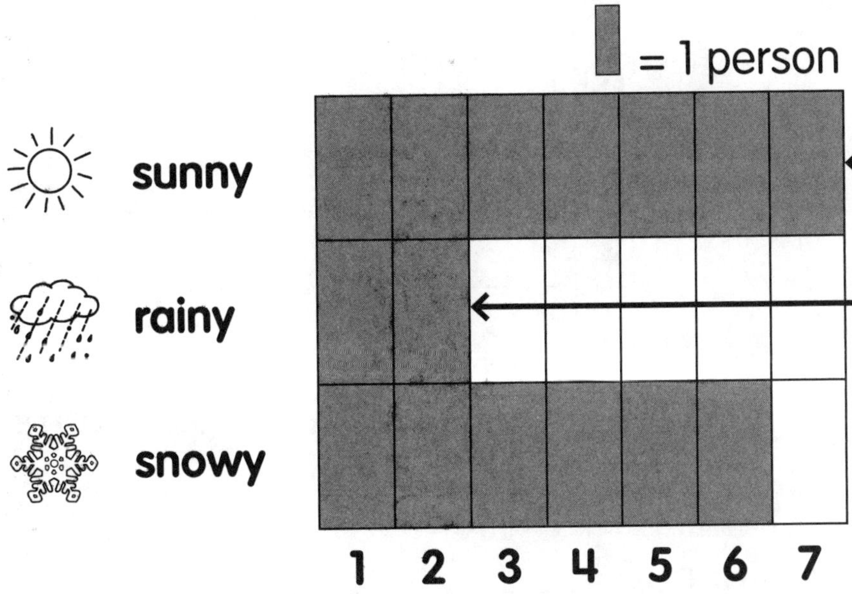

Most of Marie's friends said sunny weather was their favorite.

Fewer people liked rainy than sunny or snowy weather.

15 friends in all named their favorite weather.

How many fewer friends liked rainy weather than sunny weather? Explain your thinking.

Organize, represent, and interpret data with up to three categories.

Name ______________________________

Read the word problem. Color to complete the bar graph. Then answer the questions.

➤ Mrs. Garcia asked her students if they like the beach or the forest best. 8 students said they like the beach. 12 students said they like the forest.

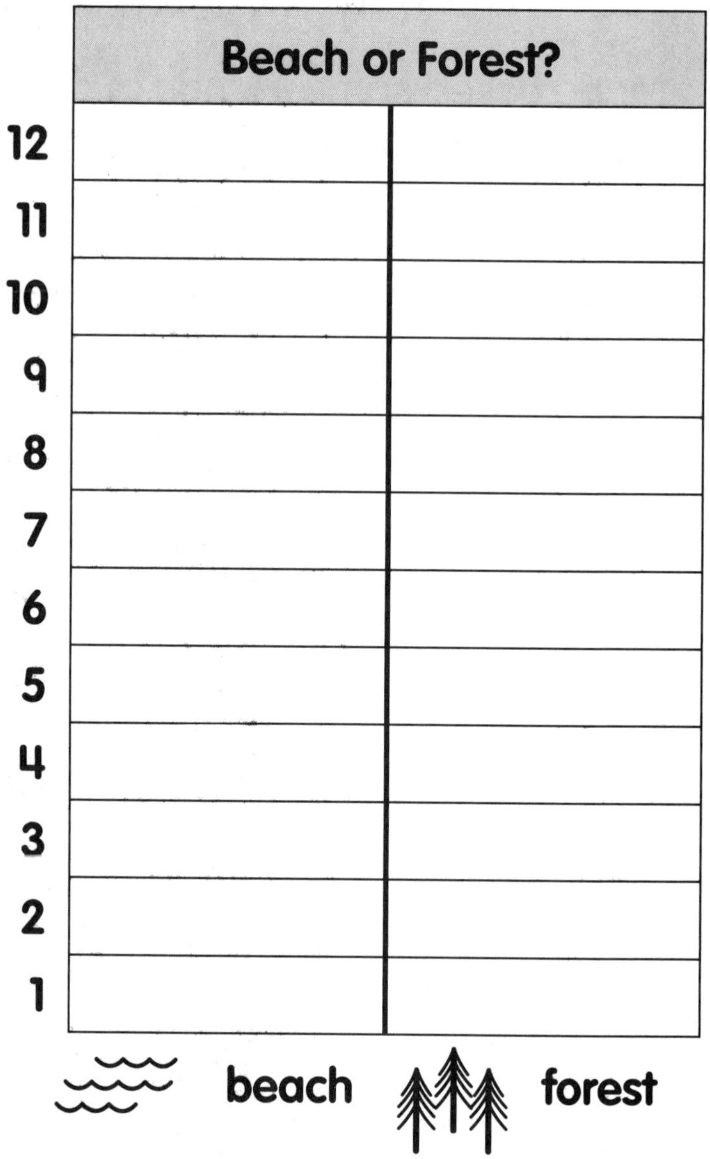

❶ Color one ▭ to show what each student likes best.

❷ What is this bar graph about? ______________________________

____

❸ How many more students chose the forest than the beach?

_____ more students

Name ____________________

Read the word problem. Color to complete the bar graph. Then answer the questions.

Farmer Tom has hens. Each hen lays one egg every day. Farmer Tom finds 3 white, 4 brown, and 5 spotted eggs every day.

1. Color one ▭ for each egg laid.

Eggs Laid Every Day					
white					
brown					
spotted					
	1	**2**	**3**	**4**	**5**

2. What is this bar graph about? ______________________________

____

3. How many fewer white eggs than spotted eggs are laid each day? _____ fewer white eggs

4. How many eggs are laid each day in all? _____ eggs

Organize, represent, and interpret data with up to three categories.

Name ______________________________

Read the Problem and Complete the Graph

Mr. Black trains dogs. How many of each size dog does he train?

Use this data:
4 small dogs
7 medium dogs
2 large dogs

Dog Sizes

	small	medium	large
7			
6			
5			
4			
3			
2			
1			

1. Complete the bar graph.

Think About It

2. What is this bar graph about?

____

Interpret the Graph

3. How many more medium dogs than large dogs does Mr. Black train? _____ more medium dogs

4. How many dogs does he train altogether? _____ dogs

Check Your Work

5. Do your answers make sense? ○ yes ○ no

Money

Unit Contents

Math Process Skills in This Unit

Make sense of problems and persevere in solving them: *pages 175, 179, 184*

Reason abstractly and quantitatively: *pages 172, 173, 174, 176, 177, 178, 179, 180, 181, 182, 183, 184*

Construct viable arguments and critique the reasoning of others: *pages 172, 176, 180*

Model with mathematics: *pages 175, 179, 184*

Attend to precision: *pages 172, 175, 176, 179, 180, 184*

Look for and make use of structure: *pages 172, 173, 174, 175, 176, 177, 178, 179, 180, 181, 182, 183, 184*

You can identify pennies, nickels, dimes, and quarters. Each coin has a different size, look, and value.

What it looks like	What it is called	Its value
	penny	1¢
	nickel	5¢
	dime	10¢
	quarter	25¢

Look at the chart. Would you rather have **2 quarters** or **2 nickels**? Explain your thinking.

Name ______________________________

Circle the value of each coin.

Examples

5¢

25¢ (circled)

1¢

10¢ (circled)

❶ 

5¢

25¢

❷ 

25¢

10¢

❸ 

1¢

5¢

❹ 

10¢

1¢

❺ 

25¢

10¢

❻ 

5¢

1¢

Name ____________________

Draw a line from each coin to its name and/or value.

1		•	• dime
2		•	• 25¢
3		•	• penny
4		•	• 5¢
5		•	• nickel
6		•	• 10¢

Name ______________________

Read the Problem

Marci has 3 coins.
The values of her coins are 25 cents, 10 cents, and 1 cent.
What are the names of each of Marci's coins?

Think About It

1. You will write the _____ of Marci's coins.
   - ○ value ○ names ○ total

Solve the Problem

Use the word box to help you write your answers.

penny	nickel	dime	quarter

2. Marci has a ____________, a ____________,
   and a ____________.

Check Your Work

3. Do your answers make sense? ○ yes ○ no

Math Models

Writing the value of coins

You can use ¢ to write the value of coins.

Front and Back

We say, "A penny equals one cent."
We write: **1¢**

We say, "A nickel equals five cents."
We write: **5¢**

We say, "A dime equals ten cents."
We write: **10¢**

We say, "A quarter equals 25 cents."
We write: **25¢**

Why is it important to use **¢** when you write numbers about money? Explain your thinking.

Name ______________________

Write the value of each coin.

Examples

5¢

10¢

❶

______

❷

______

❸

______

❹

______

❺

______

❻

______

Name ____________________

Circle the name of each coin. Then write its value.

1. 

dime

quarter

25¢

2. 

nickel

dime

______

3. 

dime

quarter

______

4. 

penny

nickel

______

5. 

nickel

quarter

______

6. 

penny

dime

______

Name ______________________

Read the Problem

Jack has a nickel. Teera has a quarter. Mike has a dime.
How much money does each child have?

Think About It

1. You will find out how much money ____.
   - ○ in all ○ each child has ○ is left

2. Mark the other way to write "cents."
   - ○ $ ○ ? ○ ¢

Solve the Problem

3. Use this work space.

4. Jack has ____.

5. Teera has ____.

6. Mike has ____.

Check Your Work

7. Do your answers make sense? ○ yes ○ no

Math Models

Counting coins

You can use counting on to find the value of groups of pennies, nickels, and dimes.

You can **count on** for groups of matching coins.
These are some examples:

5¢ 10¢ 15¢ 20¢ **= 20¢**

10¢ 20¢ 30¢ 40¢ **= 40¢**

You can **count on** for groups of coins that don't match, too.
Count in order from the largest value to the smallest value coins.

10¢ 20¢ 25¢ 26¢ **= 26¢**

If you had 3 pennies, 1 nickel, and 2 dimes, what order should you use to **count on**? Explain your thinking.

Name ____________________

Count on for each group of coins. Write the values.

Examples

5¢ 10¢ 15¢ = 15¢

❶  = ____

____ ____ ____ ____ ____ ____

❷  = ____

____ ____ ____ ____ ____ ____

❸  = ____

____ ____ ____ ____ ____

Name ____________________

Count on for each group of coins. Write the values.

1 

____ ____ ____ ____ = ____

2 

____ ____ ____ ____ = ____

3 

____ ____ ____ ____ ____ = ____

4 

____ ____ ____ ____ = ____

Name ______________________

Money
Counting coins

7

Count on for each group of coins. Write the value.

1

______

2

______

3

______

4

______

Name ______________________________

Read the Problem

Anna has 2 dimes, 1 nickel, and 3 pennies.
How much money does Anna have?

Think About It

1. You will find out how much money Anna _____.

   ○ needs ○ lost ○ has

2. Write about your plan to solve the problem.

   ____

   ____

Solve the Problem

3. Use this work space.

4. Anna has _____.

Check Your Work

5. Do your answers make sense? ○ yes ○ no

Geometry

Unit Contents

Math Process Skills in This Unit

Make sense of problems and persevere in solving them: *pages 189, 193, 197, 201, 206*

Reason abstractly and quantitatively: *pages 189, 193, 197, 201, 206*

Construct viable arguments and critique the reasoning of others: *pages 186, 190, 194, 197, 198, 202*

Model with mathematics: *pages 189, 193, 201, 206*

Attend to precision: *pages 198, 193, 197, 201, 206*

Math Models

Identifying two- and three-dimensional shapes

You can identify two- and three-dimensional shapes.

A **two-dimensional** shape is flat.
These are some examples:

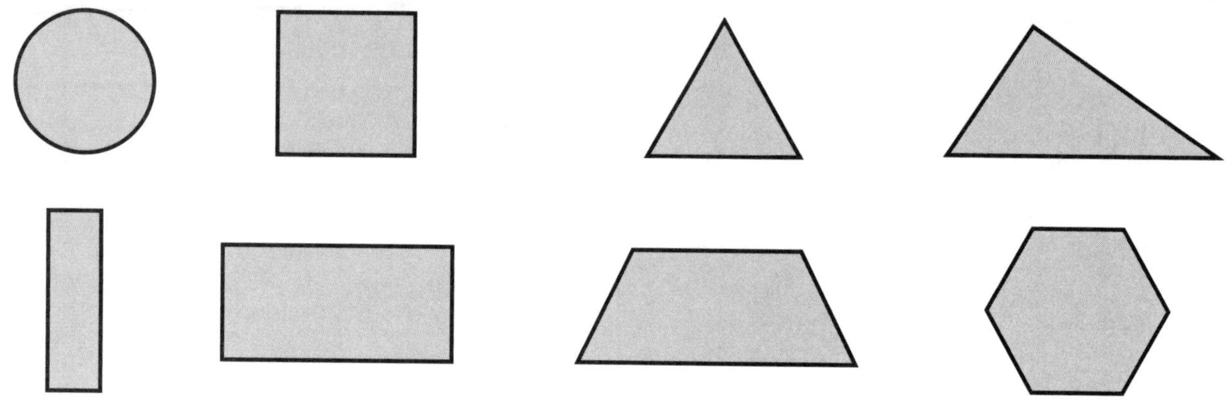

A **three-dimensional shape** has thickness.
These are some examples:

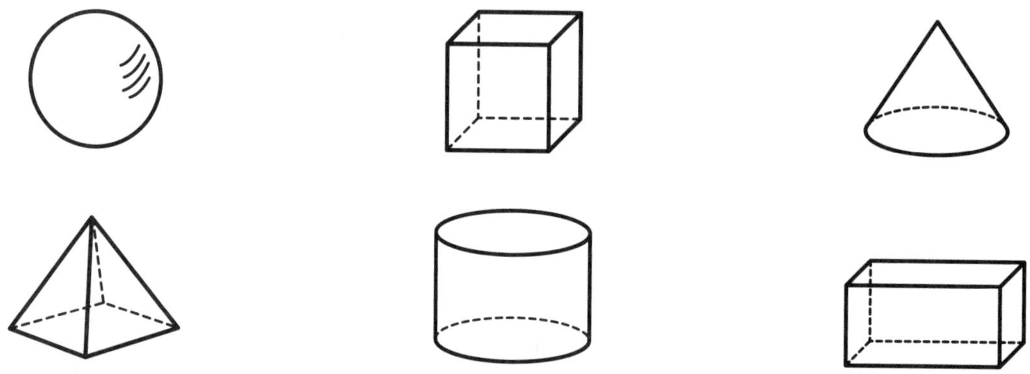

What are some differences between two- and three-dimensional shapes? Explain your thinking.

Name ____________________

Draw a line from each object to the shape it looks like.

Example

1  • 

2  • 

3 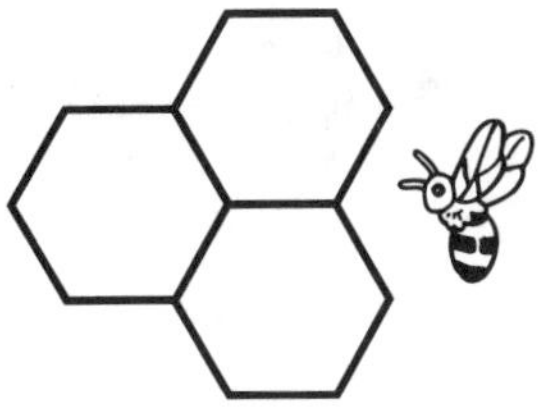 • 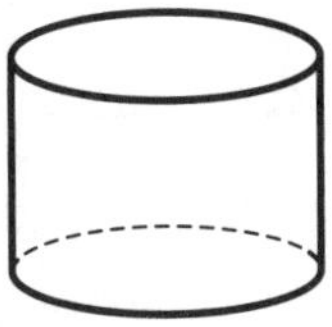

4  • 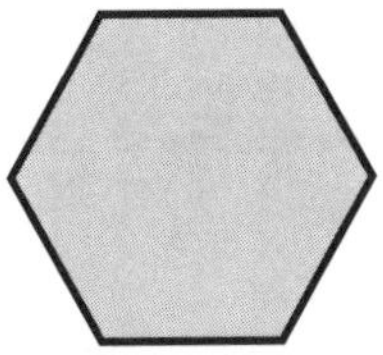

Name ______________________________

Draw a line from each object to the shape it looks like.

1 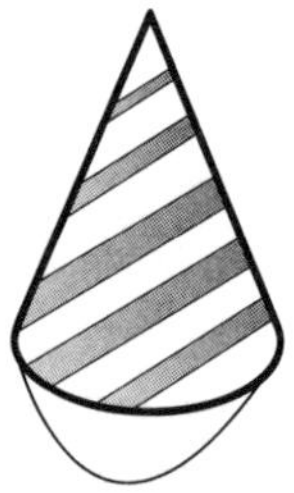 • 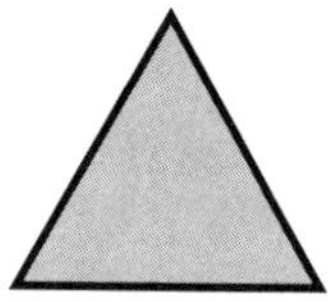

2 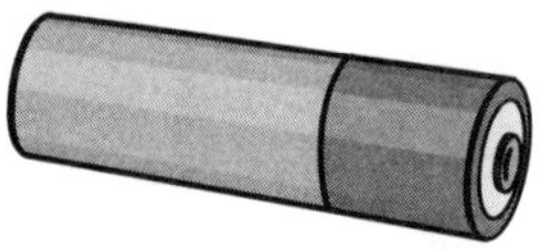 • 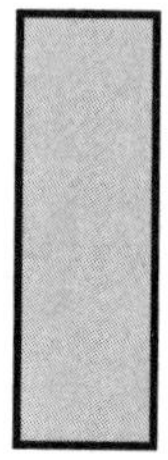

3  • 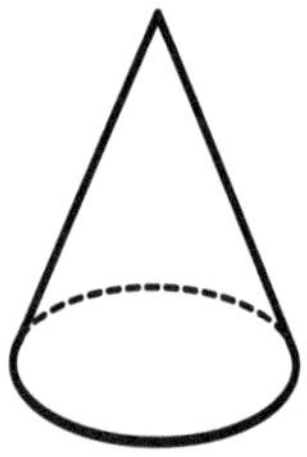

4  • 

5 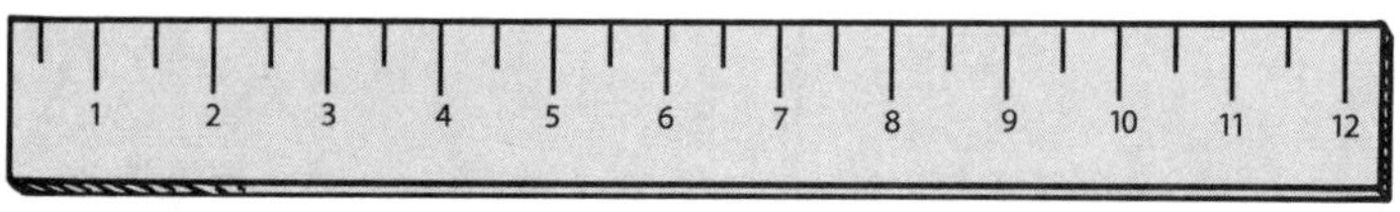

• 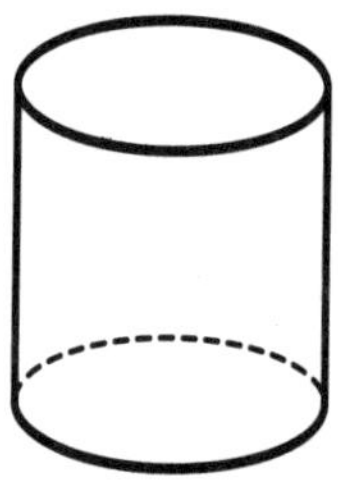

Name ______________________________

Read the Problem

Maya and her dad went for a walk to look for shapes.
They saw a house with square windows and a rectangle door.
The house had a triangle tree next to it.
Draw a picture of the house and tree Maya and her dad saw.

Think About It

1. You will draw a house with square windows and a _____ door.
   ○ triangle ○ square ○ rectangle

2. You will draw a _____ tree next to the house.
   ○ square ○ rectangle ○ triangle

Solve the Problem

3. Draw the house and tree that Maya and her dad saw.

Check Your Work

4. Do your answers make sense? ○ yes ○ no

Math Models

Identifying defining and nondefining attributes

You can identify a shape by looking at what it has.

This is an example:

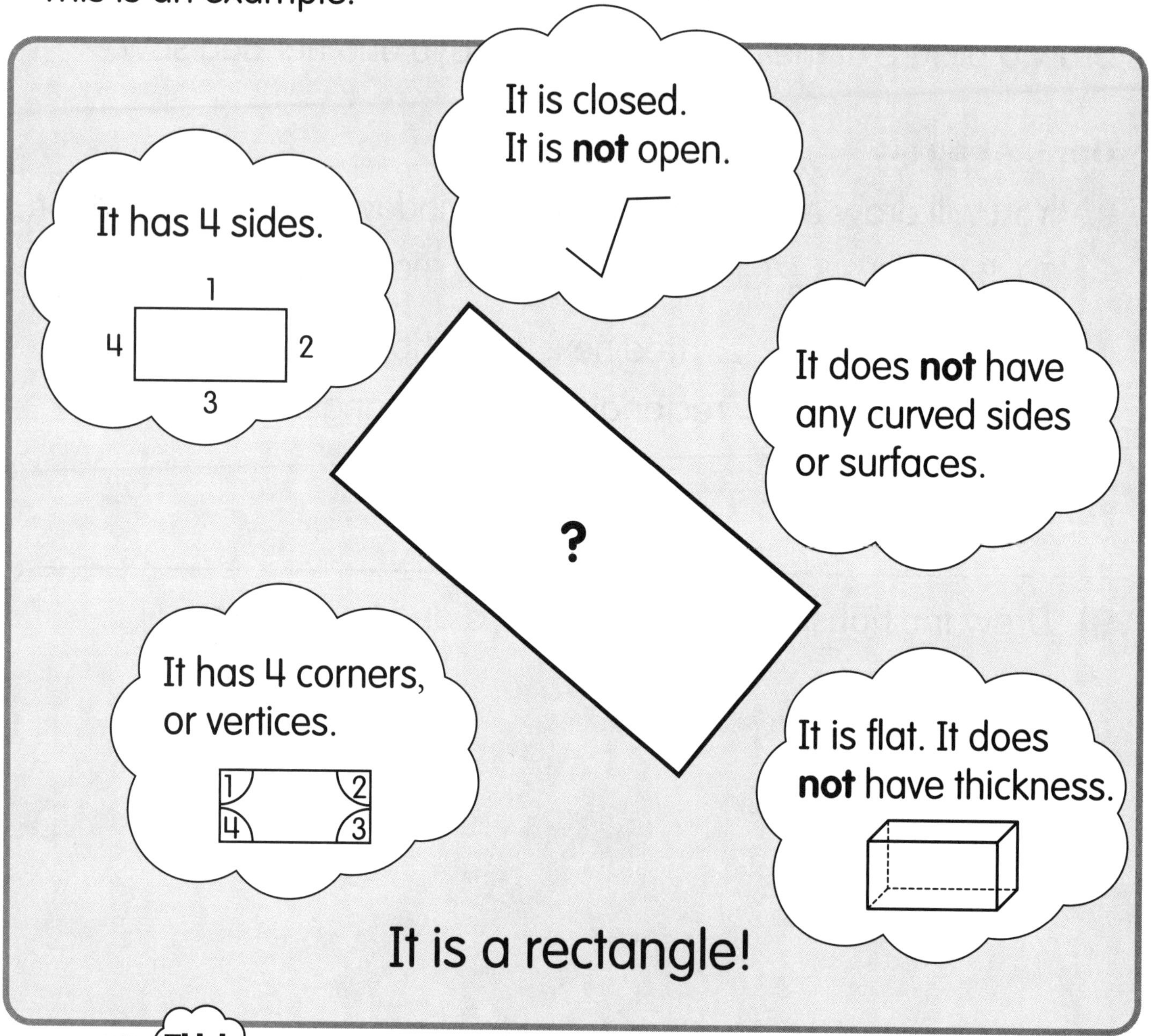

If the rectangle was smaller, colored, or turned, would it still be a rectangle? Explain your answer.

 Distinguish between attributes that compose two- or three-dimensional shapes.

Name ____________________

Trace each shape. Write the number of sides and corners.

Example

3 sides

3 corners

triangle

❶

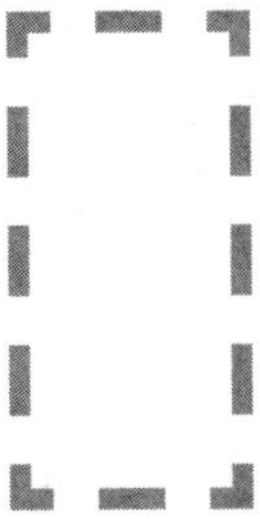

____ sides

____ corners

rectangle

❷

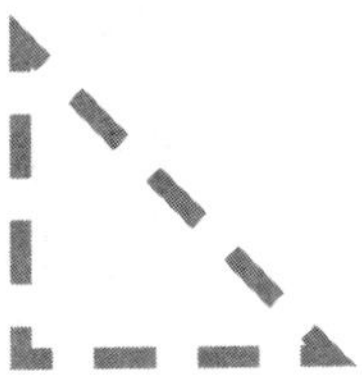

____ sides

____ corners

triangle

❸

____ sides

____ corners

square

❹

____ sides

____ corners

trapezoid

❺

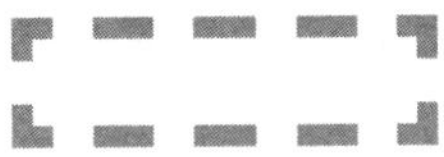

____ sides

____ corners

rectangle

Distinguish between attributes that compose two- or three-dimensional shapes.

Write the number of flat or curved surfaces for each shape.

1

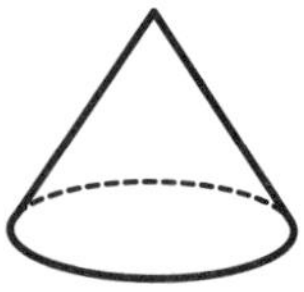

_____ flat

_____ curved

cone

2

_____ flat

_____ curved

sphere

3

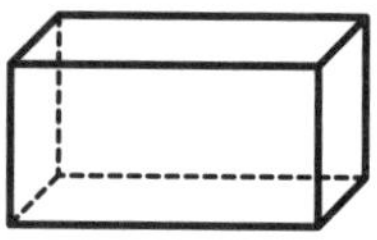

_____ flat

_____ curved

rectangular prism

4

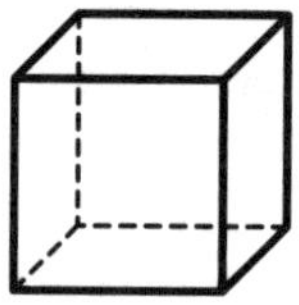

_____ flat

_____ curved

cube

5

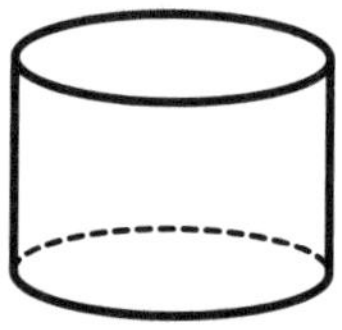

_____ flat

_____ curved

cylinder

6

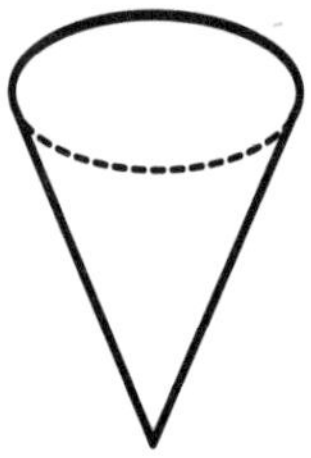

_____ flat

_____ curved

cone

Name ______________________________

Read the Problem

Brian has a set of blocks. He can't find one of the blocks. It has 1 flat and 1 curved surface. Circle the missing block.

Think About It

1. You will circle the block that has _____ surface.
   ○ 1 flat ○ 1 curved ○ 1 flat and 1 curved

2. The block will _____.
   ○ be flat ○ have thickness ○ have 4 sides

Solve the Problem

3. Circle the missing block.

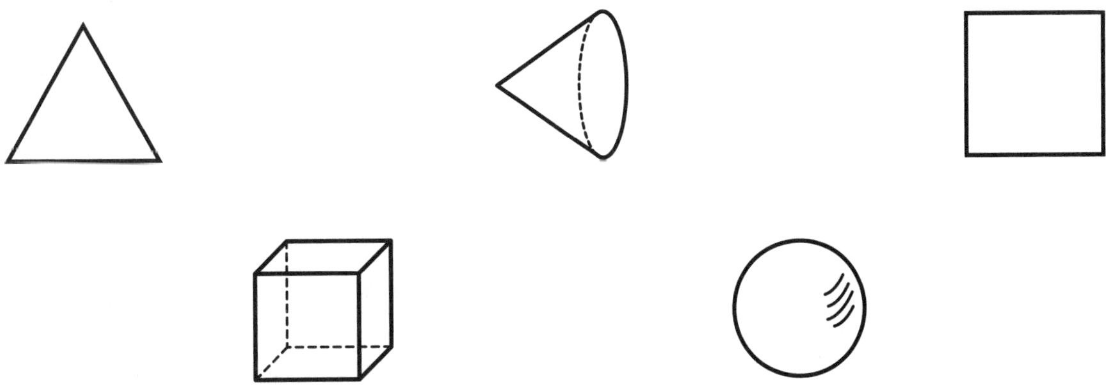

Check Your Work

4. Do your answers make sense? ○ yes ○ no

You can combine shapes to make new shapes.

These are some examples:

Shapes Used | **New Shape**

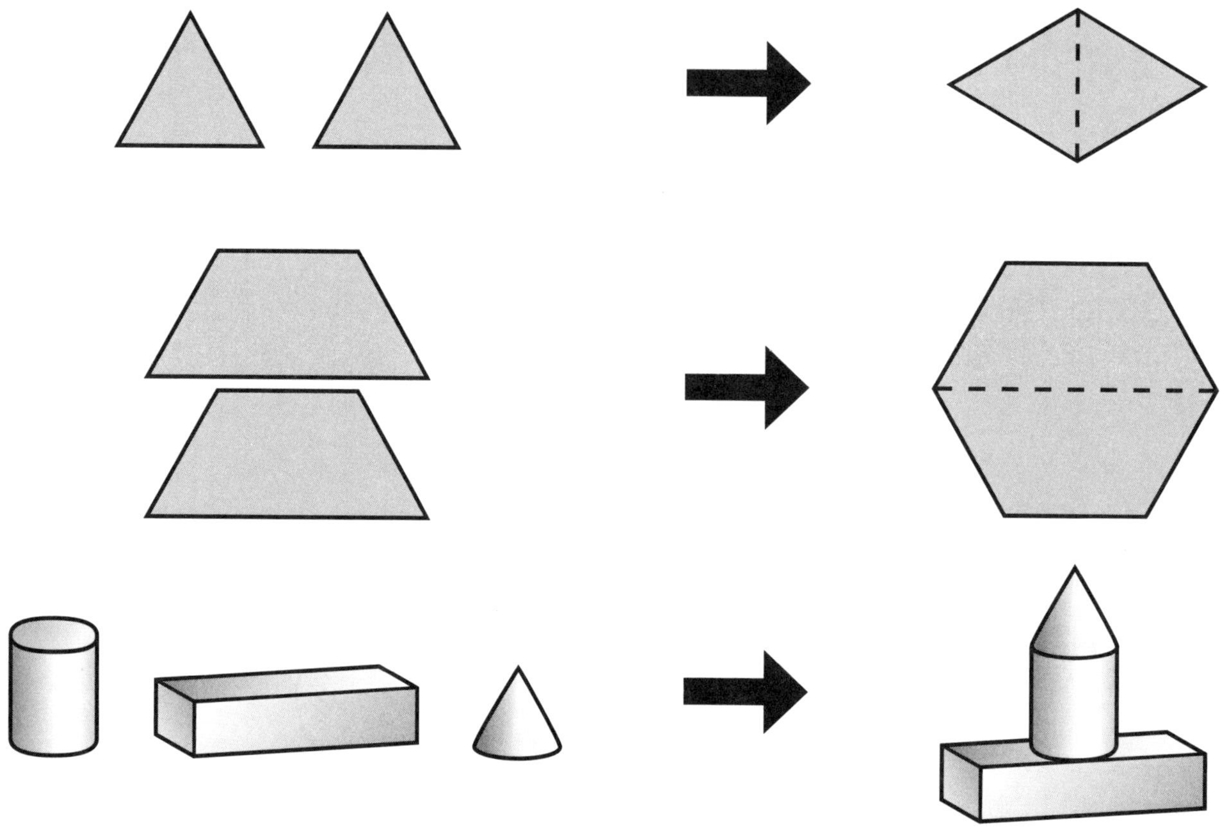

What shapes do you need to build ?
Explain your thinking.

Circle the smaller shapes that can be used to make the bigger shape.

Example

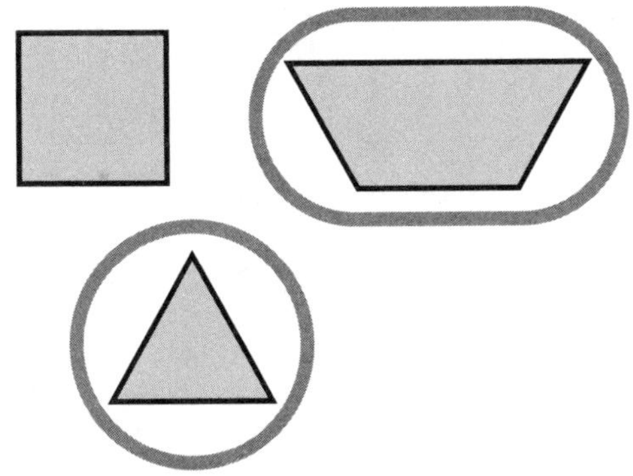

can make

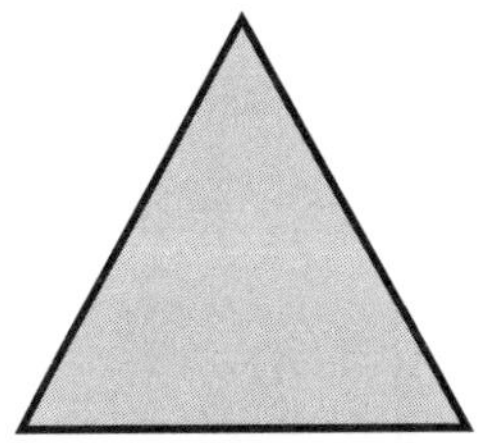

❶

can make

❷

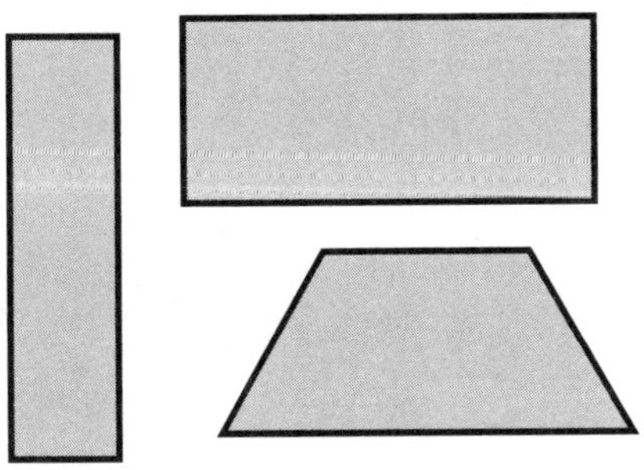

can make

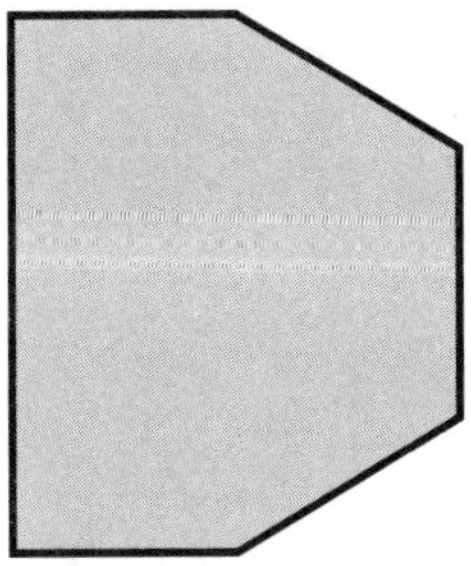

❸

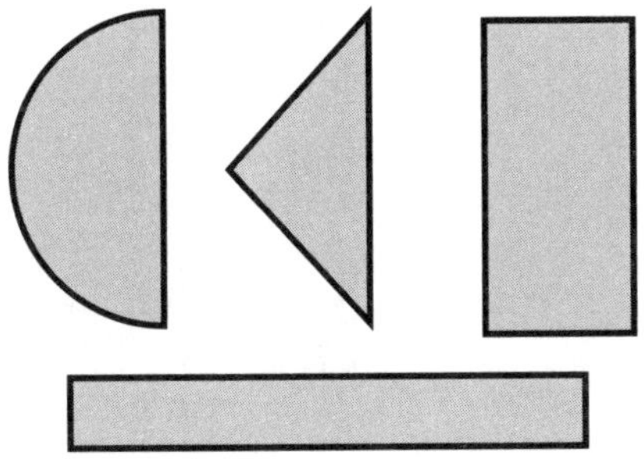

can make

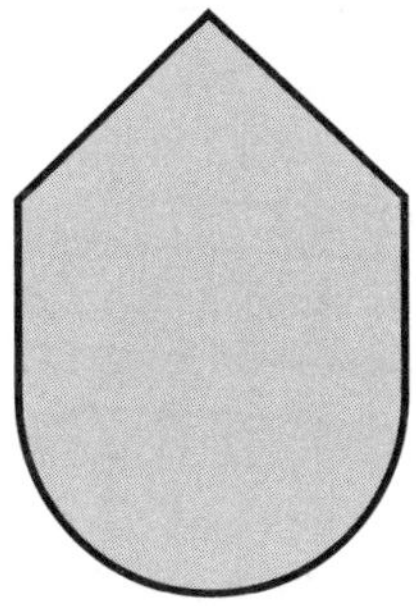

Draw a line from each group of shapes to the new shape you can make.

1 

2 

3 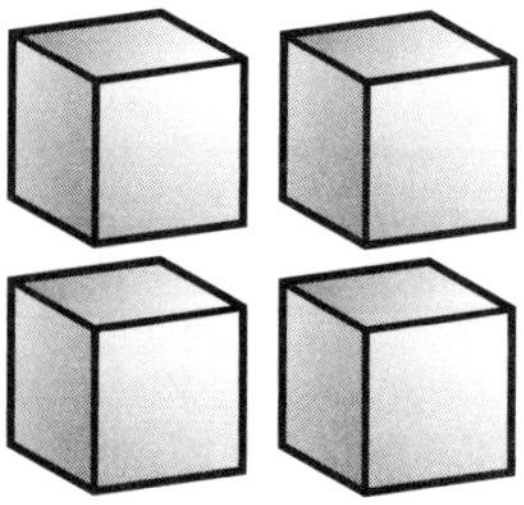

4 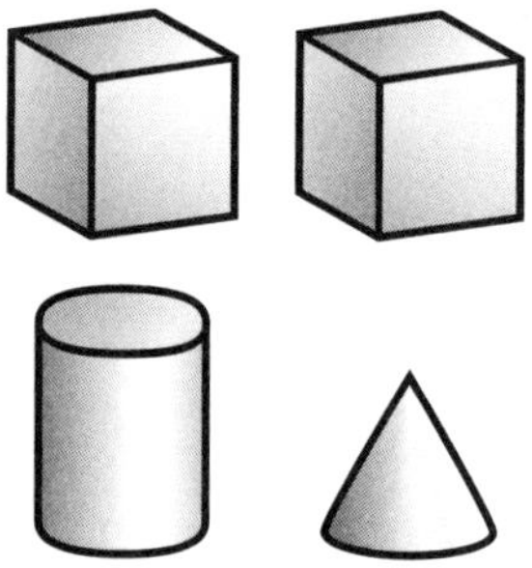

5 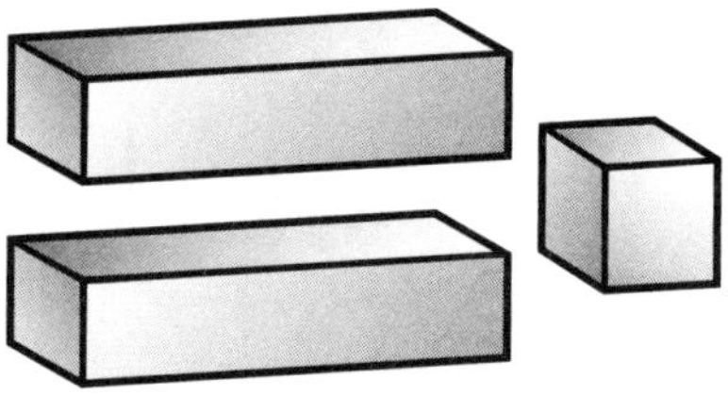

• 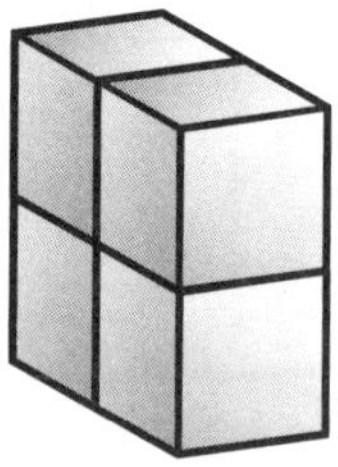

• 

• 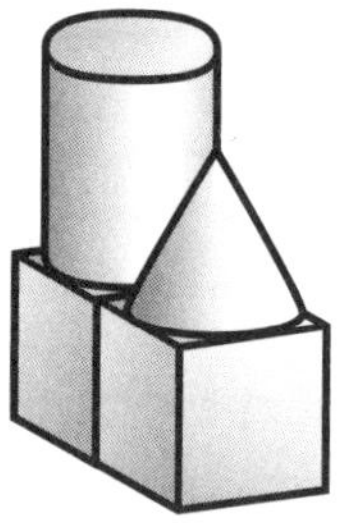

• 

• 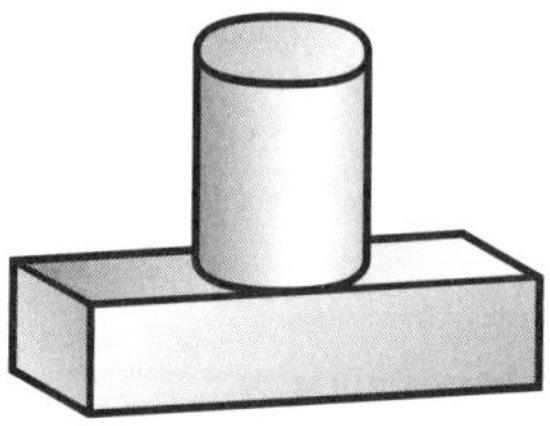

 Compose two-dimensional or three-dimensional shapes to create composite shapes.

Read the Problem

Matt sees 8 s in the big shape.
Zoey said, "I see more than 8 s."
How many s are there?

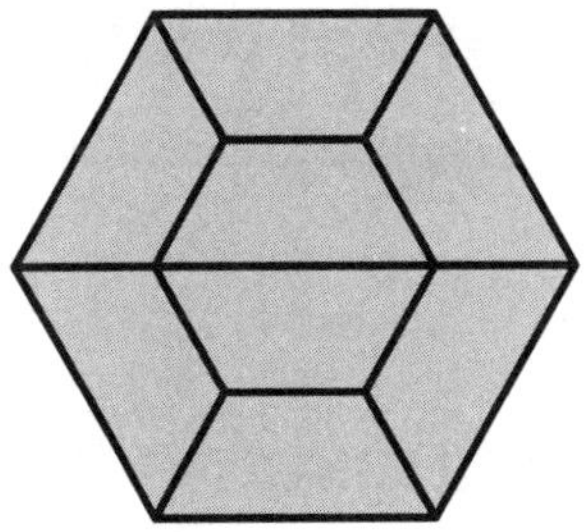

Think About It

❶ You will find out how many _____ compose the big shape.

○ s ○ s ○ s

❷ Zoey says that there are _____.

○ more than 8 ○ fewer than 8 ○ 8

Solve the Problem

❸ There are _____ s in the shape.

Check Your Work

❹ Do your answers make sense? ○ yes ○ no

Compose two-dimensional or three-dimensional shapes to create composite shapes.

Math Models

Partitioning shapes into equal shares

You can tell if shares, or parts, of a whole are equal or not equal.

These are some examples:

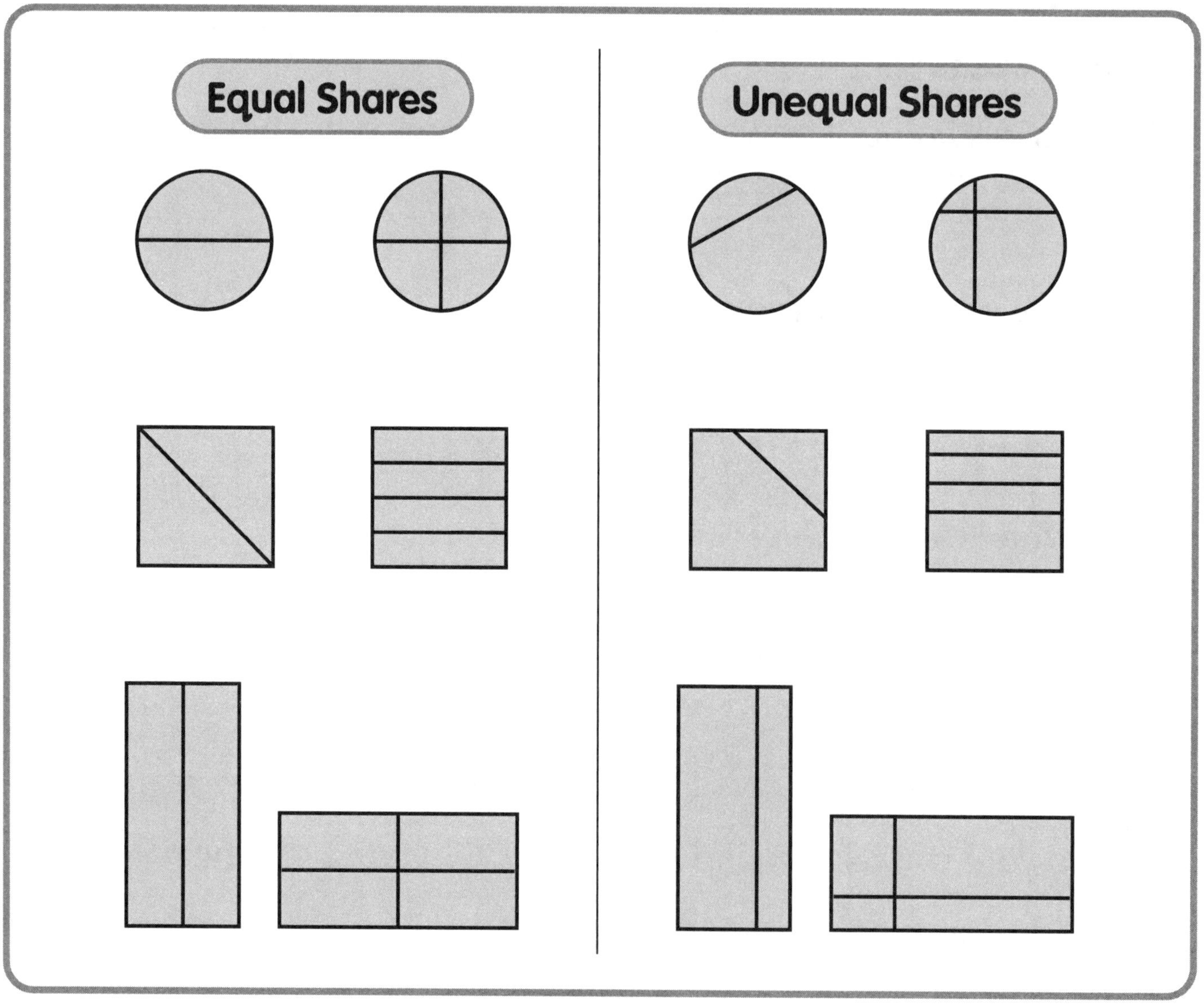

If you are cutting pizza for friends, is it important to cut equal shares? Explain your thinking.

Name ______________________________

Circle ☺ if the shape has **equal** shares, or parts.

Circle ☹ if the shape has **unequal** shares, or parts.

Examples

☺ equal (circled)

☹ unequal

☺ equal

☹ unequal (circled)

1. 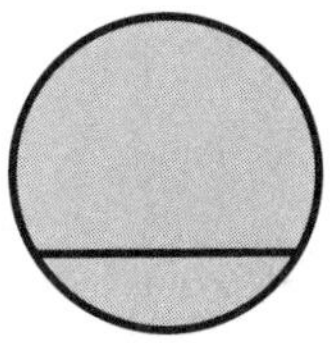

☺ equal

☹ unequal

4. 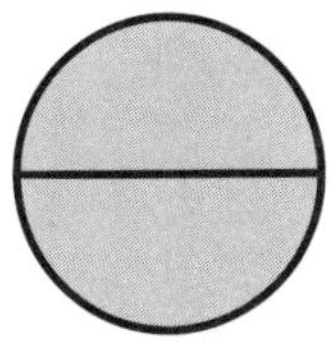

☺ equal

☹ unequal

2. 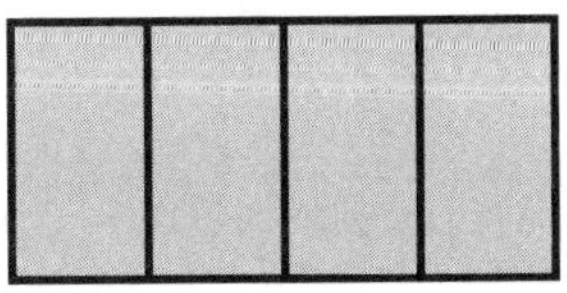

☺ equal

☹ unequal

5. 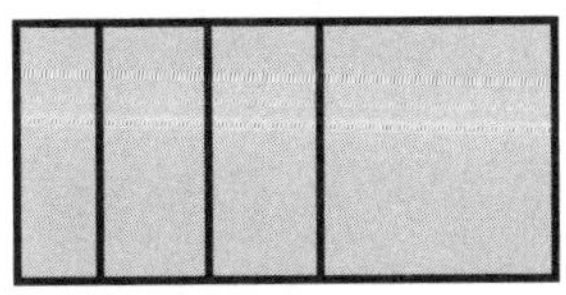

☺ equal

☹ unequal

3. 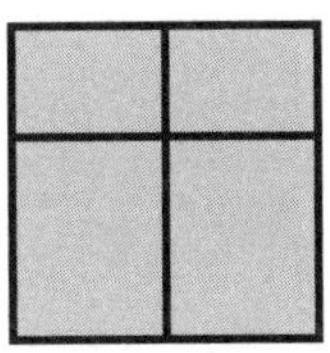

☺ equal

☹ unequal

6. 

☺ equal

☹ unequal

Partition circles and rectangles into two and four equal shares.

Name ______________________________

Circle the shapes that show **equal** shares, or parts.

1 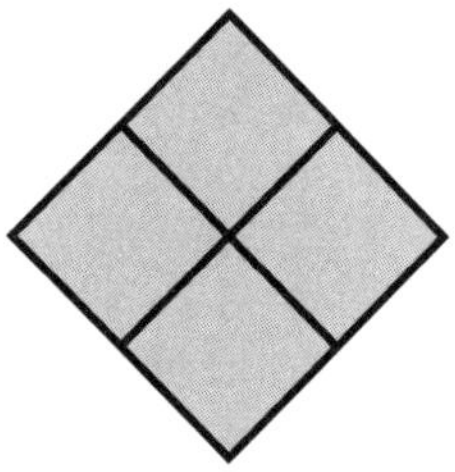

2 

3 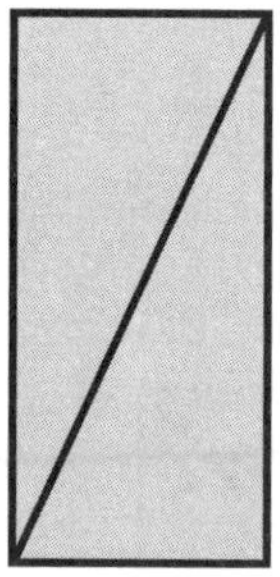

4 

5 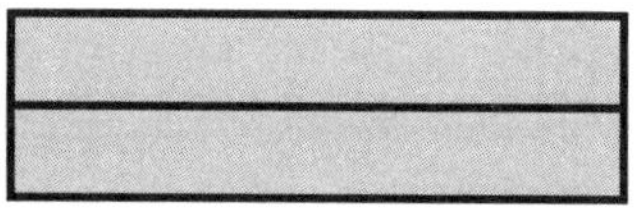

6 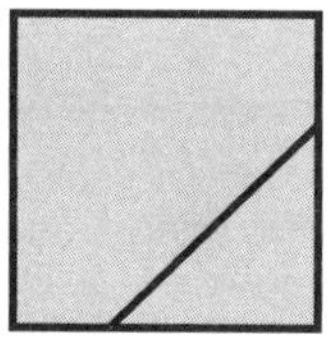

7 

8 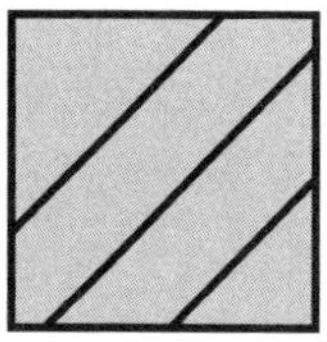

9 

Name ______________________________

Read the Problem

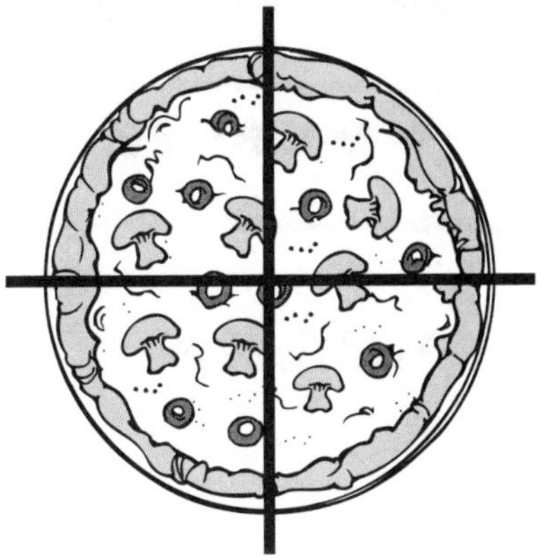

Tami cut a pizza into four equal shares. It looked like this. Circle the shape below that shows one equal share of Tami's pizza.

Think About It

1. You will find the shape that is 1 of _____ equal shares.
   ○ 2 ○ 3 ○ 4

2. A circle has a _____ side.
   ○ curved ○ straight ○ zigzag

Solve the Problem

3. Circle the shape that shows one equal share of Tami's pizza.

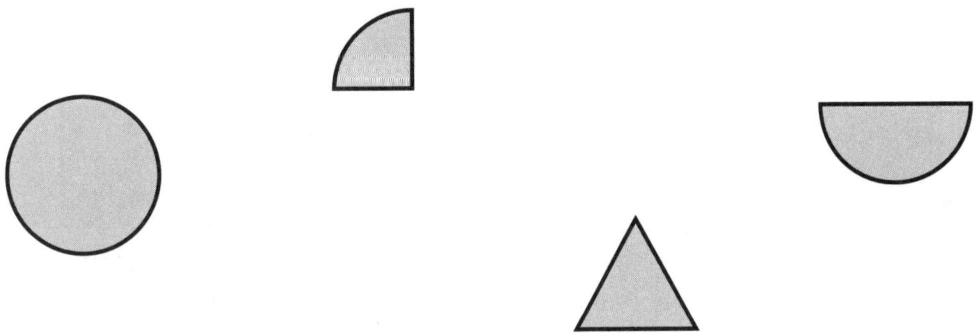

Check Your Work

4. Do your answers make sense? ○ yes ○ no

You can show how a fraction is an equal part of a whole shape.

Halves are two equal shares of a whole shape.

Examples

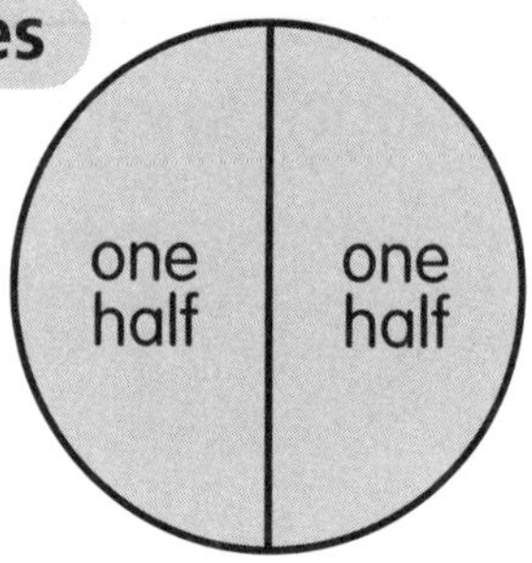

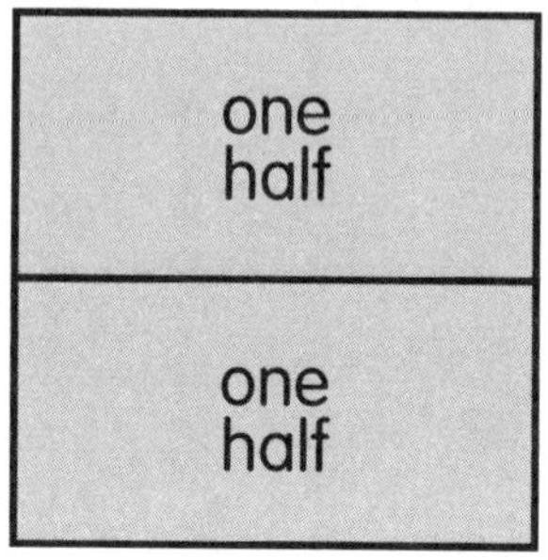

Fourths are four equal shares of a whole shape.
Another name for a fourth is a **quarter**.

Examples

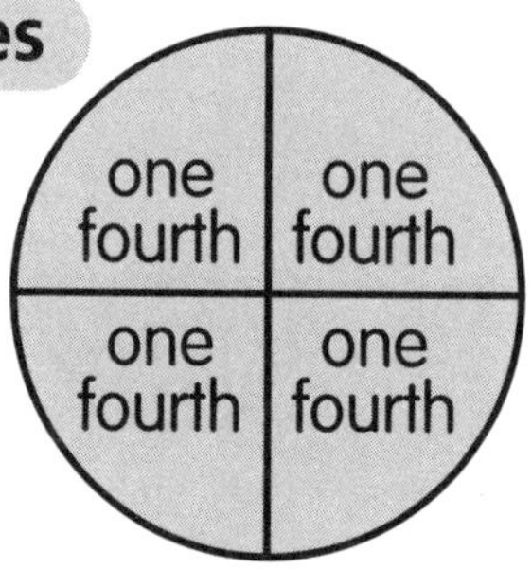

Which is more, **one half** of a pie or **one fourth** of that pie? Explain your thinking.

Name ________________________________

Circle the shape in each row that shows **halves**.

Example

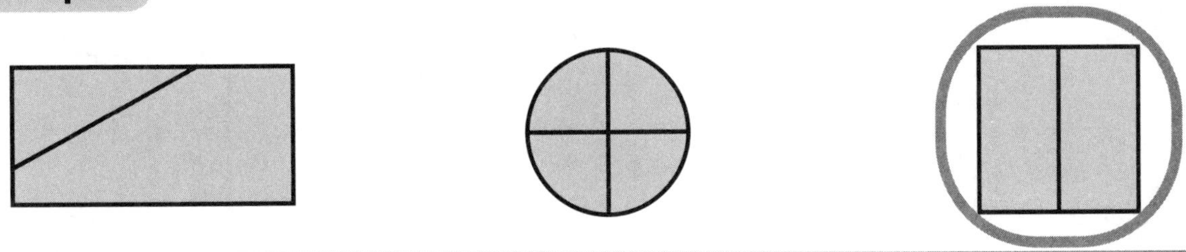

1 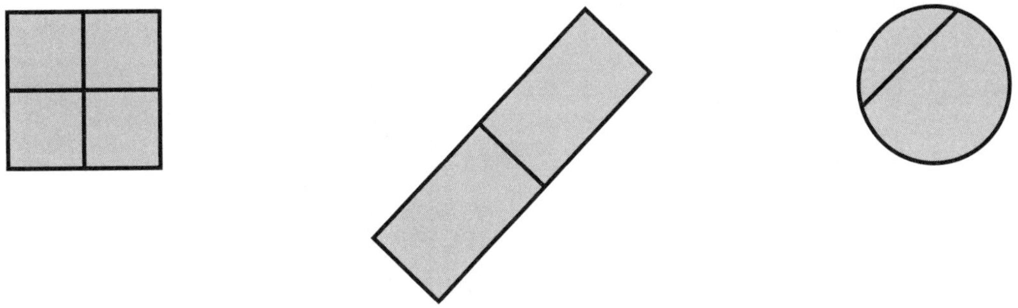

2 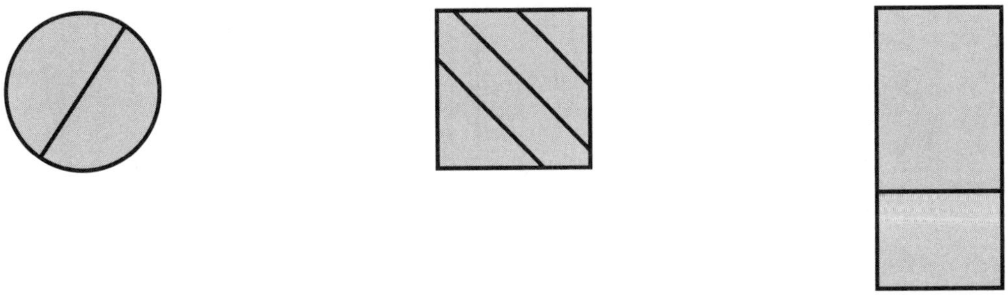

3 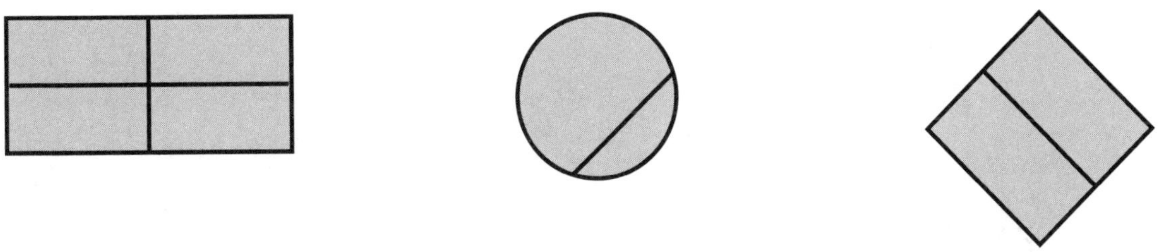

Name ______________________________

Circle the shape in each row that shows **fourths**.

Example

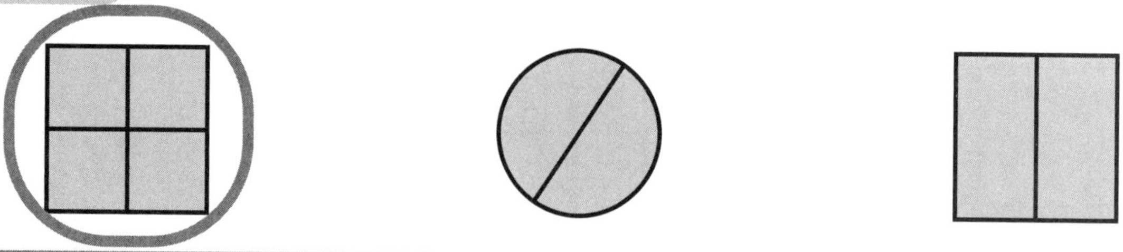

1

2

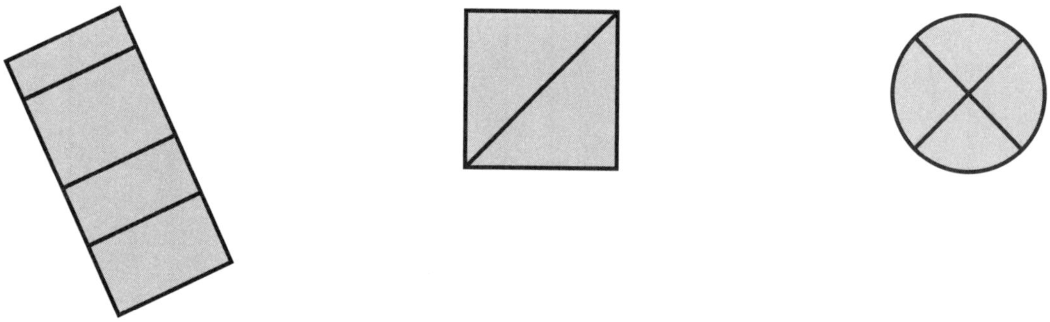

3

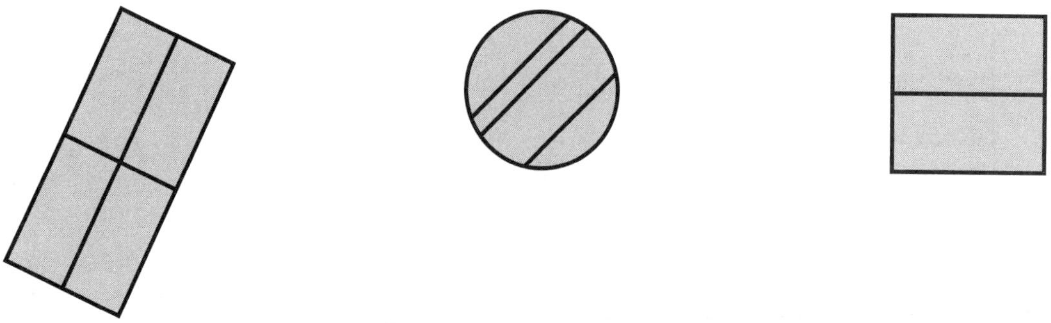

Name ____________________

Circle the name of the shaded part of each shape.

❶

whole

half

fourth

❷
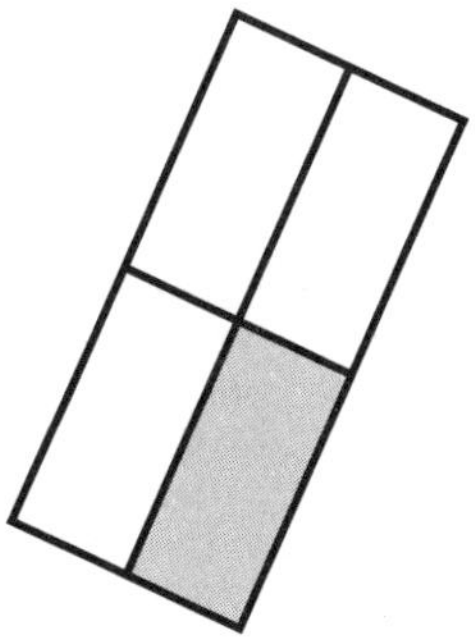

whole

half

fourth

❸
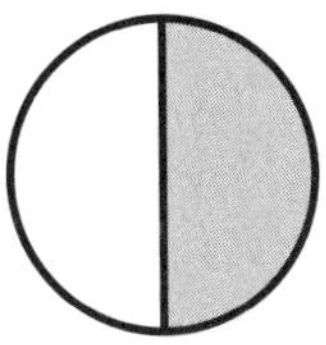

whole

half

fourth

❹

whole

half

fourth

❺
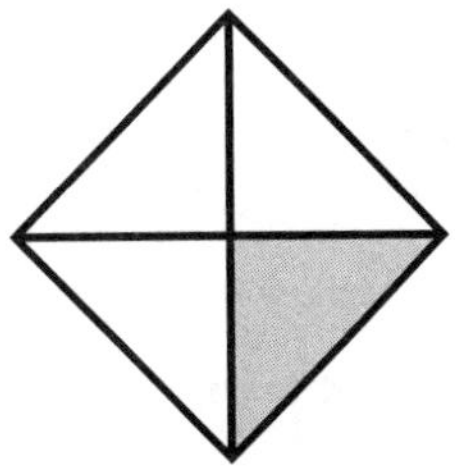

whole

half

fourth

❻
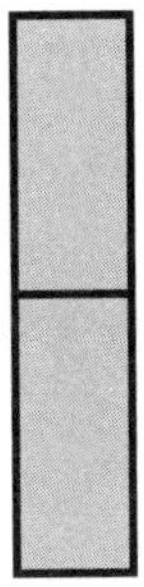

whole

half

fourth

Name ________________________________

Read the Problem

Two friends want to share a square sandwich.
How many ways can it be cut into 2 equal shares?
Draw all the ways in the work space.

Think About It

1 You will find ways to cut a square into _____.

○ halves ○ fourths ○ quarters

2 You will _____ the ways.

○ read ○ draw ○ cut

Solve the Problem

3 Use this work space.

4 There are _____ ways to cut the sandwich into 2 equal shares.

Check Your Work

5 Do your answers make sense? ○ yes ○ no

Answer Key

Page 13

Name ______________________ **Word Problems** Adding within 20 (1)

Read the example. Then solve the problem.

Example

6 ants sat on a log.
4 more ants came.
How many ants were there in all? 10 ants

These are some ways to solve the problem:

Draw a picture.	Draw a diagram.	Write a number sentence.
	10, 6, ?	6 + 4 = ?

Read the word problem.
Show one way to solve the problem by adding.

Luis has 8 fish. Tia has 7 fish.
How many fish do they have in all?

1. Use this work space. **Answers will vary.**
2. They have 15 fish in all.

Page 14

Name ______________________ **Word Problems** Adding within 20 (2)

Read each word problem.
Show one way to solve each problem by adding.

There were 3 girls and 9 boys at Emma's party.
How many children were at the party?

1. Use this work space. **Answers will vary.**
2. 12 children were at the party.

Liz had 10 crayons. I gave her 5 more.
How many crayons does Liz have now?

3. Use this work space. **Answers will vary.**
4. Liz has 15 crayons.

Page 15

Name ______________________ **Word Problems** Adding within 20

Read the Problem

Lily saw children flying kites at the park.
She counted 6 yellow and 7 blue kites.
How many kites did she see altogether?

Think About It

1. You will find out how many ____ Lily saw.
○ children ○ parks ● kites
2. Mark the number sentence that tells about the problem.
○ 7 − 6 = ? ● 6 + 7 = ? ○ 6 + ? = 7

Solve the Problem

3. Use this work space. **Answers will vary.**
4. Lily saw 13 kites altogether.

Check Your Work **Answers will vary.**

5. Do your answers make sense? ○ yes ○ no

Page 17

Name ______________________ **Word Problems** Subtracting within 20 (3)

Read the example. Then solve the problem.

Example

10 ants sat on a log.
4 ants went away.
How many ants were left? 6 ants

These are some ways to solve the problem:

Draw a picture.	Draw a diagram.	Write a number sentence.
	10, 6, ?	10 − 4 = 6

Read the word problem.
Show one way to solve the problem by subtracting.

Mike had 15 fish. He gave 7 fish to Jan.
How many fish does Mike have now?

1. Use this work space. **Answers will vary.**
2. Mike has 8 fish.

Page 18

Name ______________________ **Word Problems** Subtracting within 20 (4)

Read each word problem.
Show one way to solve each problem by subtracting.

There were 12 children at Alisa's party. 9 children played games. How many children did **not** play games?

1. Use this work space. **Answers will vary.**
2. 3 children did **not** play games.

Carlos had 15 crayons. He lost 2 crayons.
How many crayons does Carlos have left?

3. Use this work space. **Answers will vary.**
4. Carlos has 13 crayons left.

Page 19

Name ______________________ **Word Problems** Subtracting within 20

Read the Problem

At the park, Harold saw 13 kites flying.
Then 3 kites got stuck in trees.
How many kites were still flying?

Think About It

1. You will find out how many ____ were still flying.
● kites ○ trees ○ birds
2. Mark the number sentence that tells about the problem.
○ ? − 13 = 3 ○ 13 + 3 = ? ● 13 − 3 = ?

Solve the Problem

3. Use this work space. **Answers will vary.**
4. 10 kites were still flying.

Check Your Work **Answers will vary.**

5. Do your answers make sense? ○ yes ○ no

Page 21

Name ______________________ **Word Problems** Choosing addition or subtraction to solve word problems (5)

Read the problem. Choose to put together, take apart, or compare.
Draw a model or write a number sentence to solve the problem.

Example

Mom saw 18 ants on Monday. She saw 12 ants on Tuesday. How many more ants did Mom see on Monday? 6 more ants

Choose. ○ put together + ○ take apart − ● compare −

Draw a model or write a number sentence. 18 − 12 = 6

1. Teri has 8 fish. She got 6 new fish.
How many fish does she have now? 14 fish
2. Choose. ● put together + ○ take apart − ○ compare −
3. Draw a model or write a number sentence. **Answers will vary.**

Page 22

Name ______________________ **Word Problems** Choosing addition or subtraction to solve word problems (6)

Read each word problem. Choose to put together, take apart, or compare.
Draw a model or write a number sentence to solve the problem.

1. Dad made 18 cupcakes for the party.
After the party, there were 7 cupcakes left.
How many cupcakes were eaten? 11 cupcakes
2. Choose. ○ put together + ● take apart − ○ compare −
3. Draw a model or write a number sentence. **Answers will vary.**
4. Clay has 13 crayons. A box holds 16 crayons. How many more crayons can fit in the box? 3 more crayons
5. Choose. ○ put together + ○ take apart − ● compare −
6. Draw a model or write a number sentence. **Answers will vary.**

Page 23

Name ______________________ **Word Problems** Choosing addition or subtraction to solve word problems

Read the Problem

Tracy is making cards for 14 of her friends.
So far, she has made 9 cards.
How many more cards does Tracy need to make?

Think About It

1. You will find out ____ cards Tracy needs to make.
○ what kind of ● how many more
2. Mark the number sentence that tells about the problem.
● 14 − 9 = ? ○ 14 + 9 = ? ○ ? = 14 + 9

Solve the Problem

3. Use this work space. **Answers will vary.**
4. Tracy needs to make 5 more cards.

Check Your Work **Answers will vary.**

5. Do your answers make sense? ○ yes ○ no

Page 25

Name ____________________ **Word Problems** Comparing numbers **7**

Read the example. Then solve the problem.

Example

There are 10 black ants. There are 7 red ants.
How many more black ants are there than red ants?
__3__ more black ants

These are some ways to solve the problem:

Draw a picture. 3

Draw a chart. 3

Write a number sentence. 10 – 7 = 3

Read the word problem. Show one way to solve the problem by comparing numbers to find the difference.

➤ Michelle had 15 fish. She gave 7 fish to Tan. How many fish does Michelle have now?

❶ Use this work space.

Answers will vary.

❷ Michelle has __8__ fish.

© Evan-Moor Corporation • EMC 3081 • Math Fundamentals 25

Page 26

Name ____________________ **Word Problems** Comparing numbers **8**

Read each word problem. Show one way to solve each problem by comparing numbers to find the difference.

➤ At Keisha's party, 4 children ate cake. 8 children ate pie. How many more children ate pie than cake?

❶ Use this work space.

Answers will vary.

❷ __4__ more children ate pie.

➤ Meg has 20 crayons. Liza has 13 crayons. How many fewer crayons does Liza have?

❸ Use this work space.

Answers will vary.

❹ Liza has __7__ fewer crayons.

26 Math Fundamentals • EMC 3081 • © Evan-Moor Corporation

Page 27

Name ____________________ **Word Problems** Comparing numbers

Read the Problem

19 children met at a park.
13 of them were flying kites.
How many children were **not** flying kites?

Think About It

❶ You will find out how many children ____.
○ were at a park ● were not flying kites

❷ Mark the number sentence that tells about the problem.
● 19 – 13 = ? ○ 19 + 13 = ? ○ ? = 19 + 13

Solve the Problem

❸ Use this work space.

Answers will vary.

❹ __6__ children were **not** flying kites.

Check Your Work **Answers will vary.**

❺ Do your answers make sense? ○ yes ○ no

© Evan-Moor Corporation • EMC 3081 • Math Fundamentals 27

Page 29

Name ____________________ **Word Problems** Adding three whole numbers **9**

Read the example. Then solve the problem.

Example

Leon saw 3 ants in the garden. He saw 7 ants in the grass. He saw 5 ants in the dirt. How many ants did Leon see?
__15__ ants

These are some ways to solve the problem:

Use counters. | Draw a diagram. | Write a number sentence.

3 + 7 + 5 = ?
10 + 5 = ?
10 + 5 = 15

Read the word problem. Show one way to solve the problem by adding three numbers.

➤ Tina has many pet fish. She has 4 striped, 8 blue, and 2 gray fish. How many fish does Tina have altogether?

❶ Use this work space.

Answers will vary.

❷ Tina has __14__ fish altogether.

© Evan-Moor Corporation • EMC 3081 • Math Fundamentals 29

Page 30

Name ____________________ **Word Problems** Adding three whole numbers **10**

Read each word problem.
Show one way to solve each problem by adding three numbers.

➤ Caleb went to Emma's party. He saw 1 red, 6 blue, and 6 green balloons. How many balloons did Caleb see?

❶ Use this work space.

Answers will vary.

❷ Caleb saw __13__ balloons.

➤ Melita found 3 old boxes of crayons. The first box had 7 crayons. The second box had 8 crayons. The third box had 5 crayons. How many crayons did Melita find?

❸ Use this work space.

Answers will vary.

❹ Melita found __20__ crayons.

30 Math Fundamentals • EMC 3081 • © Evan-Moor Corporation

Page 31

Name ____________________ **Word Problems** Adding three whole numbers

Read the Problem

Lisa and her dad rode their bikes 5 blocks to buy a book. Next, they rode 2 more blocks to the park. Then they rode 7 blocks back home. How many blocks did they ride?

Think About It

❶ You will find out how many ____.
○ parks they saw ● blocks they rode

❷ Mark the number sentence that tells about the problem.
○ 5 + 2 + ? = 7 ● 5 + 2 + 7 = ? ○ 7 – 2 – 5 = ?

Solve the Problem

❸ Use this work space.

Answers will vary.

❹ Lisa and her dad rode __14__ blocks.

Check Your Work **Answers will vary.**

❺ Do your answers make sense? ○ yes ○ no

© Evan-Moor Corporation • EMC 3081 • Math Fundamentals 31

Page 33

Name ____________________ **Word Problems** Unknowns in all positions **11**

Read the example. Then solve the problem.

Example

17 ants went walking.
It started to rain.
10 ants ran under a rock.
How many ants were still walking? __7__ ants

17 – ? = 10 | 17 – 10 = ? | ? = 17 – 10

Read the word problem. Use **?** as the unknown number.
Write 3 number sentences that can help you solve the problem.

❶ Adam has 14 pet fish.
8 of his fish swim together in a group.
How many fish do **not** swim in the group? __6__ fish

❷ ❸ ❹ **Answers will vary.**

© Evan-Moor Corporation • EMC 3081 • Math Fundamentals 33

Page 34

Name ____________________ **Word Problems** Unknowns in all positions **12**

Read each word problem. Use **?** as the unknown number.
Write 3 number sentences that can help you solve the problem.

❶ At Jessica's party, 7 children sang songs. 6 children danced. How many children sang and danced? __13__ children

❷ ❸ ❹ **Answers will vary.**

❺ A small box has 8 crayons. A bigger box has 16 crayons. How many fewer crayons are in the small box? __8__ fewer crayons

❻ ❼ ❽ **Answers will vary.**

34 Math Fundamentals • EMC 3081 • © Evan-Moor Corporation

Page 35

Name ____________________ **Word Problems** Unknowns in all positions **13**

Read each word problem. Use **?** as the unknown number.
Write 3 number sentences that can help you solve the problem.

❶ My dog Gus had 14 bones. He hid 6 of them. How many bones were **not** hidden? __8__ bones

❷ ❸ ❹ **Answers will vary.**

❺ At the park, Tami jumped 15 times. Pat did 3 more jumps than Tami. How many jumps did Pat do? __18__ jumps

❻ ❼ ❽ **Answers will vary.**

© Evan-Moor Corporation • EMC 3081 • Math Fundamentals 35

Page 36

Name ______

Word Problems
Unknowns in all positions

Read the Problem

Ed went to the park 15 times in May. He went 8 times with Dad. The other times he went with Mom. How many times did Ed go to the park with Mom?

Think About It

1. You will find out how many times Ed went to the park ______.
   ○ with Dad ● with Mom ○ in a car
2. Mark the number sentence that tells about the problem.
   ○ 8 − 15 = ? ○ 15 + 8 = ? ● ? = 15 − 8

Solve the Problem

3. Use this work space.
   Answers will vary.
4. Ed went to the park __7__ times with Mom.

Check Your Work **Answers will vary.**

5. Do your answers make sense? ○ yes ○ no

36 · Math Fundamentals • EMC 3081 • © Evan-Moor Corporation

Page 39

Name ______

Operations and Number Relationships
Commutative property
1

Add. Write a new number sentence by changing the order of the addends.

Example

Add. 7 + 3 = __10__ Change the order. 3 + 7 = __10__

	Add	Change the Order
1	4 + 12 = __16__	__12__ + __4__ = __16__
2	10 + 7 = __17__	__7__ + __10__ = __17__
3	5 + 11 = __16__	__11__ + __5__ = __16__
4	80 + 1 = __81__	__1__ + __80__ = __81__

© Evan-Moor Corporation • EMC 3081 • Math Fundamentals · 39

Page 40

Name ______

Operations and Number Relationships
Commutative property
2

Add. Then write a new number sentence by changing the order of the addends.

1. If 10 + 6 = __16__, then __6__ + __10__ = __16__.
2. If 7 + 8 = __15__, then __8__ + __7__ = __15__.
3. If 9 + 4 = __13__, then __4__ + __9__ = __13__.
4. If 17 + 3 = __20__, then __3__ + __17__ = __20__.
5. If 1 + 69 = __70__, then __69__ + __1__ = __70__.
6. If 100 + 10 = __110__, then __10__ + __100__ = __110__.

40 · Math Fundamentals • EMC 3081 • © Evan-Moor Corporation

Page 41

Name ______

Operations and Number Relationships
Commutative property

Read the Problem

Carl has 8 blue socks and 4 white socks.
Ali has 4 blue socks and 8 white socks.
How many socks does Carl have?
How many socks does Ali have?

Think About It

1. You will find out how many socks Carl and Ali have ______.
   ○ altogether ● each ○ left over
2. Mark the **two** number sentences that have the same sum.
   ● 8 + 4 = ? ○ 8 + 8 = ? ● 4 + 8 = ?

Solve the Problem

3. Use this work space.
   Answers will vary.
4. Carl has __12__ socks.
5. Ali has __12__ socks.

Check Your Work **Answers will vary.**

6. Do your answers make sense? ○ yes ○ no

© Evan-Moor Corporation • EMC 3081 • Math Fundamentals · 41

Page 43

Name ______

Operations and Number Relationships
Associative property
3

Add. Then add again in a different order.

Example

(3 + 7) + 4 = __?__ 3 + (7 + 4) = __?__
10 + 4 = __14__ 3 + 11 = __14__

1. 5 + (10 + 2) = __17__ (5 + 10) + 2 = __17__
2. (15 + 5) + 0 = __20__ 15 + (5 + 0) = __20__
3. 20 + (5 + 5) = __30__ (20 + 5) + 5 = __30__
4. (80 + 0) + 1 = __81__ 80 + (0 + 1) = __81__

© Evan-Moor Corporation • EMC 3081 • Math Fundamentals · 43

Page 44

Name ______

Operations and Number Relationships
Associative property
4

Add. Draw a line around the numbers you chose to add first.

1. 10 + (4 + 5) = __19__
2. 7 + 3 + 7 = __17__
3. 8 + 3 + 6 = __17__
4. 9 + 1 + 5 = __15__
5. 2 + 8 + 10 = __20__
6. 20 + 10 + 30 = __60__

44 · Math Fundamentals • EMC 3081 • © Evan-Moor Corporation

Page 45

Name ______

Operations and Number Relationships
Associative property

Read the Problem

The kids saw 6 tigers, 4 bears, and 8 zebras at the zoo. How many animals did the kids see?

Think About It

1. You will find out how many ______ were seen.
   ● animals ○ zoos ○ lions
2. Mark the grouping you like best. **Answers will vary.**
   ○ (6 + 4) + 8 = ? ○ 6 + (4 + 8) = ? ○ (6 + 8) + 4 = ?

Solve the Problem

3. Use this work space.
   Answers will vary.
4. The kids saw __18__ animals.

Check Your Work **Answers will vary.**

5. Do your answers make sense? ○ yes ○ no

© Evan-Moor Corporation • EMC 3081 • Math Fundamentals · 45

Page 47

Name ______

Operations and Number Relationships
Using the unknown addend
5

Find the unknown addend first. Then use the unknown addend to help you find the difference.

Example

First, add. 3 + __10__ = 13
Then subtract. 13 − 3 = __10__

1. First, add. 7 + __8__ = 15
   Then subtract. 15 − 7 = __8__
2. First, add. __11__ + 9 = 20
   Then subtract. 20 − 9 = __11__
3. First, add. __7__ + 5 = 12
   Then subtract. 12 − 5 = __7__
4. First, add. 10 + __30__ = 40
   Then subtract. 40 − 10 = __30__

© Evan-Moor Corporation • EMC 3081 • Math Fundamentals · 47

Page 48

Name ______

Operations and Number Relationships
Using the unknown addend
6

Find the unknown addend.
Use the unknown addend to help you find the difference.

1. Add. 7 + __10__ = 17 Subtract. 17 − 7 = __10__
2. Add. __9__ + 6 = 15 Subtract. 15 − __9__ = 6
3. Add. 11 + __9__ = 20 Subtract. 20 − 11 = __9__
4. Add. __10__ + 20 = 30 Subtract. 30 − __10__ = 20
5. Add. 20 + 80 = __100__ Subtract. 80 = 100 − __20__

48 · Math Fundamentals • EMC 3081 • © Evan-Moor Corporation

Page 49

Name ______________

Operations and Number Relationships
Using the unknown addend
7

Mark the addition number sentence that can help you solve each subtraction number sentence. Then write the answer.

Example
15 − 5 = 10 ○ 15 + 5 = 20 ● 10 + 5 = 15

1. 21 − 1 = **20** ● 1 + 20 = 21 ○ 10 + 11 = 21
2. 18 − 9 = **9** ● 9 + 9 = 18 ○ 6 + 3 = 9
3. 14 − 8 = **6** ○ 4 + 4 = 8 ● 8 + 6 = 14
4. 50 − 10 = **40** ○ 50 + 10 = 60 ● 10 + 40 = 50

© Evan-Moor Corporation • EMC 3081 • Math Fundamentals — Understand subtraction as an unknown-addend problem. 49

Page 50

Name ______________

Operations and Number Relationships
Using the unknown addend

Read the Problem
Cam saw 13 books on the table. She put 6 of them away. How many books were left on the table?

Think About It
1. Mark the subtraction number sentence that tells about the problem.
○ 6 − 3 = ? ● 13 − 6 = ? ○ 31 − 6 = ?
2. Mark the addition number sentence that can help you.
○ 13 + 6 = 19 ○ 13 + 7 = 20 ● 6 + 7 = 13

Solve the Problem
3. Use this work space.
Answers will vary.
4. **7** books were left on the table.

Check Your Work **Answers will vary.**
5. Do your answers make sense? ○ yes ○ no

50 Understand subtraction as an unknown-addend problem. — Math Fundamentals • EMC 3081 • © Evan-Moor Corporation

Page 53

Name ______________

Add and Subtract Within 20
Counting on to add
1

Look at each number sentence. Show one way to solve with counting on.

Example
9 + 2 = ?
Use a diagram. | Draw counters. 9 + 2 = 11 | Use a number line. 9 10 11

1. 7 + 1 = **8**
Answers will vary.
2. 12 + 3 = **15**
3. 10 + 2 = **12**
4. 2 + 14 = **16**

© Evan-Moor Corporation • EMC 3081 • Math Fundamentals — Relate counting to addition. Use counting on to add. 53

Page 54

Name ______________

Add and Subtract Within 20
Counting on to add
2

Look at each number sentence. Show one way to solve with counting on.

1. 8 + 3 = **11**
Answers will vary.
2. 2 + 17 = **19**
3. 15 + 1 = **16**
4. 6 + 3 = **9**
5. 13 + 1 = **14**
6. 18 + 2 = **20**

54 Relate counting to addition. Use counting on to add. — Math Fundamentals • EMC 3081 • © Evan-Moor Corporation

Page 55

Name ______________

Add and Subtract Within 20
Counting on to add

Read the Problem
Dad ate 7 grapes.
Then he ate 2 more.
How many grapes did Dad eat?

Think About It
1. You will find out how many grapes Dad ____.
○ picked ○ gave away ● ate
2. To solve the problem, you will ____.
● count on from 7 ○ count on from 2

Solve the Problem
3. Use this work space.
Answers will vary.
4. Dad ate **9** grapes.

Check Your Work **Answers will vary.**
5. Do your answers make sense? ○ yes ○ no

© Evan-Moor Corporation • EMC 3081 • Math Fundamentals — Relate counting to addition. Use counting on to add. 55

Page 57

Name ______________

Add and Subtract Within 20
Counting back to subtract
3

Look at each number sentence. Show one way to solve with counting back.

Example
8 − 3 = ?
Use a diagram. 7 6 5 ← Count back 3 | Draw counters. Count back 3 7 6 5 8 − 3 = 5 | Use a number line. 3 2 1 ← Count back 3 5 6 7 8

1. 9 − 1 = **8**
Answers will vary.
2. 15 − 3 = **12**
3. 11 − 2 = **9**
4. 20 − 1 = **19**

© Evan-Moor Corporation • EMC 3081 • Math Fundamentals — Relate counting to subtraction. 57

Page 58

Name ______________

Add and Subtract Within 20
Counting back to subtract
4

Look at each number sentence. Show one way to solve with counting back.

1. 12 − 1 = **11**
Answers will vary.
2. 18 − 3 = **15**
3. 14 − 2 = **12**
4. 13 − 2 = **11**
5. 16 − 1 = **15**
6. 17 − 3 = **14**

58 Relate counting to subtraction. — Math Fundamentals • EMC 3081 • © Evan-Moor Corporation

Page 59

Name ______________

Add and Subtract Within 20
Counting back to subtract

Read the Problem
Jan had 12 pencils.
She gave 2 pencils to Kai.
How many pencils did Jan have left?

Think About It
1. You will find out how many pencils Jan ____.
○ gave to Kai ● had left ○ will get
2. To solve the problem, you will ____.
○ count back from 2 ● count back from 12

Solve the Problem
3. Use this work space.
Answers will vary.
4. Jan had **10** pencils left.

Check Your Work **Answers will vary.**
5. Do your answers make sense? ○ yes ○ no

© Evan-Moor Corporation • EMC 3081 • Math Fundamentals — Relate counting to subtraction. 59

Page 61

Name ______________

Add and Subtract Within 20
Making a ten
5

Look at each number sentence. Show one way to solve by making a ten.

Example
8 + 5 = ?
Use a ten frame. 8 + 5 = ? (8 + 2) + 3 = 13 | Draw a chart. 8 + 5 = ? (8 + 2) + 3 = 13

1. 6 + 7 = **13**
Answers will vary.
2. 9 + 4 = **13**
3. 7 + 8 = **15**
4. 5 + 11 = **16**

© Evan-Moor Corporation • EMC 3081 • Math Fundamentals — Use making a ten as a strategy to add. 61

Page 62

Name ______________ **Add and Subtract Within 20** Making a ten 6

Look at each number sentence. Show one way to solve by making a ten.

❶ 5 + 9 = 14
Answers will vary.

❷ 6 + 5 = 11

❸ 11 + 3 = 14

❹ 12 + 7 = 19

❺ 8 + 9 = 17

❻ 13 + 6 = 19

62 Use making a ten as a strategy to add. Math Fundamentals • EMC 3081 • © Evan-Moor Corporation

Page 63

Name ______________ **Add and Subtract Within 20** Making a ten

Read the Problem

Ron likes hats.
He has 7 baseball caps.
He has 6 cowboy hats.
How many hats does Ron have?

Think About It

❶ You will find out how many hats Ron ____.
○ lost ● has ○ gave away

❷ Mark the number sentence that makes a ten to add.
● (7 + 3) + 3 ○ (7 + 4) + 2 ○ (7 + 5) + 1

Solve the Problem

❸ Use this work space.
Answers will vary.

❹ Ron has 13 hats.

Check Your Work **Answers will vary.**

❺ Do your answers make sense? ○ yes ○ no

© Evan-Moor Corporation • EMC 3081 • Math Fundamentals Use making a ten as a strategy to add. 63

Page 65

Name ______________ **Add and Subtract Within 20** Leading to a ten 7

Look at each number sentence. Show one way to lead to a ten to subtract.

Example

13 − 4 = ?

Use a ten frame. (13 − 3) − 1 = 9; 13 − 4 = 9

Draw a chart. 13 − 4 = ? (13 − 3) − 1 = 9; 10 − 1 = 9

❶ 12 − 5 = 7
Answers will vary.

❷ 15 − 6 = 9

❸ 11 − 3 = 8

❹ 14 − 9 = 5

© Evan-Moor Corporation • EMC 3081 • Math Fundamentals Use decomposing a number leading to a ten to subtract. 65

Page 66

Name ______________ **Add and Subtract Within 20** Leading to a ten 8

Look at each number sentence. Show one way to subtract by leading to a ten.

❶ 13 − 7 = 6
Answers will vary.

❷ 17 − 8 = 9

❸ 15 − 9 = 6

❹ 16 − 7 = 9

❺ 11 − 4 = 7

❻ 12 − 4 = 8

66 Use decomposing a number leading to a ten to subtract. Math Fundamentals • EMC 3081 • © Evan-Moor Corporation

Page 67

Name ______________ **Add and Subtract Within 20** Leading to a ten

Read the Problem

16 children were painting.
Then 9 of them went out to play.
How many children were still painting?

Think About It

❶ You will find out how many children were ____.
● still painting ○ still playing ○ painting outside

❷ Mark the number sentence that leads to a ten.
○ (16 − 4) − 5 = ? ○ (16 − 5) − 4 = ? ● (16 − 6) − 3 = ?

Solve the Problem

❸ Use this work space.
Answers will vary.

❹ 7 children were still painting.

Check Your Work **Answers will vary.**

❺ Do your answers make sense? ○ yes ○ no

© Evan-Moor Corporation • EMC 3081 • Math Fundamentals Use decomposing a number leading to a ten to subtract. 67

Page 69

Name ______________ **Add and Subtract Within 20** Using equivalent or known sums 9

Look at each number sentence. Use a math fact that you already know to help you solve it.

Example

9 + 8 = ? I know 10 + 8 = 18. So, (10 − 1) + 8 = 17. 9 + 8 = 17

14 − 8 = ? I know 14 − 7 = 7. So, 14 − (7 + 1) = 6. 14 − 8 = 6

❶ 6 + 7 = ? I know So, 6 + 7 = 13

❷ 15 − 9 = ? I know So, 15 − 9 = 6

Answers will vary.

© Evan-Moor Corporation • EMC 3081 • Math Fundamentals Use equivalent or known sums to add or subtract. 69

Page 70

Name ______________ **Add and Subtract Within 20** Using equivalent or known sums 10

Look at each number sentence. Use a math fact that you already know to help you solve it.

❶ 6 + 5 = ? I know 5 + 5 = 10 So, (5 + 1) + 5 = 11. 6 + 5 = 11

❷ 9 + ? = 16 I know So, 9 + 7 = 16

❸ 14 − 6 = ? I know So, 14 − 6 = 8

❹ 19 − 8 = ? I know So, 19 − 8 = 11

Answers will vary.

70 Use equivalent or known sums to add or subtract. Math Fundamentals • EMC 3081 • © Evan-Moor Corporation

Page 71

Name ______________ **Add and Subtract Within 20** Using equivalent or known sums 11

Write the missing number to complete each number sentence. Mark the number sentence that can help you solve it.

Example

6 + 7 = 13 ● 6 + 6 = 12 ○ 13 + 7 = 20

❶ 15 − 7 = 8 ● 7 + 8 = 15 ○ 7 + 1 = 8

❷ 8 + 9 = 17 ○ 9 + 3 = 12 ● 8 + 8 = 16

❸ 5 + 6 = 11 ● 5 + 5 = 10 ○ 5 + 1 = 6

❹ 20 − 11 = 9 ○ 4 + 5 = 9 ● 10 + 10 = 20

© Evan-Moor Corporation • EMC 3081 • Math Fundamentals Use equivalent or known sums to add or subtract. 71

Page 72

Name ______________ **Add and Subtract Within 20** Using equivalent or known sums

Read the Problem

Mom picked 12 apples.
She used 7 apples to make a pie.
How many apples were left?

Think About It

❶ You will find out how many apples were ____.
○ used ● left ○ picked

❷ Mark **two** number sentences that can help you.
○ 12 + 7 = 19 ● 6 + 6 = 12 ● 12 − 6 = 6

Solve the Problem

❸ Use this work space.
Answers will vary.

❹ 5 apples were left.

Check Your Work **Answers will vary.**

❺ Do your answers make sense? ○ yes ○ no

72 Use equivalent or known sums to add or subtract. Math Fundamentals • EMC 3081 • © Evan-Moor Corporation

Page 75

Name ______

Equivalency and Unknown Numbers
Determining equivalency
1

Look at each number sentence.
Circle true ☺ or false ☹.

Example

12 = 6 + 7
12 = 13
true ☺ false ☹ (circled: false)

1. 15 = 15 — true (circled)
2. 5 + 8 = 4 + 10 — false (circled)
3. 18 − 9 = 6 + 3 — true (circled)

© Evan-Moor Corporation • EMC 3081 • Math Fundamentals — 75

Page 76

Name ______

Equivalency and Unknown Numbers
Determining equivalency
2

Look at each number sentence.
Circle true ☺ or false ☹.

1. 16 = 61 — false (circled)
2. 2 + 11 = 11 + 2 — true (circled)
3. 5 + 2 = 17 − 10 — true (circled)
4. 8 + 6 = 7 + 7 — true (circled)

76 — Math Fundamentals • EMC 3081 • © Evan-Moor Corporation

Page 77

Name ______

Equivalency and Unknown Numbers
Determining equivalency

Read the Problem

Pat has 3 pink shirts and 4 white shirts.
Fran has 5 pink shirts and 2 white shirts.
Do Pat and Fran have the same number of shirts?

Think About It

1. You will find out if Pat and Fran have ______.
   ○ more pink than white shirts ● the same number of shirts
2. Mark the number sentence that tells about the problem.
   ○ 3 + 4 = 5 − 2 ● 3 + 4 = 5 + 2 ○ 4 − 3 = 5 − 2

Solve the Problem

3. Use this work space.
   Answers will vary.
4. Pat and Fran have the same number of shirts.
   ● yes ○ no

Check Your Work

Answers will vary.

5. Do your answers make sense? ○ yes ○ no

© Evan-Moor Corporation • EMC 3081 • Math Fundamentals — 77

Page 79

Name ______

Equivalency and Unknown Numbers
Finding unknown numbers
3

Mark the number that makes each number sentence true.
Show your work.

Example

6 + _?_ = 14
● 8 ○ 9
(14 → 6, 8 unknown number)

Work Space

1. _?_ + 7 = 11 — ○ 3 ● 4
2. 8 + 9 = _?_ — ● 17 ○ 18
3. 10 = 15 − _?_ — ○ 4 ● 5

© Evan-Moor Corporation • EMC 3081 • Math Fundamentals — 79

Page 80

Name ______

Equivalency and Unknown Numbers
Finding unknown numbers
4

Mark the number that makes each number sentence true.
Show your work.

Work Space

1. 3 + _?_ = 15 — ○ 11 ● 12
2. 19 = _?_ + 8 — ○ 10 ● 11
3. _?_ + 7 = 12 — ● 5 ○ 6
4. 6 + 5 = _?_ — ○ 10 ● 11

80 — Math Fundamentals • EMC 3081 • © Evan-Moor Corporation

Page 81

Name ______

Equivalency and Unknown Numbers
Finding unknown numbers
5

Write the unknown number that makes each number sentence true.
Mark the model that tells about the number sentence.

Example

6 + _4_ = 10

1. _5_ + 11 = 16
2. 15 − 9 = _6_
3. 20 = _12_ + 8

© Evan-Moor Corporation • EMC 3081 • Math Fundamentals — 81

Page 82

Name ______

Equivalency and Unknown Numbers
Finding unknown numbers

Read the Problem

Travis had 12 rocks in his pocket. Some rocks fell out.
Travis had 7 rocks left. How many rocks fell out?

Think About It

1. You will find out how many rocks ______.
   ● fell out ○ Travis had ○ in all
2. Mark **two** number sentences that are true.
   ● 12 = 7 + 5 ○ 12 + 5 = 16 ● 12 − 5 = 7

Solve the Problem

3. Use this work space.
   Answers will vary.
4. _5_ rocks fell out.

Check Your Work

Answers will vary.

5. Do your answers make sense? ○ yes ○ no

82 — Math Fundamentals • EMC 3081 • © Evan-Moor Corporation

Page 85

Name ______

Counting and Number Sequences
Counting from zero
1

Show some ways to count things.

Examples

Count to 13.
Draw a picture. | Draw a chart. | Draw a number line.
0 1 2 3 4 5 6 7 8 9 10 11 12 13

Count to 20.

1. Draw a picture.
2. Draw a chart.
3. Draw a number line.

Answers will vary.

© Evan-Moor Corporation • EMC 3081 • Math Fundamentals — 85

Page 86

Name ______

Counting and Number Sequences
Counting from zero
2

Count how many. Write the number.

1. _7_ dots
2. _9_ butterflies
3. 0 1 2 3 4 5 6 7 — _7_ balls
4. _22_ hearts
5. _53_ dots

86 — Math Fundamentals • EMC 3081 • © Evan-Moor Corporation

Page 87

Name ______ **Counting and Number Sequences** Counting from zero 3

Look at the picture next to each item. Count how many in the picture above. Color or mark each item you count. Write the number on the line.

1. 10
2. 7
3. 1
4. 15
5. 5
6. 0

Page 88

Name ______ **Counting and Number Sequences** Counting from zero

Read the Problem

Count the chairs in your classroom.
Draw a model in the work space below.
Write the number that tells how many.

Think About It

1. The problem says to ____.
   ○ sit on the chairs ● count the chairs
2. What kind of model will you draw? **Answers will vary.**
   ○ picture ○ chart ○ number line ○ other

Solve the Problem

3. Use this work space.

Answers will vary.

4. There are ____ chairs.

Check Your Work **Answers will vary.**

5. Do your answers make sense? ○ yes ○ no

Page 90

Name ______ **Counting and Number Sequences** Counting on: 1 to 50 4

Count on to tell how many. Write the numbers.

Examples

10 11 12 13 — 13 marbles
10 11 12 13 — 13 marbles
10 11 12 13 — 13 marbles

1. 12 13 14 15 — 15 eggs
2. 40 41 42 43 44 — 44 cubes
3. 20 21 22 23 24 25 26 27 — 27 dots

Page 91

Name ______ **Counting and Number Sequences** Counting on: 1 to 50 5

Count on to tell how many. Write the numbers.

1. 6 7 8 — 8 fish
2. 10 11 12 13 14 — 14 cups
3. 40 41 42 43 44 45 — 45 ants

Page 92

Name ______ **Counting and Number Sequences** Counting on: 1 to 50

Read the Problem

A frog needs help finding its pond. Count on from 4.
Write the missing numbers from 1 to 50.

Think About It

1. The problem says to ____.
   ○ count on from 1 ● count on from 4
2. You will write the missing numbers. ● yes ○ no

Solve the Problem

3.

Check Your Work **Answers will vary.**

4. Do your answers make sense? ○ yes ○ no

Page 94

Name ______ **Counting and Number Sequences** Counting on: 51 to 120 6

Count on from each number. Write the numbers.

Examples

100 101 102 103 — 100 101 102 103 — 100 101 102 103

1. 81 82 83 84 85 86 87 88 89 90
2. 105 106 107 108 109 110
3. 111 112 113 114 115 116

Page 95

Name ______ **Counting and Number Sequences** Counting on: 51 to 120 7

Count on from each number. Write the numbers.

1. 50 51 52 53 54 — 54 paper clips
2. 74 75 76 77 78 79 80
3. 65 66 67 68
4. 99 100 101 102 103 104 105

Page 96

Name ______ **Counting and Number Sequences** Counting on: 51 to 120

Read the Problem

A bird needs help finding the way to its nest.
Color the boxes that count in order from 90 to 120.

Think About It

1. I need to find numbers that ____.
   ● count from 90 to 120 ○ count from 19 to 100

Solve the Problem

2.

90	91	92	93	60	43	29	74	52	80
44	19	40	94	95	96	97	98	99	61
30	98	36	79	63	68	51	43	100	39
109	108	107	106	105	104	103	102	101	37
110	77	64	65	54	42	84	50	25	79
111	112	113	114	115	116	117	118	119	120

Check Your Work **Answers will vary.**

3. Do your answers make sense? ○ yes ○ no

Page 98

Name ______ **Counting and Number Sequences** Skip counting 8

Skip count by tens, fives, or twos. Write the missing numbers.

Examples

I see groups of two eyes. I can count by twos. 2 4 6 8 10 12

1. 5 10 15 20 25 30
2. 10 20 30 40 50 60
3. 2 4 6 8 10 12

Page 99

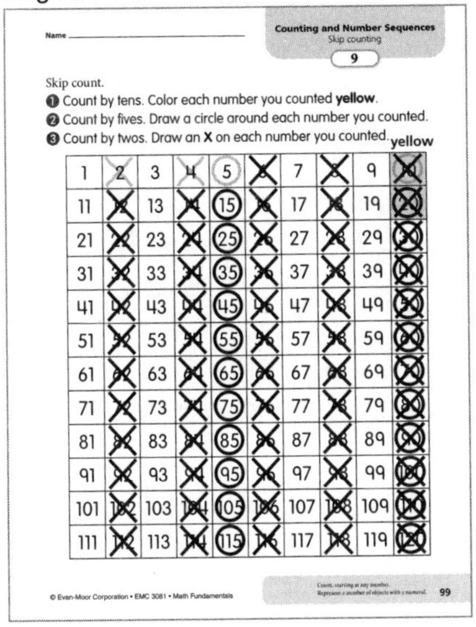

Name ____________

Counting and Number Sequences
Skip counting
9

Skip count.
1. Count by tens. Color each number you counted **yellow**.
2. Count by fives. Draw a circle around each number you counted.
3. Count by twos. Draw an **X** on each number you counted.

yellow

1	2	3	4	5	6	7	8	9	10
11	12	13	14	15	16	17	18	19	20
21	22	23	24	25	26	27	28	29	30
31	32	33	34	35	36	37	38	39	40
41	42	43	44	45	46	47	48	49	50
51	52	53	54	55	56	57	58	59	60
61	62	63	64	65	66	67	68	69	70
71	72	73	74	75	76	77	78	79	80
81	82	83	84	85	86	87	88	89	90
91	92	93	94	95	96	97	98	99	100
101	102	103	104	105	106	107	108	109	110
111	112	113	114	115	116	117	118	119	120

© Evan-Moor Corporation • EMC 3081 • Math Fundamentals 99

Page 100

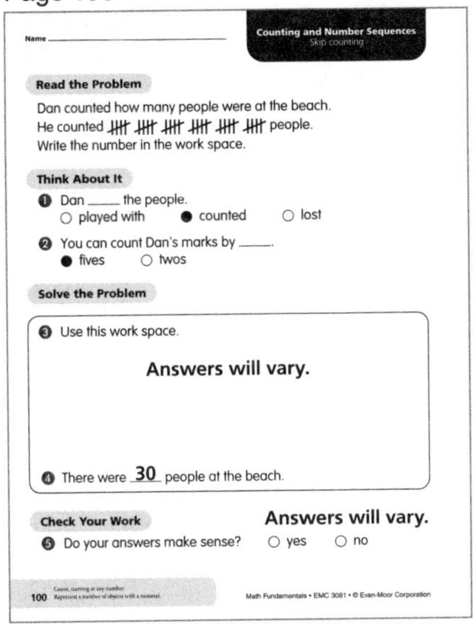

Name ____________

Counting and Number Sequences
Skip counting

Read the Problem

Dan counted how many people were at the beach.
He counted 𝍸 𝍸 𝍸 𝍸 𝍸 𝍸 people.
Write the number in the work space.

Think About It

1. Dan ____ the people.
   ○ played with ● counted ○ lost
2. You can count Dan's marks by ____.
   ● fives ○ twos

Solve the Problem

3. Use this work space.

   Answers will vary.

4. There were **30** people at the beach.

Check Your Work **Answers will vary.**

5. Do your answers make sense? ○ yes ○ no

100 Math Fundamentals • EMC 3081 • © Evan-Moor Corporation

Page 102

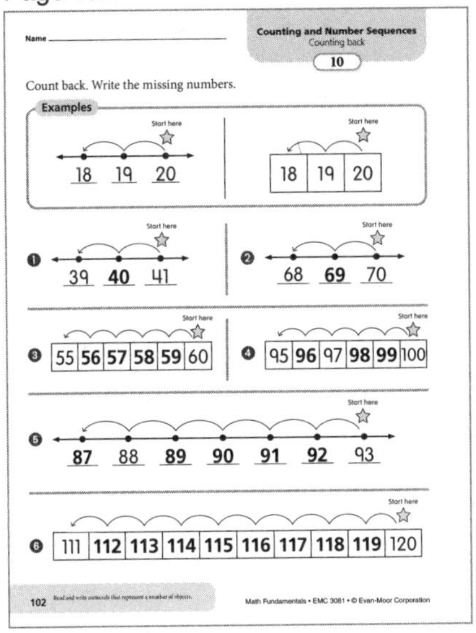

Name ____________

Counting and Number Sequences
Counting back
10

Count back. Write the missing numbers.

Examples: Start here — 18 19 20; 18 | 19 | 20

1. 39 **40** 41
2. 68 **69** 70
3. 55 **56** **57** **58** **59** 60
4. 95 **96** 97 **98** **99** 100
5. **87** 88 **89** **90** **91** **92** 93
6. 111 **112** **113** **114** **115** **116** **117** **118** **119** 120

102 Math Fundamentals • EMC 3081 • © Evan-Moor Corporation

Page 103

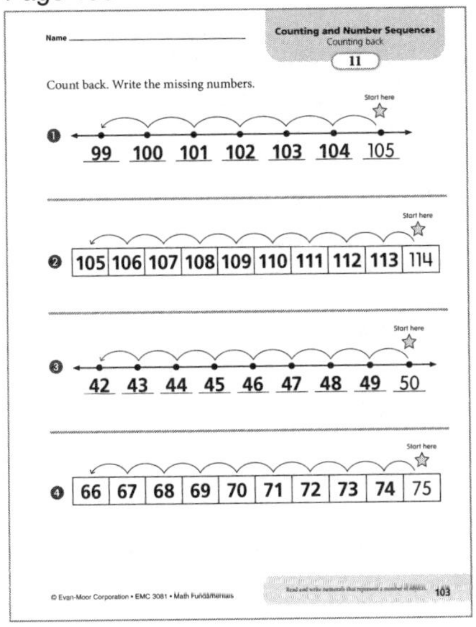

Name ____________

Counting and Number Sequences
Counting back
11

Count back. Write the missing numbers.

1. **99** **100** **101** **102** **103** **104** 105
2. 105 **106** **107** **108** **109** **110** **111** **112** **113** 114
3. **42** **43** **44** **45** **46** **47** **48** **49** 50
4. **66** **67** **68** **69** **70** **71** **72** **73** **74** 75

© Evan-Moor Corporation • EMC 3081 • Math Fundamentals 103

Page 104

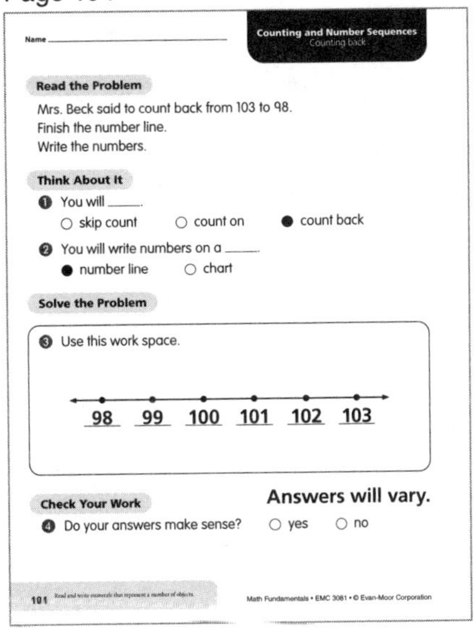

Name ____________

Counting and Number Sequences
Counting back

Read the Problem

Mrs. Beck said to count back from 103 to 98.
Finish the number line.
Write the numbers.

Think About It

1. You will ____.
   ○ skip count ○ count on ● count back
2. You will write numbers on a ____.
   ● number line ○ chart

Solve the Problem

3. Use this work space.

   98 **99** **100** **101** **102** **103**

Check Your Work **Answers will vary.**

4. Do your answers make sense? ○ yes ○ no

104 Math Fundamentals • EMC 3081 • © Evan-Moor Corporation

Page 107

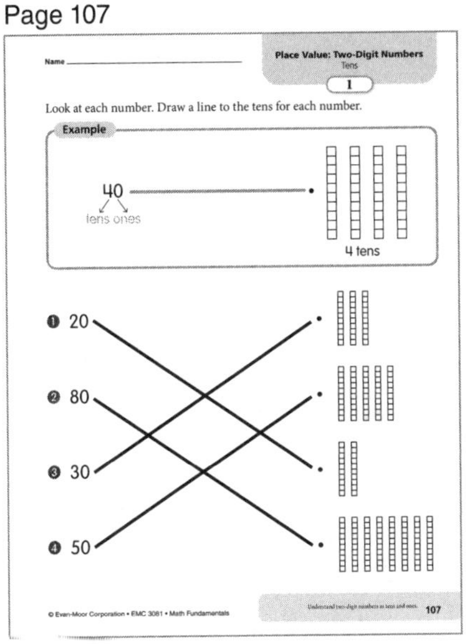

Name ____________

Place Value: Two-Digit Numbers
Tens
1

Look at each number. Draw a line to the tens for each number.

Example: 40 (tens ones) — 4 tens

1. 20
2. 80
3. 30
4. 50

© Evan-Moor Corporation • EMC 3081 • Math Fundamentals 107

Page 108

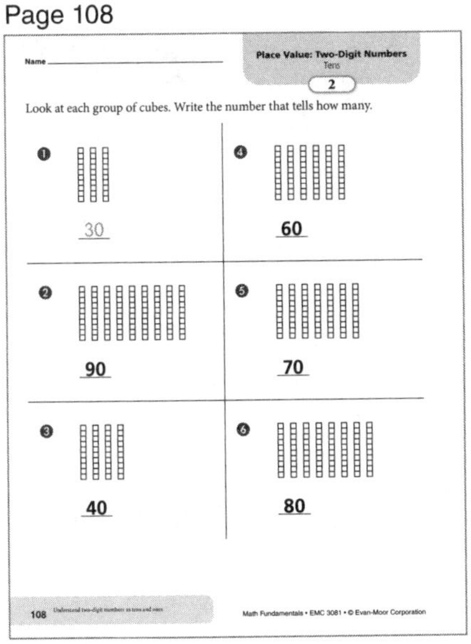

Name ____________

Place Value: Two-Digit Numbers
Tens
2

Look at each group of cubes. Write the number that tells how many.

1. 30
2. **90**
3. **40**
4. **60**
5. **70**
6. **80**

108 Math Fundamentals • EMC 3081 • © Evan-Moor Corporation

Page 109

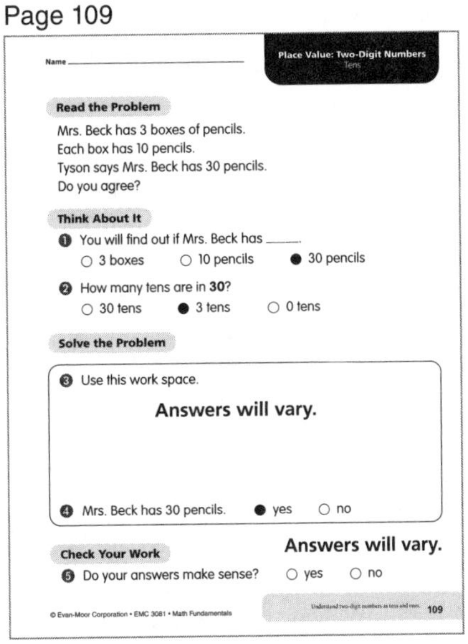

Name ____________

Place Value: Two-Digit Numbers
Tens

Read the Problem

Mrs. Beck has 3 boxes of pencils.
Each box has 10 pencils.
Tyson says Mrs. Beck has 30 pencils.
Do you agree?

Think About It

1. You will find out if Mrs. Beck has ____.
   ○ 3 boxes ○ 10 pencils ● 30 pencils
2. How many tens are in **30**?
   ○ 30 tens ● 3 tens ○ 0 tens

Solve the Problem

3. Use this work space.

   Answers will vary.

4. Mrs. Beck has 30 pencils. ● yes ○ no

Check Your Work **Answers will vary.**

5. Do your answers make sense? ○ yes ○ no

© Evan-Moor Corporation • EMC 3081 • Math Fundamentals 109

Page 111

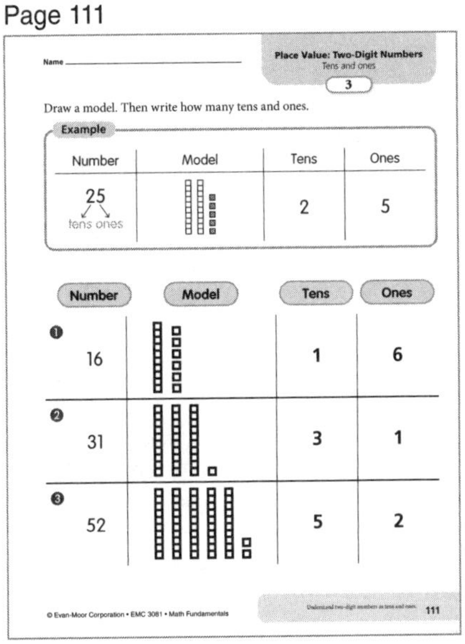

Name ____________

Place Value: Two-Digit Numbers
Tens and ones
3

Draw a model. Then write how many tens and ones.

Example:

Number	Model	Tens	Ones
25 (tens ones)		2	5

	Number	Model	Tens	Ones
1	16		**1**	**6**
2	31		**3**	**1**
3	52		**5**	**2**

© Evan-Moor Corporation • EMC 3081 • Math Fundamentals 111

Page 112

Name ______________ **Place Value: Two-Digit Numbers** Tens and ones **4**

Mark the value of each underlined digit.

1. 1<u>9</u> — ● 9 ones ○ 9 tens
2. <u>5</u>8 — ○ 5 ones ● 5 tens
3. 9<u>0</u> — ● 0 ones ○ 9 tens
4. <u>8</u>3 — ○ 3 ones ● 8 tens
5. <u>3</u>0 — ○ 3 ones ● 3 tens
6. 6<u>2</u> — ● 2 ones ○ 2 tens
7. 7<u>5</u> — ● 5 ones ○ 7 tens
8. <u>4</u>9 — ○ 9 ones ● 4 tens

112 Math Fundamentals • EMC 3081 • © Evan-Moor Corporation

Page 113

Name ______________ **Place Value: Two-Digit Numbers** Tens and ones

Read the Problem

Mr. Lau said, "Guess my number!
It has 5 tens and 9 ones.
What number is it?"

Think About It

1. You will find out what number ____.
   ● has 5 tens and 9 ones ○ has 5 ones and 9 tens
2. Mr. Lau's number has ____.
   ○ one digit ● two digits ○ three digits

Solve the Problem

3. Use this work space.
   Answers will vary.
4. The number is 59.

Check Your Work **Answers will vary.**

5. Do your answers make sense? ○ yes ○ no

© Evan-Moor Corporation • EMC 3081 • Math Fundamentals 113

Page 115

Name ______________ **Place Value: Two-Digit Numbers** Comparing two-digit numbers **5**

Write >, =, or < to make a true number sentence. Then draw a model.

Examples

23 (<) 32

1. 15 (=) 15 **Models will vary.**
2. 27 (<) 32
3. 31 (>) 21

© Evan-Moor Corporation • EMC 3081 • Math Fundamentals 115

Page 116

Name ______________ **Place Value: Two-Digit Numbers** Comparing two-digit numbers **6**

Write >, =, or < to make a true number sentence. Then draw a model.

1. 32 (>) 23 **Models will vary.**
2. 16 (<) 61
3. 40 (>) 39
4. 52 (=) 52

116 Math Fundamentals • EMC 3081 • © Evan-Moor Corporation

Page 117

Name ______________ **Place Value: Two-Digit Numbers** Comparing two-digit numbers **7**

Write a **two-digit** number to complete each number sentence.
Then draw a model.

1. 12 = 12
2. 43 > ____ **Answers will vary.**
3. 50 = 50
4. ____ > 12 **Answers will vary.**
5. 43 < ____ **Answers will vary.**
6. ____ < 50 **Answers will vary.**

© Evan-Moor Corporation • EMC 3081 • Math Fundamentals 117

Page 118

Name ______________ **Place Value: Two-Digit Numbers** Comparing two-digit numbers

Read the Problem

Chris read 59 books. Dan read 61 books.
Use >, =, or <.
Write a number sentence to compare **59** and **61**.

Think About It

1. You will write a ____.
   ○ word problem ● number sentence ○ math book
2. Mark the symbol that you can **not** use.
   ○ > greater than ● = equal to ○ < less than

Solve the Problem

3. Use this work space.
   Answers will vary.
4. Number sentence: 59 (<) 61 **OR 61 > 59**

Check Your Work **Answers will vary.**

5. Do your answers make sense? ○ yes ○ no

118 Math Fundamentals • EMC 3081 • © Evan-Moor Corporation

Page 121

Name ______________ **Place Value: Addition and Subtraction** Adding two-digit numbers within 100 **1**

Add. Compose a ten if you need to.

Example

36 + 17 = 53

40 + 13 (I need to compose a ten.)
40 + 10 + 3
50 + 3 = 53

Work Space

1. 42 + 20 = 62
2. 61 + 17 = 78
3. 57 + 15 = 72

© Evan-Moor Corporation • EMC 3081 • Math Fundamentals 121

Page 122

Name ______________ **Place Value: Addition and Subtraction** Adding two-digit numbers within 100 **2**

Add. Compose a ten if you need to.

Work Space

1. 60 + 27 = 87
2. 28 + 36 = 64
3. 91 + 6 = 97
4. 59 + 23 = 82

122 Math Fundamentals • EMC 3081 • © Evan-Moor Corporation

Page 123

Name ______________ **Place Value: Addition and Subtraction** Adding two-digit numbers within 100

Read the Problem

26 girls and 25 boys rode on the bus.
How many children rode on the bus altogether?

Think About It

1. You will find out how many children ____.
   ○ were girls ○ got off the bus ● rode on the bus
2. Will you need to compose a ten?
   ● yes ○ no

Solve the Problem

3. Use this work space.
   Answers will vary.
4. 51 children rode on the bus altogether.

Check Your Work **Answers will vary.**

5. Do your answers make sense? ○ yes ○ no

© Evan-Moor Corporation • EMC 3081 • Math Fundamentals 123

Page 125

Name ____________

Place Value: Addition and Subtraction
Ten more or ten less
3

Look at each number. Write ten more or ten less.

Examples

Ten More	Ten Less
27	13
37	23

Ten More

1. 60 / **70**
2. 31 / **41**
3. 76 / **86**
4. 58 / **68**

Ten Less

5. **9** / 19
6. **14** / 24
7. **37** / 47
8. **72** / 82

© Evan-Moor Corporation • EMC 3081 • Math Fundamentals — Given a two-digit number, mentally find 10 more or 10 less than the number. 125

Page 126

Name ____________

Place Value: Addition and Subtraction
Ten more or ten less
4

Look at each number. Write ten more or ten less.

Ten More

1. 11 **21**
2. 27 **37**
3. 63 **73**
4. 75 **85**

Ten Less

5. **2** 12
6. **43** 53
7. **26** 36
8. **89** 99

126 Given a two-digit number, mentally find 10 more or 10 less than the number. — Math Fundamentals • EMC 3081 • © Evan-Moor Corporation

Page 127

Name ____________

Place Value: Addition and Subtraction
Ten more or ten less

Read the Problem

I planted 25 seeds in the garden.
Mom planted 10 more seeds than I did.
How many seeds did Mom plant?

Think About It

1. You will find out how many seeds ____.
   ● Mom planted ○ I planted
2. Mark the number sentence that tells about the problem.
   ○ 25 – 10 = ? ○ ? + 10 = 25 ● 25 + 10 = ?

Solve the Problem

3. Use this work space.
   Answers will vary.
4. Mom planted **35** seeds.

Check Your Work **Answers will vary.**

5. Do your answers make sense? ○ yes ○ no

© Evan-Moor Corporation • EMC 3081 • Math Fundamentals — Given a two-digit number, mentally find 10 more or 10 less than the number. 127

Page 129

Name ____________

Place Value: Addition and Subtraction
Subtracting multiples of ten
5

Subtract. Show your work.

Example

70 – 30 = **40**

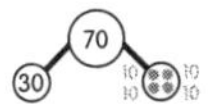

Work Space

1. 50 – 40 = **10**
2. 60 – 20 = **40**
3. 90 – 80 = **10**

© Evan-Moor Corporation • EMC 3081 • Math Fundamentals — Subtract multiples of ten from multiples of ten. Show a model or strategy and explain the reasoning. 129

Page 130

Name ____________

Place Value: Addition and Subtraction
Subtracting multiples of ten
6

Complete each number sentence. Show your work.

Work Space

1. 80 – **20** = 60
2. **40** – 10 = 30
3. 30 = 90 – **60**
4. 70 – **50** = 20

130 Subtract multiples of ten from multiples of ten. Show a model or strategy and explain the reasoning. — Math Fundamentals • EMC 3081 • © Evan-Moor Corporation

Page 131

Name ____________

Place Value: Addition and Subtraction
Subtracting multiples of ten
7

Draw a line from each number sentence to the model that can help you solve the problem. Write the answer.

1. 90 – 70 = **20**
2. 40 – **20** = 20
3. 60 – 40 = **20**
4. **50** – 10 = 40

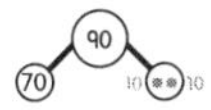

20 + 20 = 40

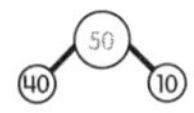

© Evan-Moor Corporation • EMC 3081 • Math Fundamentals — Subtract multiples of ten from multiples of ten. Show a model or strategy and explain the reasoning. 131

Page 132

Name ____________

Place Value: Addition and Subtraction
Subtracting multiples of ten

Read the Problem

The store had 60 apples.
20 apples were sold.
How many apples were left?

Think About It

1. You will find out how many apples were ____.
   ○ sold ● left ○ big
2. Mark the number sentence that tells about the problem.
   ● ? = 60 – 20 ○ ? = 60 + 20 ○ ? = 80 – 20

Solve the Problem

3. Use this work space.
   Answers will vary.
4. **40** apples were left.

Check Your Work **Answers will vary.**

5. Do your answers make sense? ○ yes ○ no

132 Subtract multiples of ten from multiples of ten. Show a model or strategy and explain the reasoning. — Math Fundamentals • EMC 3081 • © Evan-Moor Corporation

Page 135

Name ____________

Measuring Length
Ordering objects by length
1

Follow the directions to number each group of things in order by length.

Example

Number the worms from **longest** to **shortest**.

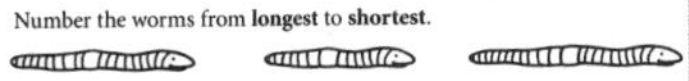

2 **3** **1**

1. Number the dogs from **tallest** to **shortest**.

2 **1** **3**

2. Number the bones from **shortest** to **longest**.

3 **1** **2**

© Evan-Moor Corporation • EMC 3081 • Math Fundamentals — Order three objects by length. 135

Page 136

Name ____________

Measuring Length
Ordering objects by length
2

Follow the directions to number each group of things in order by length.

1. Number the crayons from **longest** to **shortest**.

2 **1** **3**

2. Number the sticks from **shortest** to **longest**.

2 **1** **3**

3. Number the trees from **tallest** to **shortest**.

2 **3** **1**

136 Order three objects by length. — Math Fundamentals • EMC 3081 • © Evan-Moor Corporation

Page 137

Name ______________ **Measuring Length** Ordering objects by length

Read the Problem

Mike has 3 leaves.
He wants to put them in order from **shortest** to **tallest**.
Mark the group that shows how he put the leaves in that order.

Think About It

1. You will mark three leaves that are in order from ____.
   ○ tallest to shortest ● shortest to tallest
2. The tallest leaf will be ____.
   ○ first ○ in the middle ● last

Solve the Problem

3. Mark the group that is in order from **shortest** to **tallest**.
   ○ ○ ●

Check Your Work **Answers will vary.**

4. Do your answers make sense? ○ yes ○ no

© Evan-Moor Corporation • EMC 3081 • Math Fundamentals — Order three objects by length. 137

Page 139

Name ______________ **Measuring Length** Measuring and writing the length of objects (3)

Look at the paper clips to measure each item. Write the length.

Example: 4 paper clips

1. 2 paper clips
2. 3 paper clips
3. 1 paper clips

© Evan-Moor Corporation • EMC 3081 • Math Fundamentals — 139

Page 140

Name ______________ **Measuring Length** Measuring and writing the length of objects (4)

Look at the cubes to measure each item. Write the length.

1. 10 cubes
2. 8 cubes
3. 6 cubes
4. 4 cubes

140 — Math Fundamentals • EMC 3081 • © Evan-Moor Corporation

Page 141

Name ______________ **Measuring Length** Measuring and writing the length of objects (5)

Cut out the sticks. Use the sticks to measure the trees.

1. About how tall is the **tallest** tree?
   5 sticks tall
2. About how tall is the apple tree?
   3 sticks tall
3. About how tall is the **shortest** tree?
   2 sticks tall

© Evan-Moor Corporation • EMC 3081 • Math Fundamentals — 141

Page 142

Name ______________ **Measuring Length** Measuring and writing the length of objects

Read the Problem

Sara used her shoe to measure desks.
Her desk was 5 shoes tall.
Mr. Hall's desk was 4 shoes taller than Sara's desk.
How many shoes tall was Mr. Hall's desk?

Think About It

1. You will find out how many shoes tall ____ was.
   ○ Sara's desk ○ Mr. Hall ● Mr. Hall's desk
2. Mark the number sentence that tells about the problem.
   ○ 5 − 4 = ? ● 5 + 4 = ? ○ 5 + 5 = ?

Solve the Problem

3. Use this work space.
   Answers will vary.
4. Mr. Hall's desk was 9 shoes tall.

Check Your Work **Answers will vary.**

5. Do your answers make sense? ○ yes ○ no

142 — Math Fundamentals • EMC 3081 • © Evan-Moor Corporation

Page 145

Name ______________ **Time** Telling time by the hour (1)

Look at the time on the analog clock. Draw a line to the digital clock with the same time.

Example: 3:00

1:00 2:00 12:00 5:00 11:00 8:00

© Evan-Moor Corporation • EMC 3081 • Math Fundamentals — Tell and write time in hours using analog and digital clocks. 145

Page 146

Name ______________ **Time** Telling time by the hour (2)

Look at the time on the analog clock. Write the time on the digital clock.

1. 9 : 00
2. 4 : 00
3. 6 : 00
4. 10 : 00

146 — Math Fundamentals • EMC 3081 • © Evan-Moor Corporation

Page 147

Name ______________ **Time** Telling time by the hour

Read the Problem

The school day ends at 3:00.
A baseball game begins an hour later.
At what time does the game begin?

Think About It

1. You will find out what time ____.
   ○ the school day ends ● the game begins
2. To find out the answer, you will ____.
   ● go ahead one hour ○ go back one hour

Solve the Problem

3. Use this work space.
   Answers will vary.
4. The game begins at 4 : 00

Check Your Work **Answers will vary.**

5. Do your answers make sense? ○ yes ○ no

© Evan-Moor Corporation • EMC 3081 • Math Fundamentals — 147

Page 149

Name ______________ **Time** Telling time by the half-hour (3)

Look at the time on the analog clock. Draw a line to the digital clock with the same time.

Example: 3:30

12:30 6:30 4:30 10:30 8:30 1:30

© Evan-Moor Corporation • EMC 3081 • Math Fundamentals — 149

Page 150

Name ______________ **Time** Telling time by the half-hour 4

Look at the time on the analog clock. Write the time on the digital clock.

1. 11 : 30
2. 2 : 30
3. 5 : 30
4. 9 : 30

150 Tell and write time in half-hours using analog and digital clocks. Math Fundamentals • EMC 3081 • © Evan-Moor Corporation

Page 151

Name ______________ **Time** Telling time by the half-hour 5

Fill in the circle below the digital clock that shows the same time as the analog clock.

1. ○ 5:30 ● 4:30
2. ● 12:30 ○ 1:30
3. ● 6:30 ○ 7:30
4. ○ 9:30 ● 8:30

© Evan-Moor Corporation • EMC 3081 • Math Fundamentals Tell and write time in half-hours using analog and digital clocks. 151

Page 152

Name ______________ **Time** Telling time by the half-hour

Read the Problem

Jason reads every night at 8:00.
He reads a half-hour before he goes to bed.
At what time does Jason go to bed?

Think About It

1. You will find out what time Jason ______.
○ reads ● goes to bed
2. To find the answer, you will ______.
● go ahead a half-hour ○ go back a half-hour

Solve the Problem

3. Use this work space.
Answers will vary.
4. Jason goes to bed at 8 : 30

Check Your Work **Answers will vary.**

5. Do your answers make sense? ○ yes ○ no

152 Tell and write time in half-hours using analog and digital clocks. Math Fundamentals • EMC 3081 • © Evan-Moor Corporation

Page 155

Name ______________ **Charts and Graphs** Understanding charts and graphs 1

Look at the tally chart. Answer the questions.

卌 = 5

Our Favorite Lunch	
sandwiches	卌 I
pizza	卌 II
tacos	卌 卌 I

Answers will vary—Example:

1. What is this chart about? **This chart tells about people's favorite lunches.**
2. Which food was picked by the most people?
○ sandwiches ○ pizza ● tacos
3. How many people like sandwiches the best?
6 people
4. How many more people picked tacos than pizza?
4 more people picked tacos

© Evan-Moor Corporation • EMC 3081 • Math Fundamentals 155

Page 156

Name ______________ **Charts and Graphs** Understanding charts and graphs 2

Look at the picture graph. Answer the questions.

(picture) = 1 person

Do you want to go to the beach?

Yes	No	Maybe
4	3	2

Answers will vary—Example:

1. What is this picture graph about? **This graph tells how many people want to go to the beach or not.**
2. How many people do **not** want to go?
○ 5 people ● 3 people ○ 2 people
3. How many people answered the question?
9 people

156 Math Fundamentals • EMC 3081 • © Evan-Moor Corporation

Page 157

Name ______________ **Charts and Graphs** Understanding charts and graphs 3

Look at the bar graph. Answer the questions.

How do you go to school?

	Number
car	3
bike	2
walk	5

Answers will vary—Example:

1. What is this bar graph about? **This graph tells how students go to school.**
2. How many more children walk than ride a bike?
3 more children
3. How do the most children go to school?
○ car ○ bike ● walk
4. How many children answered the question? 10 children

© Evan-Moor Corporation • EMC 3081 • Math Fundamentals Interpret data with up to three categories. 157

Page 158

Name ______________ **Charts and Graphs** Understanding charts and graphs

Read the Problem and Complete the Graph

Last summer, Kate and her friends made a graph to show when each of them lost a tooth. Look at the graph. Answer the questions.

(tooth) = 1 tooth

Lost Teeth		
June	July	August
2	2	4

Answers will vary—Example:

Think About It

1. What is this graph about?
This graph shows how many teeth Kate and her friends lost.
2. You will look at each ______.
○ tally ● picture ○ bar

Interpret the Graph

3. The children lost the most teeth in the month of **August**.
4. How many more teeth were lost in August than in June?
2 more teeth
5. How many teeth were lost in all? 10 teeth lost in all

Check Your Work **Answers will vary.**

6. Do your answers make sense? ○ yes ○ no

158 Interpret data with up to three categories. Math Fundamentals • EMC 3081 • © Evan-Moor Corporation

Page 160

Name ______________ **Charts and Graphs** Tally charts 4

Read the word problem. Use the data to complete the tally chart. Then answer the questions.

➤ Tim asked some children, "Have you ever been on an airplane?" 6 children said "Yes." 9 children said "No."

卌 = 5

1.

Have you ever been on an airplane?	
Yes	卌 I
No	卌 IIII

Answers will vary—Example:

2. What is this tally chart about? **This chart tells how many children have or have not been on an airplane.**
3. Have most of the children been on a plane?
○ yes ● no
4. How many children answered the question? 15 children

160 Organize, represent, and interpret data with up to three categories. Math Fundamentals • EMC 3081 • © Evan-Moor Corporation

Page 161

Name ______________ **Charts and Graphs** Tally charts 5

Read the word problem. Use the data to complete the tally chart. Then answer the questions.

➤ Mrs. Soto's class voted for the game they like best. The data shows how the children voted.

卌 = 5

1.

Use this data:	
soccer	8
baseball	7
4-square	3

Our Favorite Game	
soccer	卌 III
baseball	卌 II
4-square	III

2. Which game got the most votes? **soccer**
3. How many more children chose soccer than 4-square?
5 more children
4. How many children voted? 18 children

© Evan-Moor Corporation • EMC 3081 • Math Fundamentals Organize, represent, and interpret data with up to three categories. 161

Page 162

Name ______________________ **Charts and Graphs** Tally charts

Read the Problem and Complete the Chart

1. Read the chart. Look at the total votes for each apple. Write the tally marks to complete the chart. Then answer the questions.

Apples We Like		
Color	Tallies	Total
red	𝍸 𝍸 I	11
green	𝍸	5
yellow	IIII	4

Think About It

2. This chart is about which color apples children like.
● yes ○ no

3. You completed the chart with ____.
● tally marks ○ pictures ○ bars

Interpret the Chart

4. The least favorite apple is **yellow**.

5. How many more children voted for red apples than yellow?
7 more children

6. How many children voted in all? **20** children

Check Your Work **Answers will vary.**

7. Do your answers make sense? ○ yes ○ no

162 Organize, represent, and interpret data with up to three categories. Math Fundamentals • EMC 3081 • © Evan-Moor Corporation

Page 164

Name ______________________ **Charts and Graphs** Picture graphs 6

Read the word problem. Draw to complete the picture graph. Then answer the questions.

➤ Keli asked some friends if they like funny or scary movies. 7 friends like funny movies. 3 friends like scary movies.

1. Write ☺ for what each friend likes.

☺ = 1 friend

Do you like funny or scary movies?	
funny	☺☺☺☺☺☺☺
scary	☺☺☺

Answers will vary—Example:

2. What is this picture graph about? **This graph shows how many friends like funny or scary movies.**

3. Most of the friends like ____ movies.
● funny ○ scary

4. How many friends answered the question? **10** friends

164 Organize, represent, and interpret data with up to three categories. Math Fundamentals • EMC 3081 • © Evan-Moor Corporation

Page 165

Name ______________________ **Charts and Graphs** Picture graphs 7

Read the word problem. Draw to complete the picture graph. Then answer the questions.

➤ Each sports team has a different color flag. Players on one team voted for a new flag color. 4 voted for yellow. 6 voted for green. 3 voted for red.

1. Draw one ⚑ for each vote.

New Flag Colors		
	⚑	
	⚑	
⚑	⚑	
⚑	⚑	⚑
⚑	⚑	⚑
⚑	⚑	⚑
yellow	green	red

Answers will vary—Example:

2. What is this picture graph about? **This graph tells what color flag the players voted for.**

3. Which flag color got the most votes? **green**

© Evan-Moor Corporation • EMC 3081 • Math Fundamentals Organize, represent, and interpret data with up to three categories. 165

Page 166

Name ______________________ **Charts and Graphs** Picture graphs

Read the Problem and Complete the Graph

A family voted for their favorite fruit.

Use this data:
5 voted for bananas
4 voted for plums
3 voted for grapes

Fruit		
🍌		
🍌	plum	
🍌	plum	grapes
🍌	plum	grapes
🍌	plum	grapes
bananas	plums	grapes

1. Draw banana, plum, and grapes to complete the picture graph.

Think About It **Answers will vary—Example:**

2. What is this picture graph about? **This graph is about a family's favorite fruits.**

Interpret the Graph

3. Which fruit was the favorite of most family members?
bananas

4. How many family members voted? **12** family members

Check Your Work **Answers will vary.**

5. Do your answers make sense? ○ yes ○ no

166 Organize, represent, and interpret data with up to three categories. Math Fundamentals • EMC 3081 • © Evan-Moor Corporation

Page 168

Name ______________________ **Charts and Graphs** Bar graphs 8

Read the word problem. Color to complete the bar graph. Then answer the questions.

➤ Mrs. Garcia asked her students if they like the beach or the forest best. 8 students said they like the beach. 12 students said they like the forest.

1. Color one ▬ to show what each student likes best.

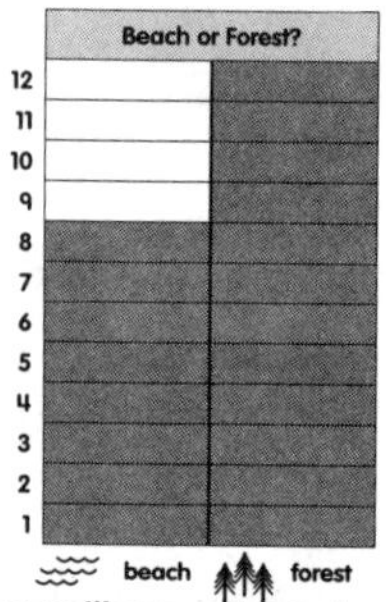

Answers will vary—Example:

2. What is this bar graph about? **This graph tells how many students chose the beach or the forest.**

3. How many more students chose the forest than the beach?
4 more students

168 Organize, represent, and interpret data with up to three categories. Math Fundamentals • EMC 3081 • © Evan-Moor Corporation

Page 169

Name ______________________ **Charts and Graphs** Bar graphs 9

Read the word problem. Color to complete the bar graph. Then answer the questions.

➤ Farmer Tom has hens. Each hen lays one egg every day. Farmer Tom finds 3 white, 4 brown, and 5 spotted eggs every day.

1. Color one ▮ for each egg laid.

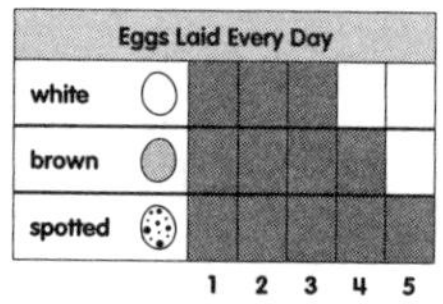

Answers will vary—Example:

2. What is this bar graph about? **This graph tells how many eggs the hens lay every day.**

3. How many fewer white eggs than spotted eggs are laid each day? **2** fewer white eggs

4. How many eggs are laid each day in all? **12** eggs

© Evan-Moor Corporation • EMC 3081 • Math Fundamentals Organize, represent, and interpret data with up to three categories. 169

Page 170

Name ______________________ **Charts and Graphs** Bar graphs

Read the Problem and Complete the Graph

Mr. Black trains dogs. How many of each size dog does he train?

Use this data:
4 small dogs
7 medium dogs
2 large dogs

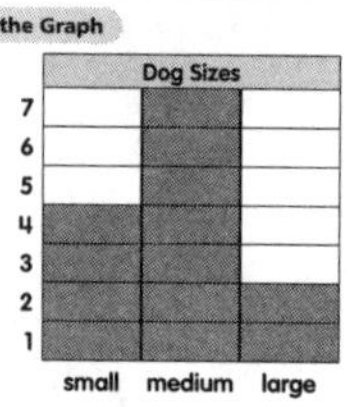

1. Complete the bar graph.

Think About It **Answers will vary—Example:**

2. What is this bar graph about?
This graph shows how many of each size dog Mr. Black trains.

Interpret the Graph

3. How many more medium dogs than large dogs does Mr. Black train? **5** more medium dogs

4. How many dogs does he train altogether? **13** dogs

Check Your Work **Answers will vary.**

5. Do your answers make sense? ○ yes ○ no

170 Organize, represent, and interpret data with up to three categories. Math Fundamentals • EMC 3081 • © Evan-Moor Corporation

Page 173

Name ______________________ **Money** Identifying coins 1

Circle the value of each coin.

Examples

quarter: 5¢ / **(25¢)**	dime: 1¢ / **(10¢)**
1. **(5¢)** / 25¢	4. 10¢ / **(1¢)**
2. **(25¢)** / 10¢	5. 25¢ / **(10¢)**
3. 1¢ / **(5¢)**	6. 5¢ / **(1¢)**

© Evan-Moor Corporation • EMC 3081 • Math Fundamentals Identify coins. 173

Page 174

Name ______________________ **Money** Identifying coins 2

Draw a line from each coin to its name and/or value.

1.	dime
2.	25¢
3.	penny
4.	5¢
5.	nickel
6.	10¢

174 Identify coins. Math Fundamentals • EMC 3081 • © Evan-Moor Corporation

Page 175

Name ______

Money
Identifying coins

Read the Problem

Marci has 3 coins.
The values of her coins are 25 cents, 10 cents, and 1 cent.
What are the names of each of Marci's coins?

Think About It

1. You will write the ____ of Marci's coins.
   ○ value ● names ○ total

Solve the Problem

Use the word box to help you write your answers.

penny nickel dime quarter

2. Marci has a **quarter**, a **dime**, and a **penny**.

Check Your Work

3. Do your answers make sense? ○ yes ○ no
   Answers will vary.

© Evan-Moor Corporation • EMC 3081 • Math Fundamentals — Identify coins. 175

Page 177

Name ______

Money
Writing the value of coins
3

Write the value of each coin.

Examples: 5¢ 10¢

1. 25¢
2. 10¢
3. 1¢
4. 5¢
5. 1¢
6. 25¢

© Evan-Moor Corporation • EMC 3081 • Math Fundamentals — Write the value of coins. 177

Page 178

Name ______

Money
Writing the value of coins
4

Circle the name of each coin. Then write its value.

1. dime / (quarter) — 25¢
2. nickel / (dime) — 10¢
3. dime / (quarter) — 25¢
4. (penny) / nickel — 1¢
5. (nickel) / quarter — 5¢
6. penny / (dime) — 10¢

178 Write the value of coins. — Math Fundamentals • EMC 3081 • © Evan-Moor Corporation

Page 179

Name ______

Money
Writing the value of coins

Read the Problem

Jack has a nickel. Teera has a quarter. Mike has a dime.
How much money does each child have?

Think About It

1. You will find out how much money ____.
   ○ in all ● each child has ○ is left
2. Mark the other way to write "cents."
   ○ $ ○ ? ● ¢

Solve the Problem

3. Use this work space.
   Answers will vary.
4. Jack has **5¢**
5. Teera has **25¢**
6. Mike has **10¢**

Check Your Work

7. Do your answers make sense? ○ yes ○ no
   Answers will vary.

© Evan-Moor Corporation • EMC 3081 • Math Fundamentals — Identify coins. 179

Page 181

Name ______

Money
Counting coins
5

Count on for each group of coins. Write the values.

Examples: 5¢ 10¢ 15¢ = 15¢

1. 1¢ 2¢ 3¢ 4¢ 5¢ 6¢ = 6¢
2. 10¢ 20¢ 30¢ 40¢ 50¢ 60¢ = 60¢
3. 5¢ 10¢ 15¢ 20¢ 25¢ = 25¢

© Evan-Moor Corporation • EMC 3081 • Math Fundamentals — Count coins. 181

Page 182

Name ______

Money
Counting coins
6

Count on for each group of coins. Write the values.

1. 10¢ 15¢ 16¢ 17¢ = 17¢
2. 10¢ 20¢ 25¢ 30¢ = 30¢
3. 5¢ 10¢ 15¢ 16¢ 17¢ = 17¢
4. 10¢ 20¢ 30¢ 31¢ = 31¢

182 Count coins. — Math Fundamentals • EMC 3081 • © Evan-Moor Corporation

Page 183

Name ______

Money
Counting coins
7

Count on for each group of coins. Write the value.

1. 36¢
2. 45¢
3. 27¢
4. 51¢

© Evan-Moor Corporation • EMC 3081 • Math Fundamentals — Count coins. 183

Page 184

Name ______

Money
Counting coins

Read the Problem

Anna has 2 dimes, 1 nickel, and 3 pennies.
How much money does Anna have?

Think About It

1. You will find out how much money Anna ____.
   ○ needs ○ lost ● has
2. Write about your plan to solve the problem.
   Answers will vary.

Solve the Problem

3. Use this work space.
   Answers will vary.
4. Anna has **28¢**

Check Your Work

5. Do your answers make sense? ○ yes ○ no
   Answers will vary.

184 Count coins. — Math Fundamentals • EMC 3081 • © Evan-Moor Corporation

Page 187

Name ______

Geometry
Identifying two- and three-dimensional shapes
1

Draw a line from each object to the shape it looks like.

Example

1. 2. 3. 4.

© Evan-Moor Corporation • EMC 3081 • Math Fundamentals — Identify two- and three-dimensional shapes. 187

Page 188

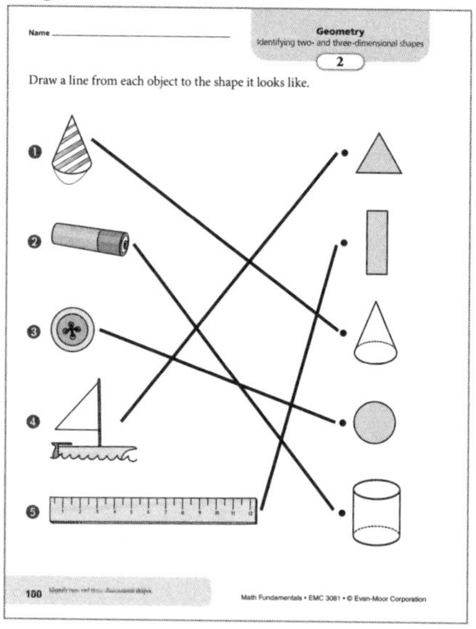
Name

Geometry
Identifying two- and three-dimensional shapes

2

Draw a line from each object to the shape it looks like.

100

Math Fundamentals • EMC 3081 • © Evan-Moor Corporation

Page 189

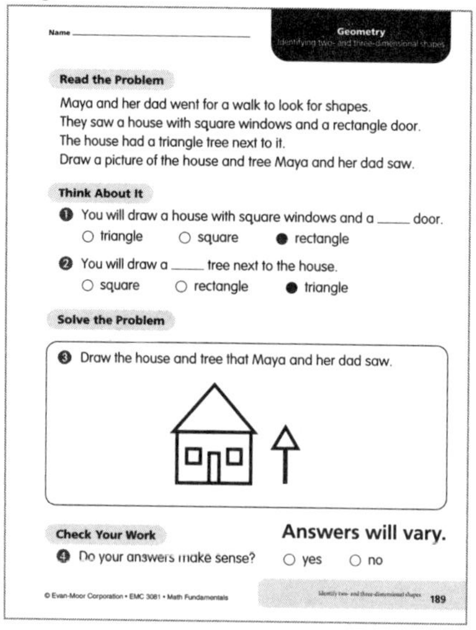
Name

Geometry
Identifying two- and three-dimensional shapes

Read the Problem

Maya and her dad went for a walk to look for shapes.
They saw a house with square windows and a rectangle door.
The house had a triangle tree next to it.
Draw a picture of the house and tree Maya and her dad saw.

Think About It

1. You will draw a house with square windows and a ____ door.
   ○ triangle ○ square ● rectangle
2. You will draw a ____ tree next to the house.
   ○ square ○ rectangle ● triangle

Solve the Problem

3. Draw the house and tree that Maya and her dad saw.

Check Your Work

Answers will vary.

4. Do your answers make sense? ○ yes ○ no

© Evan-Moor Corporation • EMC 3081 • Math Fundamentals

189

Page 191

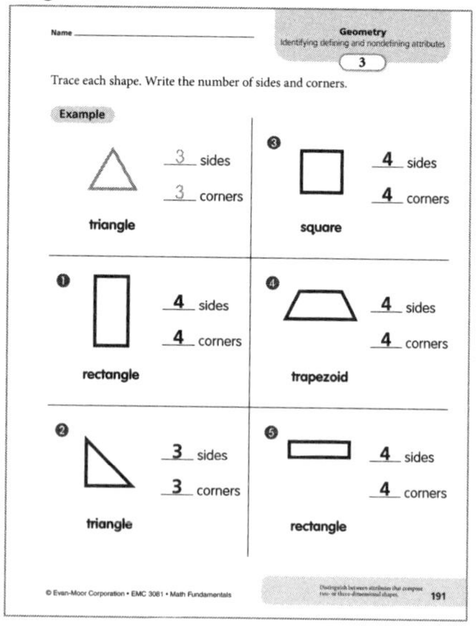
Name

Geometry
Identifying defining and nondefining attributes

3

Trace each shape. Write the number of sides and corners.

Example: triangle — 3 sides, 3 corners

1. rectangle — 4 sides, 4 corners
2. triangle — 3 sides, 3 corners
3. square — 4 sides, 4 corners
4. trapezoid — 4 sides, 4 corners
5. rectangle — 4 sides, 4 corners

© Evan-Moor Corporation • EMC 3081 • Math Fundamentals

191

Page 192

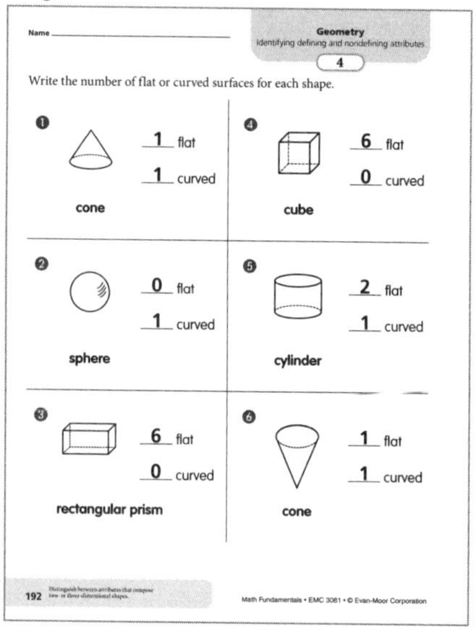
Name

Geometry
Identifying defining and nondefining attributes

4

Write the number of flat or curved surfaces for each shape.

1. cone — 1 flat, 1 curved
2. sphere — 0 flat, 1 curved
3. rectangular prism — 6 flat, 0 curved
4. cube — 6 flat, 0 curved
5. cylinder — 2 flat, 1 curved
6. cone — 1 flat, 1 curved

192

Math Fundamentals • EMC 3081 • © Evan-Moor Corporation

Page 193

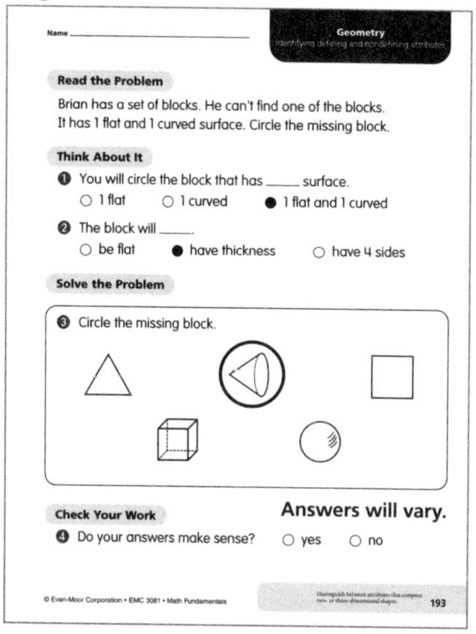
Name

Geometry
Identifying defining and nondefining attributes

Read the Problem

Brian has a set of blocks. He can't find one of the blocks.
It has 1 flat and 1 curved surface. Circle the missing block.

Think About It

1. You will circle the block that has ____ surface.
   ○ 1 flat ○ 1 curved ● 1 flat and 1 curved
2. The block will ____.
   ○ be flat ● have thickness ○ have 4 sides

Solve the Problem

3. Circle the missing block.

Check Your Work

Answers will vary.

4. Do your answers make sense? ○ yes ○ no

© Evan-Moor Corporation • EMC 3081 • Math Fundamentals

193

Page 195

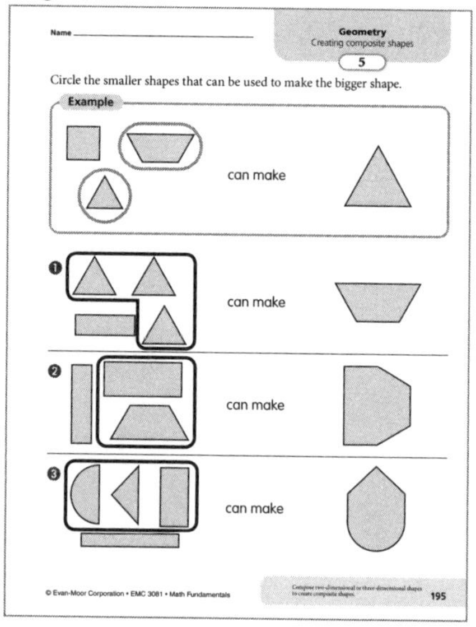
Name

Geometry
Creating composite shapes

5

Circle the smaller shapes that can be used to make the bigger shape.

Example — can make

1. can make
2. can make
3. can make

© Evan-Moor Corporation • EMC 3081 • Math Fundamentals

195

Page 196

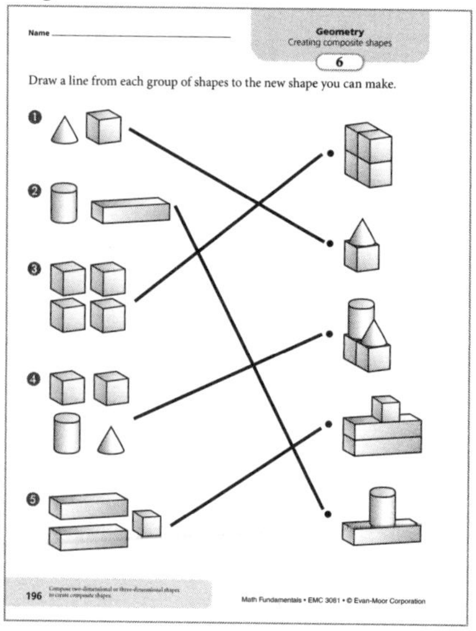
Name

Geometry
Creating composite shapes

6

Draw a line from each group of shapes to the new shape you can make.

196

Math Fundamentals • EMC 3081 • © Evan-Moor Corporation

Page 197

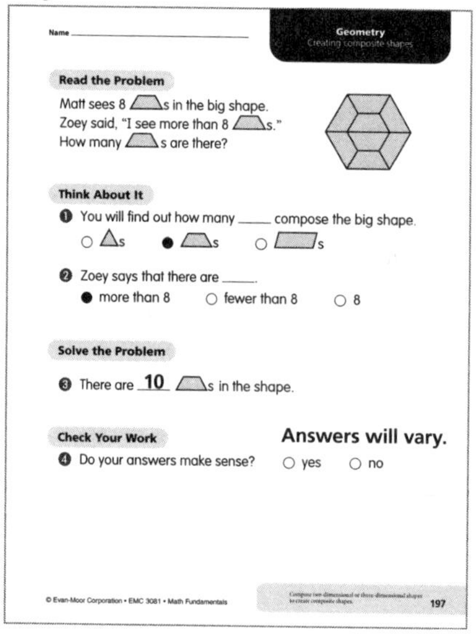
Name

Geometry
Creating composite shapes

Read the Problem

Matt sees 8 ▱s in the big shape.
Zoey said, "I see more than 8 ▱s."
How many ▱s are there?

Think About It

1. You will find out how many ____ compose the big shape.
   ○ △s ● ▱s ○ ▱s
2. Zoey says that there are ____.
   ● more than 8 ○ fewer than 8 ○ 8

Solve the Problem

3. There are 10 ▱s in the shape.

Check Your Work

Answers will vary.

4. Do your answers make sense? ○ yes ○ no

© Evan-Moor Corporation • EMC 3081 • Math Fundamentals

197

Page 199

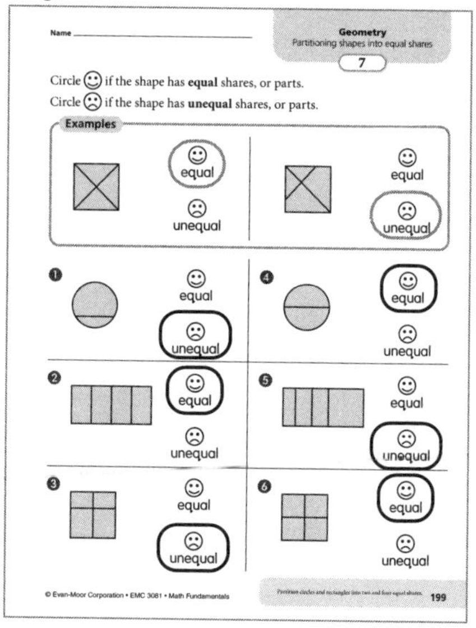
Name

Geometry
Partitioning shapes into equal shares

7

Circle ☺ if the shape has **equal** shares, or parts.
Circle ☹ if the shape has **unequal** shares, or parts.

Examples: equal (circled); unequal (circled)

1. unequal (circled)
2. equal (circled)
3. unequal (circled)
4. equal (circled)
5. unequal (circled)
6. equal (circled)

© Evan-Moor Corporation • EMC 3081 • Math Fundamentals

199

Page 200

Name ____________________

Geometry
Partitioning shapes into equal shares
8

Circle the shapes that show **equal** shares, or parts.

1 2 3
4 5 6
7 8 9

200 Partition circles and rectangles into two and four equal shares. Math Fundamentals • EMC 3081 • © Evan-Moor Corporation

Page 201

Name ____________________

Geometry
Partitioning shapes into equal shares

Read the Problem

Tami cut a pizza into four equal shares. It looked like this. Circle the shape below that shows one equal share of Tami's pizza.

Think About It

1 You will find the shape that is 1 of ____ equal shares.
○ 2 ○ 3 ● 4

2 A circle has a ____ side.
● curved ○ straight ○ zigzag

Solve the Problem

3 Circle the shape that shows one equal share of Tami's pizza.

Check Your Work **Answers will vary.**

4 Do your answers make sense? ○ yes ○ no

© Evan-Moor Corporation • EMC 3081 • Math Fundamentals Partition circles and rectangles into two and four equal shares. 201

Page 203

Name ____________________

Geometry
Partitioning shapes into fractional shares
9

Circle the shape in each row that shows **halves**.

Example

1
2
3

© Evan-Moor Corporation • EMC 3081 • Math Fundamentals Describe halves and fourths as parts of a whole. 203

Page 204

Name ____________________

Geometry
Partitioning shapes into fractional shares
10

Circle the shape in each row that shows **fourths**.

Example

1
2
3

204 Describe halves and fourths as parts of a whole. Math Fundamentals • EMC 3081 • © Evan-Moor Corporation

Page 205

Name ____________________

Geometry
Partitioning shapes into fractional shares
11

Circle the name of the shaded part of each shape.

1	whole **(half)** fourth	4	**(whole)** half fourth
2	whole half **(fourth)**	5	whole half **(fourth)**
3	whole **(half)** fourth	6	**(whole)** half fourth

© Evan-Moor Corporation • EMC 3081 • Math Fundamentals Describe halves and fourths as parts of a whole. 205

Page 206

Name ____________________

Geometry
Partitioning shapes into fractional shares

Read the Problem

Two friends want to share a square sandwich. How many ways can it be cut into 2 equal shares? Draw all the ways in the work space.

Think About It

1 You will find ways to cut a square into ____.
● halves ○ fourths ○ quarters

2 You will ____ the ways.
○ read ● draw ○ cut

Solve the Problem

3 Use this work space.

4 There are __4__ ways to cut the sandwich into 2 equal shares.

Check Your Work **Answers will vary.**

5 Do your answers make sense? ○ yes ○ no

206 Describe halves and fourths as parts of a whole. Math Fundamentals • EMC 3081 • © Evan-Moor Corporation

Daily Word Problems Math

Daily Word Problems is the perfect resource to improve students' problem-solving skills.

The all-new word problems are written to support current math standards and provide consistent spiral review of math concepts.

- 36 weeks of activities give practice of grade-level math concepts such as addition, multiplication, fractions, logic, algebra, and more.
- Monday through Thursday's activities present a one- or two-step word problem, while Friday's format is more extensive and requires multiple steps.
- The multi-step problems require students to incorporate higher-order thinking skills.
- A new day-by-day skills list helps teachers identify skills practiced.

Correlated to current standards

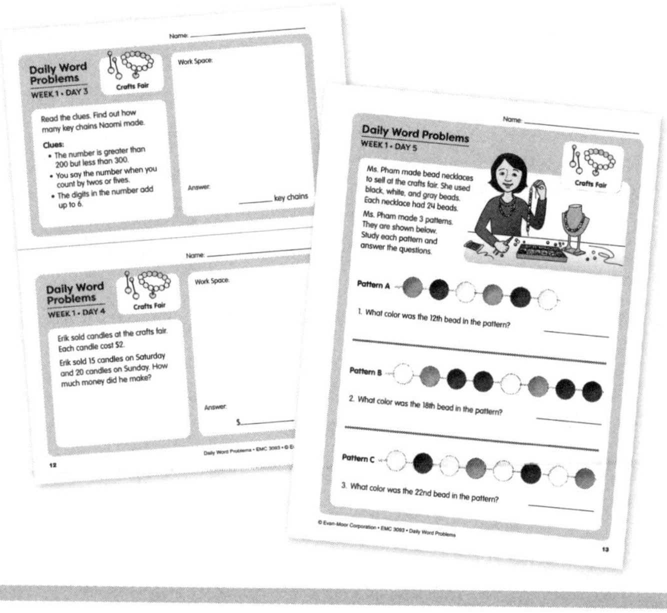

Teacher's Edition*		Student Pack (5 Student Books)	
Grade 1	EMC 3091	Grade 1	EMC 7121
Grade 2	EMC 3092	Grade 2	EMC 7122
Grade 3	EMC 3093	Grade 3	EMC 7123
Grade 4	EMC 3094	Grade 4	EMC 7124
Grade 5	EMC 3095	Grade 5	EMC 7125
Grade 6	EMC 3096	Grade 6	EMC 7126

**Available in print and e-book*